# The Arts of Korea

I (Frontispiece): MURAL, TOMB OF THE DANCERS: HUNTING SCENE (page 75).
Painting on plaster. T'ung-kou, Manchuria. Koguryo, 4th–6th century.

EVELYN McCUNE

# The Arts of Korea

## An Illustrated History

CHARLES E. TUTTLE COMPANY: PUBLISHERS

Rutland, Vermont                    Tokyo, Japan

European Representatives

For the Continent :
BOXERBOOKS, INC., Zurich

For the British Isles :
PRENTICE-HALL INTERNATIONAL INC., London

B 78200

Published by the Charles E. Tuttle Company
of Rutland, Vermont & Tokyo, Japan,
with editorial offices at
15 Edogawa-cho, Bunkyo-ku, Tokyo

Copyright in Japan, 1962
by Charles E. Tuttle Company

Library of Congress Catalog
Card No. 61-11122

First printing, 1962

Layout of illustrations by M. Kuwata
Book design and typography by Kaoru Ogimi

PRINTED IN JAPAN

To Pat and Alex

# Table of Contents

# CONTENTS

8

# List of Illustrations

*Asterisks (\*) indicate color plates*

# LIST OF ILLUSTRATIONS

# Foreword

EVELYN McCune's history of Korean art will speak for itself and therefore has little need of a foreword to recommend it. I should like, however, to take advantage of this opportunity to express my earnest hope that her book will help our foreign friends as well as our own people to discover the beauty of Korea's art and to understand the struggling soul of a nation that has been able to maintain cultural continuity during several thousands of years despite the not always easy conditions surrounding it.

The need for a new and comprehensive history of Korean art has been increasingly felt as Korea has become more and more known to the world, and we could certainly have found no better author for it than Mrs. McCune, whom we regard as one of the best of connoisseurs. Her family, the Beckers, and that of her late husband, the McCunes, came to Korea half a century ago to devote their lives to the education of Korean youth. They have become the unforgettable friends of Korea. Mrs. McCune was born and brought up in our country in the Korean atmosphere, and she understands quite well the heart of the Korean people. She is thus excellently qualified to interpret Korean culture to the West.

To write the history of a foreign people's art, one needs not only to be versed in what is genuine and beautiful in both past and present, but also to be able to interpret esthetic meanings and, above all, to appraise the esthetic merits of the art in terms of its broad human significance. Evelyn McCune possesses both of these qualifications to a high degree, and this is why we are happy to welcome this new book on Korean art by one of our true friends.

KIM CHE-WON
Director
National Museum of Korea

# Preface

THIS BOOK is designed to introduce Korean culture to those who have not come into contact with it before. The subject of art provides the main channel for such an introduction, but it is not the only one, since account has also been taken of the environment which has produced the art. An effort has been made to call attention to the humor, the subtleties, and the esthetic qualities that are to be found not only in the high tides of artistic achievement but to a degree in their ebb as well. This has been done through a chronological arrangement of the art developments of each period as they relate to the general culture. Emphasis has been placed upon the major art medium of each era; for example, the tomb murals of Koguryo, the jewelry of Silla, the sculpture of United Silla, the celadons of Koryo, and the painting of Yi. A broad scheme has first been indicated, and then details have been brought into focus, sometimes quite arbitrarily, in order to call attention to some minor but nonetheless significant style, artist, or trend. The biographies of two sixteenth-century artists, for example, are given in some detail in order to contrast the life of Madame Sin (Sa Im-dang) and her atypical, creative, *avant-garde* family—who lived in the peaceful early years of the century—with the life of Hoju, the typical conservative, well-to-do scholar-artist who was thrust into the tragedies of war and the end of an era in the later years of the same century.

This book is the first attempt in English to present a chronological account of the sweep of Korean art, and it is the first attempt to present the subject in a nonscholarly way for the use of the ordinary reader. A minimum of footnotes have been furnished, as well as a bibliographical note, in order to provide a means for further inquiry to those readers who wish to continue their study.

Romanization of Korean names and words has been arbitrarily simplified to omit diacritical marks and awkward spellings; for example, Yi Song-gye and Hyewon have been rendered as Yi Song-ge and Hewon, and no differentiation between the sounds of "o" as in *son* and *song* has been indicated. The measurements of some objects, such as those in communist North Korea, have been taken from old works but have not been verified, and the illustrations of some important items have been done from reproductions taken from early publications. None of the temples or other buildings in North Korea have been described, since no recent information about them is available.

The five chapters dealing with Yi dynasty painting were written largely around the paintings in the Chun collection. This was the suggestion of Dr. Kim Che-won, Curator of the

National Museum of Korea, who felt strongly that the most important private collection in Korea should be given the recognition that it deserves. The study was made in the summer of 1955. Dr. Kim provided me with a room in the museum in which to work, and obstacles vanished with the wonderful speed that appears when Korean energy is directed toward achieving an end of its own. Mr. Chun Hyung-pil, connoisseur and collector, was kindness itself. The reception hall of his residence in Seoul was put at my disposal. Bales and boxes of all sizes, in which treasures had been packed away during the Korean War, were brought to the veranda and unpacked. Sliding doors were rolled back to reveal storerooms crowded with screens, scrolls, and other *objets d'art*. Priceless ceramic pieces listed as national treasures, including many that later toured the United States with the Korean exhibit of 1957, were drawn from their silk and cotton-wool repositories. Buddhist reliquaries, painted fans by the score, and jewelry from the family collections were courteously displayed.

During the review of these art objects, I was impressed more than ever before with the fact that, although Korean art is founded upon Chinese tradition, it took turns of its own that merit far more than a casual look. It was possible for me to see, in this art, differences between the Koreans and their neighbors in taste, emphasis, and style. At the same time, the many general features shared by Koreans in common with their neighbors appeared to me to be the single most important fact of the study. The interplay of Korea's culture with that of neighboring countries is therefore stressed in this book both directly and by implication.

Last, but not least, notice must be taken here of the fact that there are far fewer areas in the study of Korean art that are covered by monographs than there are areas that have not been studied at all. The art historian in particular, accustomed to the rich and finished work of Western research, and to a lesser degree to Japanese and Chinese critical studies, may be irritated not to find all that he wants to know put before him in the manner that will save him time and effort. Obstacles of this sort would seem to indicate that a book of general description should be delayed, perhaps for another generation. On the other hand, much of great interest and importance has already been made available, and there is an urgent need for the people of the West to come to know more of the Korean people than war can teach. It is hoped, therefore, that this book will find its uses, both for those who wish a casual acquaintance and for those who will be stimulated to continue studies of much further range and more precise interpretation than are attempted here.

Many people have had a hand in this book. Without the generous and imaginative assistance of all, it could not have been put together. To General Maxwell Taylor, Commander of the Eighth Army in Korea, I am indebted for asking a question so difficult to answer that it started the project which turned into this book. In compiling even an elementary answer to his question, I was impressed with the nature of the difficulties in the way of any co-ordinated grasp of the Korean cultural heritage by the Westerner. Modern Korean specialists in Buddhism knew little about the history of Buddhism or its architecture; historians knew little about Buddhist doctrine; and artists knew little about any of these. Good accounts covering these various subjects as they relate to one another were almost nonexistent in any language. However, the answers were all there, if they could be pulled together. Kurt Prendergast, chief of the Time-Life office in Tokyo at the time, suggested that it was a question of "those who know don't tell, and those who tell don't know," and recommended a determined effort to break the silence of those who know. Charles Tuttle went a step further and suggested that the results of such a study be put into book form. Among those who were consulted in Korea as the project gathered way were Dr. Kim Che-won and Dr. Kim Won-yong, both of the National Museum, and Mr. Chun. Dr. George Paik, Miss Helen Kim, and Dr. Yu Chin-ho all discussed various problems with me and made suggestions. During these early stages of collecting materials, I became indebted to members of the diplomatic corps as well as to the scholarly community. Ambassador and Mrs. Ellis Briggs of the United States Embassy, Counselor of Embassy Niles Bond, and Deputy Assistant Secretary of State U. Alexis Johnson were particularly encouraging and helpful. Mr. Carl Miller of the Bank of Korea and the Conants of UNKRA, all deeply knowledgeable about the subject, contributed photographs. Miss Grace Haskell and Dallas Voran of UNKRA, interested as collectors and connoisseurs, offered valuable comments and lent slides. Dr. C. Burton Fahs of the Rockefeller Foundation, who has taken a keen interest in the preservation of Korean arts and has traveled to Korea almost yearly for fifteen years, gave me sustained and invaluable aid.

Professor Sohn Pow-key, specialist in Korean history, came to the rescue with his translations and read the entire manuscript, making valuable suggestions. Professor Kim Won-yong of the National Museum also read the first chapters, contributing important suggestions as well as answering with patience my many letters. Special thanks are due to Dr. Otto Maenchen and Professor Wolfram Eberhard of the University of California for their kindness over many years and for their reading of parts of the manuscript. Others to whom I owe thanks for reading and commenting on parts of the manuscript are Mr. James Cahill of the Freer Gallery, Professor George Rowley of Princeton University, and Mr. Robert P. Griffing, Jr., Director of the Honolulu Academy of Arts. Those who read parts of the manuscript before going to Korea in 1957 to select national treasures for the United States exhibition are Mr. Alan Priest of the Metropolitan Museum and Mr. Harold Stern of the Freer Gallery. To Professors Sueji Umehara and Kyoichi Arimitsu of Kyoto University, I am indebted for the loan of photographs and for many hours of discussion.

The young historians, Miss Chong Yang-wan and Mr. Kim Yong-sop, were especially helpful during the summer of 1955 because of their enthusiasm and interest as well as their assistance in locating books, making English translations, and discovering the meanings of obscure ideograms. Two Ehwa University students, Miss Yu Hyong-suk and Miss Han Yong-sin, did excellent work in drawing several hundred pen-and-ink designs used in the course of the project.

The difficulties that arose in connection with photographing the collections were almost insurmountable. To Colonel Henry Margeson and Lieutenant Edgar Neal of the Troop Information and Education Section goes all the credit for solving problems one after another, and to Sergeant James Culpepper the credit for photographing the Chun collection under trying conditions. Major George Posner of the Signal Corps, Mr. Dallas Voran, and Mr. Robert Kinney and Mrs. T. O. Engebretson of Torge Photos were important contributors of photographs to this book. The U.S. Army and the Department of State also gave permission for the use of some of their pictures. *Time* magazine and Mr. Junkichi Mayu-yama contributed a few of the best illustrations we were able to acquire. I also wish to thank the following museums for permission to use their materials: the Freer Gallery of Art, the Kyongju Branch of the National Museum of Korea, the Museum of Cologne, the Museum of Fine Arts of Boston, the National Museum of Korea, the Toksu Palace Museum of Fine Arts, the Tokyo National Museum, and the Yi Household Museum.

In conclusion, I wish to thank the staff of the Charles E. Tuttle Company—particularly Ralph Friedrich, Kaoru Ogimi, and Masakazu Kuwata, who accomplished with a minimum of wasted effort and a maximum of effect the difficult task of long-distance tying together of loose ends of an incredible variety. I also acknowledge with unlimited gratitude the help of my parents, who read the chapters as they were written, and of my daughters. Helen generously typed the manuscript, helped with the translations, and was a pillar of strength throughout. Heather put up with the endless nuisances occasioned by the production of an art book within the home and in the end showed extraordinary grace under pressure by voluntarily reading it.

EVELYN McCUNE

Berkeley, 1961

# Introduction

KOREAN art is difficult to assess because the Koreans have kept their art to themselves. Outsiders have therefore ranked the Korean product as a provincial variation of Chinese art—a variation, moreover, that produced no important developments of its own, such as the color print of Japan. A further difficulty has stemmed form the fact that the creative periods of Korea's past have been short-lived and most of Korea's great art has died out, leaving few traces of greatness behind it.

One of the reasons for this neglect is that modern Korean scholars have not yet had time to do the task. Much more is now known about the whole range of Korean art, from neolithic times to the present, than was known a generation ago. Archeological excavations done during the period of Japanese rule in Korea (1905–45) have brought to light a great body of fresh materials for the study of the art and archeology of ancient periods, and the despoliation of tombs since the fall of the Yi dynasty in 1910 has provided many new examples of Koryo pottery for the study of ceramics. For the study of the Choson (Yi) period, much is available in the national collections as well as in private collections, but it has been only in the last ten years that Korean scholars have had the opportunity to study this period according to modern methods of research, since that area of investigation was almost completely closed to them during Japanese rule.

The studies that have been done to date have been largely by Japanese scholars who have undoubtedly contributed to the popularization of the subject both in Japan and abroad by publishing many well-illustrated and handsomely printed books. At the same time, a number of fine specimens of pottery and painting began to filter into museums and private collections in Europe and the United States, thereby arousing further interest. One of the chief services accomplished by the Japanese publications was to establish the fact that Korea, from the fifth century on, produced masterpieces, many of which are still extant, in all the major art forms of the Far East.

Moreover, a growing appreciation of Korean art has accorded it recognition for certain qualities which have set it apart in the museums of the world as distinctly Korean. The difference, in a word, appears to have resulted from the fact that Korean artists were obliged, more often by their poverty than by their neighbors, to rely upon beauty of line and shape rather than upon costly materials. The resulting works of art were marked by elegance and refinement during periods of political stability, but during periods of war they were rustic and careless. In both extremes of refinement and rusticity, however, were to be found strength and an attractive honesty that were much admired in China and Japan—in particular by the Japanese, who imitated them. Korean artists have tended to express their major themes in contour or profile form, reinforcing the main idea by minor detail or by color. Decoration often appeared to be secondary—almost an afterthought—and materials (such as silk, paper, wood, stone, bronze, and lacquer) were used strictly according to their artistic and functional possibilities. They were also for the most part locally produced, especially during the self-imposed austerities of the Yi dynasty. It is in keeping with these preferences, then, that the Koreans did not, as did the Chinese, cultivate a taste for imported luxuries, or for the grandiose. It was as if, acknowledging inability to compete with the Chinese in magnificence, they made a virtue of necessity and proudly created lovely things out of simple materials by means of techniques of which they were masters. They aimed at strength of expression rather than brilliance and often achieved it with marked success.

Some of the art that has survived is of ancient vintage. Symbols that are older than the histories and that still carry magical impact are present on all the palaces and temples. These buildings are gradually falling into ruin, but they were the most sacred places of the kingdom only a few years ago. Today, as Korea moves into an industrial economy, the art is moving with it into commercial as well as other modern phases, but as yet, in most of the area south of the thirty-eighth parallel, the dominant tradition is still the symbolic art of the past. New art will come in with new media. Nevertheless, as long as the traditional brush-and-ink skill continues to be popular, the ancient art will stay alive with it. Calligraphy rendered in ink still has a multitude of stimulating associations for the educated Korean. If we in the West still used Latin and wrote it with the tools of the Romans, we would live more closely with our classical heritage in our daily life than we do. As it is, our fashions change so rapidly that few associations have time to form around any one tool or art medium. But the Koreans have been slow to change. This is an important clue to an understanding not only of their art but also of their whole culture. It is not because they do not like novelties that they have been slow to change, but because they have been unwilling to relinquish the emotional satisfactions connected with their old arts until they are sure that the new will bring them equal comfort. Now, of course, there is a flood tide of Western art styles to be seen in all the schools and art shows.

The satisfactions derived from the old art symbols and traditions have been useful but so elusive for outsiders to learn and understand that even other Far Easterners, like the Japanese, have had difficulty in isolating them and defining them, partly because Koreans tend to be silent on matters that show where their spiritual strength lies—where, so to speak, their hearts are. Their art furnishes one of the clues—in their painting in particular, where, by means of symbols, Korean artists were able to reveal their deepest feelings about the world they lived in; where they ran up their "flags of revolt" and captured with brush and ink those moments in life that gave them refreshment, peace of mind, and release.

Certain peculiarities which illustrate the way Koreans sought to strengthen themselves to endure with equanimity their lives of increasing austerity are mentioned below. First, there was Korean conservatism and extreme resistance to change—a resistance, however, that did yield Korean society some social and political stability. Second, there was a characteristic love of nature and outdoor living. A third trait was a pattern of response to foreign culture that allowed them to adopt without forfeiting Korean cultural identity. A fourth quality was a high respect for learning that made the Korean race exceptionally teachable. A fifth peculiarity was the development of the theory and practice of what may be called, for want of a better name, a cult of weakness that enabled Koreans to resist being swallowed up by neighboring nations of superior strength. And last, there grew up a technique of subtle means of communication, the use of silences in speech and art.

In Korea during the past five hundred years, to an even greater degree than in China, time stood still. With an economy pegged to agrarian practices dating from a prehistoric period and an educational system based upon the disorganized though poetic irrationality of the Chinese, it is not surprising to find that their intellectual development failed to progress from intuitional to rational to scientific stages, as did that of other civilizations, in which old techniques were sloughed off as new ones formed. In Korea the old never died out, and the new never quite took over. Although Korean resistance to change was secured at great cost to human rights, it was also a means by which were preserved the faculties of faith and intuition. As a primarily agricultural people for their entire historic existence, Koreans recognized little need for change in their social or economic life. There grew up an integrated, homogeneous society at whose top was a small sophisticated clique of men who could mingle with ease with the cultured gentlemen of China and Japan and at whose base was the peasantry, many of whom had a standard of living not far above the neolithic. The major binding force between these two groups was what the Koreans refer to as *aeguk* (love of the homeland), or better, *uri nara* (our land). The two groups had a profound social as well as economic effect upon one another, more intimate and vital than the relations between aristocrat and peasant in culturally diverse China or in remote and invasion-free Japan. The attachment of the average Korean to the land was and is a fundamental feature of Korean life that is obvious, and yet its composition eludes easy analysis. Even the newcomer to Korea immediately receives the impression that every Korean is a farmer at heart who has rejected in the past, consciously or unconsciously, any reforms which might threaten his use of the land according to his notions of its conservation, and that whenever a question concerning the land arises, even the scholarship of the most learned Korean becomes a thin veneer over the man who lived by raising rice and who needed for this prime objective only three things: sun, rain, and labor. This fact of economic life explains much of the Korean lack of will to change in the past.

Having noted this conservative attachment to the land, we may consider a second feature of Korean culture: the love of nature. This feeling expresses itself in important ways. For one thing, all the acts of life that can be carried on in the open air are so conducted. An open room is found in every peasant house as well as an unroofed courtyard called the *madang*. In the homes of the aristocrats a special summer room, elevated on pillars (a survival of the house on stilts or a tree house), is a universal feature. Kitchens are usually open to the weather, and most shops are open in the front. The five-day markets are held in village streets under tentlike canopies. Children are made to stay outside the house most of the day, and even schools were formerly conducted in the open when the weather permitted. The old men prefer, as much as possible, to sit outdoors to smoke or to play chess. Amusements in general were outside affairs, and music and dancing are still enjoyed al fresco in upper-class entertainments as well as in farmers' festivals. Korean outdoor life of the past was perhaps more active than that of most other civilized temperate-zone nonnomadic people in Asia. Moreover, a sort of peasant life was deliberately cultivated as an everyday way of life in Korea by ninety-nine percent of the people, and the geographic remoteness of the country from world centers of civilization has encouraged the retention of these habits to the present.

The third of the above-mentioned Korean characteristics is the inherited complex of response to foreign cultures. Korean civilization developed under waves of foreign influence. A pattern of assimilation was established long ago. First, there seems to have been an unconscious grasp by intuition, if by no other method, as a child learns the meaning of a strange importation. This was followed by efforts to master foreign techniques, and then by the attempt to interpret the imported idea for themselves and in their own way. The process is observable today. A Westerner who visits a modern art show in Korea is struck by the evidence, encountered on every side, of faithfulness to the style of Western artists—Matisse, Picasso, and so forth. The striking thing about the way this is done, however, is that there are few faithful *copies* of the foreign art. There are, on the other hand, many interpretations of its style.

The fourth aspect of Korean culture, that of respect for learning, is present today in what appears to be a remarkable thirst for education throughout the country. Korean preferences in learning are puzzling to the outsider. There is still a marked disinterest in scientific and practical courses of study and an unrealistic application to general humanistic studies such as art, music, poetry, and history. Attitudes are changing a little; practical courses are being taken by more students; and the arts are being denigrated somewhat as they are in modern America. The explanation for the dominant trend is to be found in the practice of the Yi dynasty in tying up all access to position, prestige, and wealth with the competitive examination system based upon study of Chinese classical literature. This system, in use for five hundred years, has bred an upper class which has an unusually high proportion of brilliant scholars, but it has also produced a special attitude toward the uses and abuses of education, as noted above.

The fifth characteristic of traditional Korean culture that affected Korean art is the so-called cult of weakness. No race firmly entrenched upon its own soil neglects its own defense. During the long years of foreign invasion, the Koreans developed an opposite strategy to that of militarism—a "cult of weakness" but of course with the same purpose in mind: that of defense. The methods used elude definition because, to be successful, they had to vary continually. Fluidity was the keynote: never letting the enemy know where to strike or what to anticipate. Unpredictability resulted and, in extreme situations, ungovernability. The strategy can best be explained in terms of analogy. Korean defenses, national and social, may be compared to a network of waterways in a marsh. The main currents are separate—seemingly rival and independent—but they all flow eventually into the same sea. They take devious courses and are connected by many small channels known to the initiated, unknown to the stranger.

Two main channels of Korean experience have assisted in the development of this pragmatic philosophy of weakness. One is the Koreans' experience of religion, and the other is their experience of invasion. Several foreign religions have been accepted by the Koreans during the course of their history, but they have not committed themselves completely to any one. To quote a modern Korean author: "It can be said that they hold three or more religions at the same time. The religious beliefs of the majority of Koreans are a mixture of Christianity, Confucianism, Buddhism, Shinkyo [shamanism], and one or two other faiths." Western theologians have also pointed out that Korea never enjoyed the benefits of an organized religion until Christianity was introduced, and that the Koreans regarded the three religions of Confucianism, Buddhism, and shamanism as all equally valid. Since a discussion of this matter is obviously beyond the scope of an art book, only two aspects that have bearing upon the symbols of art will be noted. The first is the surprising vitality of shamanism. Spirit worship, shamanism, even ancient fertility rites, are practices that have persisted aggressively and zestfully in Korea as they have done in no other heavily populated, civilized country in the world. The reasons for this survival are not clear, and one may easily go too far in probing for them, but it is likely that they lie in the need of the Koreans for retaining what they regard as their own form of religious outlet. Into the lower classes in Korea went the ancient magic practices and superstitions that were discarded by the most advanced members of the intellectually enlightened upper class, and there they were kept alive by the farmers and, one should add, a silently acquiescent upper class. One cause for the clinging of the more enlightened to such practices may be found in the negation that characterizes Buddhism and the repression in Confucianism, both of which were stressed in Korea at the expense of their more positive and beneficial features. Reaction in Korea against Buddhist and Confucian denials of instinctual human needs was silent but strong, and it found a quiet outlet in the sorcery of shamanism.

The influence of the negation and the repression that were general in Korea's religions was also evident in the ethics and art of the Yi dynasty. A generally inhibited way of life came gradually to be accepted. A sense of futility and fatalism spread to all classes. Passive virtues such as docility, stoicism, politeness, and other attributes of surface polish came to be valued above the more active virtues of maturity and capacity for responsibility. Nonresistance and nonviolence came to be regarded as the solutions for most conflicts. There grew up an understanding of the properties and possibilities of a sort of strong gentleness that was thought of as "the only useful quality." In art, popular folklore, with its fairies and gnomes—delightful in Korea as in every other culture in the world—still "expressed an immature conception of the supernatural in terms of fairy realms," as George Rowley observes in his *Principles of Chinese Painting,* but it offered escape to all from the intolerable restrictions that had encrusted individual development of every kind.

The other main stream of Korean experience was the country's reaction to foreign invasion and to relations with its neighbors in general. Political and military theories centering on the concept that the only useful quality was weakness were formulated and adopted. From this main stream radiated a whole delta of tactics of withdrawal, nonaction, nonresistance, and noninterference. Long experience gave the Koreans a lead among Asiatic peoples who, surrounded by stronger nations, have for their main aim the preservation of their identity. As the Swiss have been useful to the Europeans in their role of international bankers, the Koreans have been useful to other Asiatics in devising solutions for weak-nation problems. A conspicuous example of this was the great nation-wide nonviolent uprising of

23

1919, which the American historian Tyler Dennett characterized as one of the most politically naive incidents of the twentieth-century world. Whether it was as naive as it appeared to be, only history will show. "Low determines high" represents a Korean political concept that has often been tested and is symbolized, along with other related concepts, in the short and long bars on the Korean flag.

The last characteristic, the use of silences, double talk, and other tricks of communication, needs to be mentioned in relation to art practices. In Korea, unlike Japan, fluent but usually superficial speech was regarded as a valuable means of reducing human tensions, and therefore fluent speech became an art in itself—used to support the ego in the daily polite commonplaces, or by means of intricate verb endings to put a man in his place; used for enjoyment, relief, or insult, but rarely for serious matters. The form mattered, not the content. Habit and custom have hallowed the practice of silence, on the other hand, in matters of grave or dangerous import. Respect was also indicated by silence. What was deeply felt was seldom mentioned in conversation. The strategy of silence was a concept that was developed and put to work. In situations where Westerners expect reply, exact definition, statement of purpose, or a minimum commitment of some kind, a Korean often maintains a courteous but determined silence. In nine cases out of ten, the silence has meaning, but few Westerners are able to do more than guess what the meaning is. If a Korean, for example, refrains from inquiring after the health of a friend who is ill, the omission is probably not accidental but intentional and is to be construed as a sign that his relationship with the friend has deteriorated. Although to refrain from direct action and direct speech in human relationships may be found characteristic of every human group, a system of behavior based upon such restraint is not found in many. Therefore the insistence upon communication by other than verbal, or written, means has tended to load the art forms with more than ordinary significance.

PART ONE

# Early Korea

WITH PLATES  2–19

FOLLOWING PAGE  49

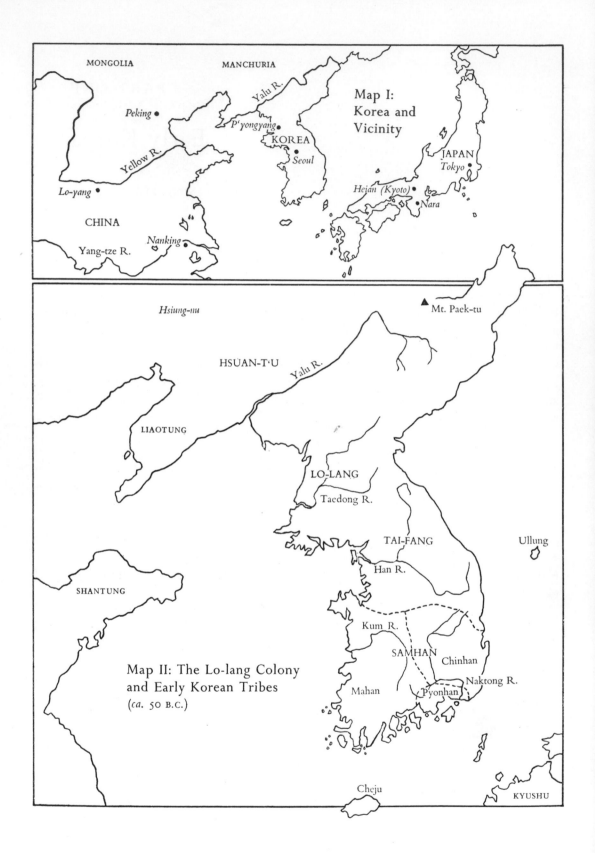

MONGOLIA          MANCHURIA

Peking ●                              Map I:
                 Yalu R.             Korea and
          P'yongyang ●               Vicinity
             KOREA
Yellow R.      ● Seoul                        JAPAN
                                              Tokyo
Lo-yang ●                          Heian (Kyoto) ●
                                              ● Nara
CHINA

Yang-tze R.    Nanking ●

Hsiung-nu                                    ▲ Mt. Paek-tu

              HSUAN-T·U
                            Yalu R.

        LIAOTUNG

                         LO-LANG

                      Taedong R.

                              TAI-FANG                    Ullung

                           Han R.

SHANTUNG

                        Kum R.

     Map II: The Lo-lang Colony        SAMHAN       Chinhan
     and Early Korean Tribes                            Naktong R.
     (ca. 50 B.C.)              Mahan        Pyonhan

                                                        Cheju                KYUSHU

# CHAPTER ONE

# Beginnings

THE OCCUPATION of the Korean peninsula by man seems to have been inexplicably late. No paleolithic remains have as yet been conclusively identified, and the neolithic artifacts do √ not appear to antedate 1000 B.C.* Nevertheless, Korean myth and legend push the story back further into prehistory by associating the origins of the race with a god-man called Tangun whose kingdom in Korea is said to have been founded in 2333 B.C. Substance is lent to the myth of such an early occupation by the fact that the Ainu, or their ancestors, an "old human stock of wavy-haired and heavily bearded races,"[1] inhabited the Korean-Japanese area for possibly several millennia before the arrival of the Mongoloid peoples, and moreover have survived to the present in a group in Japan and in individual types in Korea. The evidence of folklore and anthropology therefore leads us to suppose that a people of Caucasoid stock were possibly the first inhabitants of the Korean peninsula.

The archeological relics that remain in the form of dolmens and menhirs cannot as yet be linked to these early peoples or even with certitude to later intrusions of peoples of Tungusic and Mongol stock. That the dolmens give impressive proof of a flourishing megalithic culture in prehistoric Korea is certain, but they also raise puzzling questions. The Korean dolmens are similar to European and some Asian megaliths but not to Chinese or Japanese types, there being none at all in those general areas.† The closest in type to the Korean dolmens are to be found in west India and Syria. It should also be noted that the Korean dolmens appear to occur much later than elsewhere, some perhaps as late as the time of Christ.[2]

Tradition and Stone Age remains of prehistoric Korea offer us important clues to Korea's origins in addition to many furnished by language, customs, and religious practice, and therefore deserve more than passing attention. The founding myth of Tangun and the

* Postwar Japanese research has used carbon-14 dating to establish pre-Jomon culture in Japan as far back as the seventh or sixth millennium B.C. and possibly even further back than that. Chinese scholars have reported mesolithic sites in Manchuria which seem to antedate 5000 B.C. (See Cheng Te-k'un, "Archeology in China," in *Prehistoric China* [Cambridge, England, 1959], Vol. I, pp. 41–44, 47.) The results of both Chinese and Japanese research show affinities with known cultural remains in Korea, thus indicating that when archeological studies in Korea are made, artifacts may be identified which will more than support the dating of Korean myths. It is the theory of Professor Gordon Hewes that the sinking of western coastal lands may have submerged old neolithic sites in Korea.

† Sueji Umehara, *Chosen Kodai no Bunka* (The Ancient Culture of Korea) (Kyoto, 1946), chap. iii, pp. 34–47. Manchuria must be included in a discussion of ancient Korea. Several dolmens of the north Korean type are also found in north Manchuria.

later story about the Chinese scholar and colonizer, Kija, have become a part of the Korean heritage and should be regarded as symbolic of the facts imbedded in the account of their origins. The stories differ somewhat from founding myths current in China and Japan and should therefore be attentively examined for peculiarities that are typically Korean. The Tangun story, translated from the Korean history in which it first appeared, is as follows:

"An ancient record relates: 'In olden times there was Hang In. His son, Ung, born of his concubine, desired for himself an earthly life and wanted to be among human society. The father, knowing his son's intention, looked down upon the San We and the T'ai Po and came to the conviction that his son might bring some benefits to mankind. The father gave his son three talismans and let him go. Ung descended with three thousand followers onto the top of Mt. T'ai Po under the trees of the sacred altar, which place was called the Divine Place. He had command over the Wind Noble, the Lord of Rain, and the Lord of Clouds. Therefore he had to attend to the planting of grain, the regulation of human life, of sickness, of punishment, and he had to judge good and evil; in short, he had more than three hundred and sixty affairs to direct. In this world he regulated all metamorphosis.

" 'At this time there were a bear and a tiger who lived together in a cave. They often prayed to the god Ung [because] they wished to be transformed into human beings. Ung gave them a miraculous wormwood stalk and twenty beads of garlic. He instructed them to eat these and not to see the sunlight for one hundred days. Then they would easily acquire human form. These the bear and the tiger took and ate. They remained in seclusion for three times seven days, and the bear acquired the body of a woman. But the tiger had not been able to abstain [from looking at the daylight], and so it was not possible for him to attain a human body. The bear-woman could not find anyone to marry, whereupon under the trees of the altar she prayed to become with child. Ung changed his form and married her. She became pregnant and bore a son, and his name was Tan Gun.' "[3]

A pictorial version of this story appears in a Han dynasty tomb in Shantung (Plate 2). Here a sort of moving picture of the chief acts is presented in strip sequences on the mortuary slabs, illustrating the various dramatic episodes. In the first register at the left is represented the departure of the god Ung from the heavenly abodes. He is riding in a chariot drawn by three dragons, preceded by an honor guard of three other dragons with Spirits riding on their backs. A procession of dragons and other deities riding on curlicue-shaped clouds (Tangun's three thousand companions?) accompanies him in his descent to earth.

In the second register there appear several figures symbolizing the powers of nature: at the far left, the Lord of Wind expelling a gale from his mouth, followed by the Lord of Thunder striking two drums with his hammers; then the Lord of Rain with a water jar, and an arched dragon with a head at both ends, symbolizing the rainbow and bearing on his back the Lord of Lightning with his curling whip. Around the Lord of Lightning are several attendants, air-borne on clouds. Under the rainbow there is what appears to be a human being, a small wingless creature about to be killed by order of the Lord of Lightning. He is accompanied by two other human beings with upstanding swaths of hair. This scene supposedly illustrates the text: "He had command over the Wind Noble . . . the regulation of human life . . . he had more than three hundred and sixty affairs to direct." The number 360 doubtless refers to the affairs of the three hundred and sixty days of the agricultural year.

The third register presents a human-headed bear with a bow on his head, a sword in his left hand, and a hooking weapon in his right. There is a shield held by the bear's right foot and a spearhead or mace by his left. With the bear is another animal which is depicted with slanting eyes and feline ears and is seen drawing a tiny figure from its mouth. In the Korean story it is the bear who gives birth to Tangun. Here it appears to be the tiger. It is possible that the Korean version is a deliberate shift from tiger to bear in deference to a dominant ethnic group in Korea identified with the bear cult. The bear in the Chinese version, obviously posturing with his martial equipment, appears to be doing a ritual dance. All other figures are running towards him, possibly to watch the ceremony. The fourth register presents an agricultural and hunting scene, no doubt depicting the life on earth of Tangun's people. The god appears as their leader or chief, mounted on a horse.

On another slab in the same shrine appears the representation of the first and last scenes described above; i.e., a representation of heavenly beings coming to rest on the highest of three peaks (identified in Korea as Myohyang-san) where heaven and earth are joined, where the mountain peak is in truth "the point of juncture between the human and the spiritual world."[4]

In this story the three worlds of the divine, the human, and the subhuman are brought together in order to show in a dramatic way the mixture of all three in the origins of the Korean race.* In the reference to the tiger and the bear, which appear to serve as symbols, at least two dominant cultural components in the early composition of the Koreans seem to be acknowledged. Bear and tiger cults were widespread in north Asia in the first millennium before Christ. The bear cult is now almost extinct except among the Ainu of Japan and a few Siberian peoples. The worship of the tiger continues in vestige form in Korea, where it is now associated with the worship of the Mountain Spirit, who has a side shrine in almost every Buddhist temple in the country. Two thousand years ago, tiger worship was the chief religious activity of the Ye people living in central Korea. In China the aspect dealing with the tiger's giving birth to a human being may have been eliminated from the pantheon of the ruling classes about the time of middle Chou. Certainly the representation of the act of drawing a human figure from the tiger's mouth appears to have been a very ancient concept that disappeared from Chinese bronzes, as far as we know, after the eighth century B.C.[5] The question that arises here is naturally in relation to the interpretation of the two animals in the Korean myth.

Are the bear worshippers associated with a pre-Mongoloid people akin to the Ainu, and are the tiger worshippers associated with a people loosely defined as former inhabitants of the north China plain who, after the fall of Shang, fled eastward into the Korean peninsu-

* Some modern interpretations of the Tangun myth significantly point to Western origins for the Korean people. Professor Ryu Imanishi believed that Tangun was a Tungusic deity when Tungusic peoples occupied northwest China. See his *Chosen Shi no Shiori* (A Guide to Korean History) (Seoul, 1935). Kim Che-won, Kim Chi-yong, and others have written learned accounts pointing out that Tangun was worshipped by peoples living in central or north Asia long before he was associated in the Korean tradition with the origin of the Korean people.

la? There is little to guide us in these suppositions except the symbolism. Whatever elusiveness of evidence as to ethnological derivations this story may be subject to, it supplies us with clear clues as to the northern rather than the southern origins of the dominant Korean racial strains. Later additions to the myth are from Taoist sources (the talisman, the magic wormwood, the transformation of animals into human beings) and of shamanistic embellishment (stone altars associated with Tangun and the building of rock piles as points of contact between the spiritual and the human worlds). That educated Koreans as early as the fourteenth century brushed aside the whole myth as a fabrication designed to deceive the people regarding the divine origin of the ruling caste is well illustrated in the comments of the scholar Kwon Kun.[6]

When we turn to the information about Korean history furnished us by archeologists, we are on firmer ground. The evidence supplied by a study of neolithic artifacts, culled from village dump heaps (the shell mounds), from graves, and from ancient dwelling sites, confirms the theory of northern origins. The artifacts have been classified according to the materials from which they were made: stone, pottery, bone, or shell *(Plate 3)*. The stone implements include both polished and chipped objects, of which the latter, characteristic of neolithic culture in Siberia, are represented in Korea only in the northeast (the last area to emerge from Stone Age culture), whereas the polished implements, including the ubiquitous stone sickle, are found all over both Korea and central China.

Neolithic pottery, found in abundance in Korea, has been classified into three types roughly corresponding to three stages of neolithic culture.[7] The earliest or comb-marked pottery was of a simple shape: a bowl without handles, stand, or lid, similar to a primitive type found all over the Siberian and north European continent but strangely missing from China and Japan.* In Korea it was found in sites located along rivers or on the seacoast, indicating without doubt that the people who made it depended upon water for fishing and communication. This type of pottery was decorated with parallel wavy lines—hence the name "comb-marked." The second type in time overlapped to an important extent the comb-marked pottery. It was undecorated, was brownish in color, and had a greater range of shapes, sizes, and functions. It was found in hilly and inland sites as well as in the valleys. It was also discovered in Japan. Some scholars have associated it with the first wave of Tungusic peoples in the Korean-Japanese area. The third category of pottery, red-colored, thin-walled, and often painted with oxidized iron designs upon a polished surface, resembles Japanese Yayoi, thus indicating the possibility that the people who produced it were contemporaneous with and perhaps akin to the people who produced early Japanese Yayoi culture.

* Recently comb-marked pottery has been found in Kyushu.

# CHAPTER TWO

# The Transition Period

THE MOST striking proof of basic differences between the early cultures of China and Korea may be found in the variety and excellence of the so-called Scytho-Siberian bronzes found in many widely scattered sites in Korea which date from the period of the brief Bronze Age. "This point is of special interest," says Sir George Sansom, "because it helps to account for an important phenomenon in Far Eastern history—the preservation by Korean culture of a strong individual character despite the powerful influence and the propinquity of the advanced civilisation of Han China. It is largely because Korea was not merely a channel by which Han civilisation was passed on to Japan, but a terrain in which cultural elements from various sources were combined before they were transmitted, that from its beginnings Japanese culture presents such a marked idiosyncrasy."[1]

The transition period of roughly the first three centuries before Christ includes both the Bronze Age and the Iron Age cultures. Since most bronze artifacts were found in conjunction with iron objects, the conclusion is that Korea had no true Bronze Age at all. The theory that the Iron Age began at the time that the Chinese established Lo-lang cannot be proved. From the evidence at present available, no one can say when iron was introduced or even by whom the new technology was brought to the peninsula, but owing to the vast changes that ensued because of it, a review of the problem is included here.

Before a consideration of either the bronze or the iron remains is attempted, however, it is necessary to take note of another impressive set of early monuments which lie astride the stone and metal ages in Korea: the mysterious dolmens. They are present in sufficient numbers to testify to a flourishing and widespread dolmen-building culture, and yet they are missing from China and Japan except for areas contiguous to Korea. This is apparently another strong indication of the non-Chinese nature of prehistoric culture in Korea.[2]

Several theories have been advanced about the dates and uses of these great rock monuments. Professor Umehara's explanation is that the dolmens belong to the transition period because of the cists containing metal objects that were discovered in some of them.* He also feels that the dolmens were burial monuments for chieftains or kings. Megalithic culture in general, wherever it appeared, is thought to have developed at the close of the

* Umehara, *op. cit.,* pp. 56–57. It is possible, even probable, that the late dolmens in both north and south Korea were erected after the third century B.C. Nevertheless, a more hoary antiquity is indicated for most of the great free-standing dolmens of the north. A study on this subject has been published by Kim Won-yong: "Sokki Sidae ui Seoul" (Stone Age Seoul), *Hyant'o Seoul,* Vol. I (Seoul, 1957).

neolithic period because of man's sudden sense of power over his environment and his consequent feelings of exultation and achievement when he learned to grow and store his food and was freed from the uncertainty of a hunting and fishing economy. The fact that all dolmens are located on low ground in fertile rice-growing areas, and not in the mountains, leads us to suspect that the people who built them were settled agriculturalists rather than hunters or fishermen. Some scholars are convinced that the dolmen builders were sun worshippers who constructed these heliomegaliths as altars for worship.[3] The sun, with its paramount power over day, night, wind, rain, and other elements upon which the success or failure of the crops depended, may well have been the center of worship of a simple race who cultivated rice (some rice was raised by many neolithic peoples of the Far East) or other grains, chiefly millet. During the neolithic period the chief tool was the hoe, and the work was largely the responsibility of the women, as was the case with the North American Indian at a much later date. Then, with the introduction of the ox-drawn bronze- or iron-tipped plow during the transition period, a radical change occurred in primitive economy and culture in general.

The economy could and did sustain a vastly increased population. Patriarchal social organization began to take the place of matriarchal customs; the women, who had had charge of agriculture and sericulture of great economic value, yielded their prerogatives, and the labor force became largely male. Furthermore, labor tended to become enslaved under the domination of vigorous new rulers from the outside who doubtless took the initiative in introducing the new technology. The religious practices and customs of the primitive neolithic peoples did not, however, die out under the new economic and social systems of the Bronze and Iron ages, and the result was that, during the transitional period, the ancient sun worship appeared to blend with shamanism to produce Korea's most enduring religious institution. Modern shamanism, despite the crudity of its superstitions, continues to play a subdued part in the mores of the people. A mixture of demonology, nature worship, and magic, it is controlled by a class of women known as *mudang*. It is patronized by every class; it penetrates deeply, as we have seen; and it is as old as the memory of man. In north Korea, however, the mudang are not permitted to practice.

The relics of these ancient religious practices are of four kinds: menhirs, dolmens, rock altars, and seven-stone arrangements *(Plates 4, 5)*. Some of the monoliths retain their original shapes; others have been inscribed or carved into the likeness of the Bodhisattva Maitreya (Miruk in Korean), who is represented as a standing rather than a seated god.

The dolmen usually consists of five or more slabs of rock, of which four are arranged to form a pedestal and one, much larger than the rest, is laid as a cover across the others.* The relatively small pedestal capped by an enormous cover is common in north but not in south Korea, where a smaller, rounder capstone usually covers lower boulders arranged in a circular formation. The dolmens are sometimes arranged in groups, the most impressive of which is a Stonehenge of forty dolmens spaced at regular intervals about equal in size, facing in the same direction and extending in a line over sixteen hundred feet long.[4]

* W. Gowland, "Notes on the Dolmens and Other Antiquities of Korea," *Journal of the Anthropological Institute*, Vol. XXIV (1890), pp. 316–31. One top stone measured nearly fifteen by thirteen feet over a chamber six feet square by three feet high.

The question arises as to how the new technology—first bronze-, then iron-using—entered Korea and from where it came. Judging by archeological evidence, the probable routes by which bronze culture entered the peninsula were along the river valleys running from Manchuria into Korea. Caches of knife money of pre-Han mintage were found in at least six sites in this area. About five thousand pieces of this money were recovered.[5] Other, later sites yielded Han mirrors, coins, long daggers, and arrowheads with triangular cross-sections—all of common Han derivation. Although the sites where these objects were found were occupied by non-Chinese tribes, the objects themselves were clearly Chinese in origin, showing that an important stream of cultural advance was China-derived. We must turn to tradition and legend for other clues for this. The Kija legend, ascribing to a Shang refugee, Chi-tzu or Kija, the honor of bringing into Korea advanced methods of agriculture, architecture, and government, is by way of being a Korean acknowledgment of many other cultural borrowings such as the innovations in agriculture referred to above (wet rice culture and the ox-drawn plow, irrigation, sericulture, wheat cultivation), the construction of walled cities, introduction of wheeled vehicles, and writing.

As to when the innovations took hold in Korea, there is little sure evidence. Probably the process was gradual and scattered, wet rice cultivation coming from central and south China into southern Korea from areas outside the periphery of the Shang and Chou empires. The process must have been immensely accelerated after the Han empire came into being, and the Chinese set up direct contact with Korea through the Lo-lang (Nang-nang in Korean) colony and the other commanderies established in northeast Korea in 108 B.C. This colony unquestionably became the chief agency by which Chinese culture penetrated the Korean hinterland after that date.

The Kija legend, therefore, appears to be an interesting combination of fact and fiction. Stripped of its reference to Kija, it may be interpreted as a symbolic acknowledgment of the cultural borrowings, the waves of immigration, and direct contact through the Lo-lang colony—all rolled into one story to depict the important transmission of Chinese culture to Korean soil during Korea's "transition" period.* A significant statement in the Kija legend is to the effect that Kija and his followers did not impose the Chinese language upon the Koreans but learned the native language, which may be construed to mean that great as the debt to China was, it was not the complete or even perhaps the dominant source of Korea's culture.

In spite of their importance as civilizing agencies, the Chinese colonies, therefore, were far from being the only means by which Korean tribes obtained knowledge of technological processes of an advanced type. In fact, it is likely that the Chinese were particularly careful to keep information about the forging of metals, such as weapons, from the native tribes. How then did the Korean tribes get their technological knowledge? Abundant evidence exists to prove that some of the nomadic tribes to the north of China knew how to forge weapons as well as did the Chinese, at least to the end of the second century B.C.[6] and it is

* George M. McCune, "Notes on the History of Korea: Early Korea," *Research Monographs on Korea,* Series I, No. 1 (Ypsilanti, Michigan, 1952), p. 6. Some modern Korean scholars are inclined to dismiss the whole Kija legend as nothing but propaganda of early refugees from China.

from these Scytho-Siberian sources that the Koreans appear to have derived an important part of their early culture. Mixed with the artifacts mentioned above as showing clear Chinese derivation, were many of marked nomadic origin. Weapons, certain mirrors, kettles, horse equipment, buckles, and bells show Scytho-Siberian influence. The short daggers (as opposed to the two-foot daggers of Han make) and arrowheads of rhomboid cross-section were conspicuously non-Chinese. Kettles and other utensils show both styles.

More interesting than the weapons, perhaps, were the bronze bells. Some of them were doubtless cattle bells; others were used for war, religion, and amusement. The casting of bells, moreover, is another ancient and honorable tradition in Korea which has been maintained down to modern times.* It is worth while, therefore, to note the early appearance of bells on Korean soil. A horse bit found in south Korea had jingle-bells at either end, and an eight-pronged ornament found near it had eight bells *(Plates 6, 7)*. The decorations on these objects—saw-tooth bands and fine-line patterns in bands, medallions, and isolated curlicues—are found in every Korean art period after this time as decorations on pottery, wedding boxes, walls, bricks, mats, and other folk-craft objects in simple but characteristically Korean patterns.

An anchor-shaped object with two attached jingle-bells and a bell-shaped head made to fit the top of a wooden standard, together with a quantity of bell-shaped objects called *dotaku* by the Japanese, exhibit strongly Scytho-Siberian styles and shapes *(Plate 8)*. Moreover, all are decorated with parallel lines and saw-tooth patterns. The mysterious dotaku, often of very large size, have been found in Japan in great numbers, but not in China. The same saw-tooth design and geometric sections filled with either fine or coarse parallel lines decorate several unique bronze mirrors *(Plate 9)*. Fortunately, molds which were used in casting this type of mirror were excavated, thus testifying to the fact that they may have been produced locally *(Plate 10)*. Only about ten of these mirrors have been found. (The Han mirrors, however, come largely from Lo-lang sites, the other objects from areas inhabited by Korean tribes.) A pair of belt buckles in the Scytho-Siberian animal style were found in North Kyongsang Province *(Plate 11)*. Both buckles are about eight inches long. One represents a type of Mongol horse, the other a tiger. Both were important for their supposed prophylactic qualities as well as their function as belt clasps. The decoration on them is identical with that on the objects mentioned above. "All this proves," says Umehara, "that the bronze culture that came into Korea was not simply Chinese but Scytho-Siberian . . . it can also be found in north China."[7]

Although the metal objects from this period are the most interesting, the pottery is not to be overlooked. The plain brown pottery mentioned above as the second general type to appear in neolithic Korea persisted into the period under discussion. At the same time a third type appeared: red-colored, thin-walled, and painted—similar in range of shapes to the Yayoi pottery of Japan, as has been indicated above. A gradual development during the transition period of a fourth type of pottery—bluish wares decorated with wavy lines and crosshatching—constituted the prototypes for later Silla pottery. Funeral urns of this type were found in south Korea, but none in the Lo-lang area.[8]

Five distinct types of tombs characterize the transition period. They are the dolmen,

* Two of the largest bells in the world are still extant in Korea. See Chapter 7.

34

the cist, the cairn, the urn, and the wooden chamber. They date from different times and different areas, and all may be found elsewhere on the Eurasian continent. Each may point to a different ethnic group present in Korea at the time. There is no way at present of knowing which group built which type of tomb, but some generalizations may safely be made. The cairns were associated with nomadic culture, whereas the urn, the cist, and the dolmen appear to have belonged to agrarian cultures of north and south China, and the wooden or brick chamber to the strongly commercial classes of imperial Han.

A question naturally arises at this point about the peoples who left the remains described above. In the earliest Chinese histories all the tribes inhabiting the Mongolian plateau and the Manchurian-Korean forest were lumped together under the generic term "the nine Mo," who were supposedly Tungusic in stock. It has therefore been impossible, from early Chinese records, to identify the Mo as far as separate ethnic groups are concerned. The *Shih-ching* and the *Lun-yu* mention the Man and the Mo—the Man as being the most important savages of the Yangtze, the Mo as first among the barbarians of the northern desert. The Mo were described later as people evacuated from the Mongolian steppes and crowded eastward into Manchuria and Korea by nascent Turko-Mongolian tribes who occupied the plateau. The peoples already inhabiting central Manchuria in the two centuries preceding the Christian era called themselves "Wei," but the Chinese, regarding them as ancient Mo stock, simply referred to the resultant mixture as Wei-mo.* This term also appeared in the early Korean histories. Another vaguely related Mo people were the Sam-han in south Korea. The founder of the ruling house of Silla had the family name of Mo (read Pak in Korean).[9]

With the rise to power of Mao-tun, chief of the Hsiung-nu, and his annihilation of the only other strong confederation of tribes in Mongolia in 221 B.C., the Turko-Mongol peoples known as the Hsiung-nu grew strong on the Mongolian plateau, and the Tungusic people were crowded even farther eastward in the lowlands of Manchuria. These people retained their nomadic economy, specializing in cattle raising and, in particular, in horse breeding and were far closer to the culture of an ethnically different group on the steppes than they were to the culture of south Korea. The Mahan, for example, who at the time of Christ occupied the southwest coast of Korea, were sedentary rice growers, not herders; they lived in unwalled villages, not stockades, and they used horses sparingly, the plowing being done by oxen.

The Manchurian tribe which was destined to bring into Korea a new cultural complex, symbolized by the mounted warrior, was in close contact with similar horse-using nomads of the steppe area. Its rise to power was gradual, extending over four hundred years, and is especially interesting to historians inasmuch as these people constitute an important link between the mounted warrior of the steppe and people of the same cultural characteristics who were rising to power at this time, not only in Manchuria but also in south Korea

* The name Mo, as the Chinese used it, seems to have applied to neolithic populations in north and east Asia: peoples who still had matrilinear social structures and shamanistic religions. The name Wei seems to have been applied to Tungusic peoples already living under Shang patrilinear social organization and using bronze. The combined term Wei-mo probably roughly covered the mixture of earlier and later arrivals in the Manchuria-Korea region, as well as their descendants who, like the Koguryans, learned to use iron.

35

and Japan.[10] The four-hundred-year period of the rise to power of Koguryo coincides with the period during which both Korean and Japanese societies were apparently becoming stabilized. From all the available evidence, it appears that Koguryo played a leading role in this process, but since the records are scanty, it is necessary to piece together many scattered bits of information. The Koguryan peoples were described by Chinese travelers in the third century A.D. as lavish in the use of metals. They trafficked in prisoners; they built permanent stockaded camps; they buried their dead in huge tombs; and, in addition to breeding cattle, "they loved to travel on horseback"[11] and engaged in a form of horse worship and horse sacrifice at burials. The chief determinant in their rise to power appeared to be the knowledge of the uses of horses and iron.[12]

To summarize: sometime during the second millennium before Christ, and probably in greater momentum after 350 B.C., the various peoples living in the Korean peninsula went through a transition period in which Tungusic and Mongoloid invaders appropriated the peninsula as their chief and final home, emerged from neolithic culture, and developed rapidly under the impetus of new technical knowledge of agricultural methods and metallurgy. Closely bound by blood and way of life to Scytho-Siberian peoples and continuing to carry on a lively traffic with these restless nomads, Korean tribes at the same time developed strong and permanent ties with China.

Chinese technical contributions in the fields of agriculture and government, acknowledged by the Koreans in their Kija legend, were of paramount importance. Certain cultural characteristics associated with the Shang and the early Chou dynasties—such as partriarchal social organization as opposed to matriarchal societies, the use of bronze implements, respect for priest-kings and the city-state political organization, nature worship in which the deities were all of equal value, a sparing use of horses, rice cultivation, and a limited knowledge of writing—appeared in Korea during the transition period and were credited by Korean historians more than a thousand years later to the Shang official, Kija.

On the other hand, a strong tie with the steppe area of the north was an important feature of early Korean life. Technological contributions dealing with the forging and casting of weapons appear to have been learned from the steppe peoples rather than from the Chinese. It is not at all clear that the Chinese ever taught the primitive Koreans any skill that had to do with the production of weapons. The contrary may have been true. Iron mines and forges existed among the Koguryans, the Sienpi (Toba Tartars), and other so-called barbarians who understood iron-forging. The Koguryans, a people whose kingdom straddled south Manchuria and north Korea, were the tribe most strongly Scytho-Siberian in blood, economy, and culture, and it was they who acted as intermediaries between the steppe peoples and the sedentary populations of south Korea and Japan, which were related by blood but not by way of life.

During the transition period, then, Chinese culture took root in Korea; the Bronze Age came to a brief climax; the Iron Age developed; the amorphous and shifting tribes became organized into clearly defined political units; the separation of south Koreans from related peoples living in south Japan was completed; and the Korean race as we now know it took shape linguistically, socially, and culturally.

At least two major cultural patterns came to the top in Korea, the one linked with the non-Chinese nomadic economy of Mongolia and Manchuria and the other with the settled agricultural economy of wheat-raising north China and rice-raising south China. As time went on, these two major streams of cultural influence were reinforced by fresh contacts with both areas for many centuries. Then, in the seventeenth century, both streams were merged under the Ch'ing dynasty, and Korea was shut off at last from the invigorating free choice of cultural ties that it had enjoyed for some two thousand years before that date.

# CHAPTER THREE

# The Lo-lang Colony

IN 1913, Japanese archeologists uncovered the site of the ancient capital of Lo-lang Colony on the south bank of the Taedong River about six miles from P'yongyang. They also located on their nation-wide land-survey map more than ten thousand tombs in the general area belonging to this ancient colony. These early excavations, as well as those of other tombs uncovered during the seventy odd excavations done altogether, constitute one of the most brilliant chapters in the history of Korean archeology. The discovery of much beautifully made lacquer ware and handsome silver and gold luxury articles—the most perfectly preserved of any that had yet come to light to testify to the high achievements of Han art—formed a significant part of the finds. Five of the more famous tombs have been selected for comment below, along with a brief account of their contents.

The Chinese colonists who lived in this Korean outpost brought their families, their belongings, and their civilization with them. They also made use of local goods and materials, purchased imports of Scytho-Siberian origin, and started workshops manned by Chinese artisans and Korean helpers. Chinese and native techniques, materials, and tastes were thus gradually blended to form the foundations upon which all later Korean art was built.

Although Chinese cultural influences had undoubtedly penetrated the Korean peninsula long before the establishment of the colony, the impact upon the Koreans—then in a neolithic stage of development—must necessarily have been fragmentary. These influences, in fact, must have been a very thin trickle in comparison with the mighty flood that now began to enter Korea from Han China, which was then at the height of its new-found prosperity, vigor, and enthusiasm for all things new and different.

The effects of direct contact with this highly material culture, both upon the Korean populations living inside the boundaries of the colonies and upon those living outside, were profound and far-reaching. A flourishing trade* grew up between the Chinese colonists on the one hand and the Korean tribes on the other—Koguryo to the north, the

* Tax registers during the Former Han dynasty listed 62,812 families in Lo-lang. During the Later Han dynasty the figure stood at 61,492. (See *Ch'ien Han-shu*, 28, and *Hou Han-shu*, 33; also Alexander Slawik, "Die Chinesische Präfekturen (Kün) in Korea zur Han-, Wei-, und Tsin-zeit," *Wiener Beiträge zur Kunst- und Kultur-Geschichte Asiens*, Vol. VII [1933], pp. 5-13.) The loss of population may have been due to the absorption of runaway people by the surrounding Korean tribes. The "Han and Wei tribes became so strong and dominant that the *chun* and *hsien* [Chinese administrative divisions of Lo-lang] being unable to restrain them, the people flowed numerously into the country of the Hans [the Three Hans of south Korea, not the

fifty-four clans of Mahan to the south, and the twenty-four clans of Chinhan and Pyonhan to the east—as well as the Wo of south Japan.[1] An outpost trade of this type (in fact, strikingly analogous to it in many important particulars) was the trade and industry of the Greek cities of the Black Sea with the Sarmatians and Scythians of the hinterland, who were uncouth but eager paying customers.

That the acculturation which occurred in the Korean peninsula during the four-hundred-year life span of the colony was a slow but ultimately successful process may be deduced from the many vestiges of Han culture that may be observed in the Korean culture of the present. Han fashions in clothing, household gear, handicrafts, and even remnants of political and social institutions that came in at a moment of high achievement were gradually adopted, assimilated, and eventually made a part of Korean life. Examples of these cultural loans will be cited below. First, however, a brief outline of the history of the colony is desirable.

In 108 B.C., after a campaign that dragged on unexpectedly, the Chinese emperor Han Wu-ti overcame the small kingdom of Choson and set up in its stead four provinces or commanderies which, all together, comprised two-thirds of the area of the peninsula. This military-colonial arrangement lasted over twenty-five years. Then, after the death of Han Wu-ti, a retrenchment took place. Three of the four commanderies in Korea were discontinued, leaving only Lo-lang there and Hsuan-t'u in Manchuria. After this reorganization, which took place in 82 B.C., the situation continued substantially unchanged for the next three centuries. The colony was subject to shrinkage and expansion and periods of weakness and strength, and once a new colony was even formed to the south. However, during the first century of its life, Lo-lang's condition appears to have been one of general prosperity. In China the first century was one of peace which, only toward its close—during the usurpation of Wang Mang from 9 B.C. to A.D. 25—broke down into a period of general disorder. Border tribes like the Koguryo,* which had gradually risen in power, tested their strength by declaring their independence at the time when the central government was distracted. The death of Wang Mang, therefore, marked the end of the first

Chinese Hans]." This report from the *Wei-chih,* 30, is an important testimonial to the direction of flow of cultural dispersion.

Such a large population in the Lo-lang area did not thrive by means of agriculture alone. Had this been the case, it would not have paid the Chinese government to maintain the colony. Lo-lang was located at a crossroads of exchange with the Koreans and even with many Japanese tribes, and trade was its lifeblood. Although it was undignified for the members of the Confucian governing classes to engage directly in trade, many did so anyway, especially officials in outlying areas. (See Homer Dubs, "Wang Mang and His Economic Reforms," *T'oung Pao,* Vol. XXV [Leyden, 1940], p. 240.) The great Han Peace meant that goods could travel from Han outposts near the Persian frontier to the Han outpost of Lo-lang and from there to south Korea and Japan.

* In A.D. 12, the Koguryans refused to aid the emperor against the Hsiung-nu. The following excerpt from the Chinese annals *(Ch'ien Han-shu,* 96) gives information about the methods used by Chinese officials in dealing with independent-minded tribes within their orbit. "Yen Yu said to the Emperor Mang: 'The Mo people violated the law, have failed to fight, and their chief is Tsou. Treacherous as they are, you had better order your provincial and district officials to appease them. If you too hastily accuse them of treason, they may really revolt against you. Among the tribes of Fu-yu, there must be some who follow them blindly. At present the Hsiung-nu people have not been conquered, so if the Wei-mo should also rise against us, it would be a serious question.' " (Kurakichi Shiratori, "The Legend of King Tung-ming, the Founder of Fuyo-kuo," *Memoirs of the Research Department of the Toyo Bunko,* Series B, No. 10 [Tokyo, 1938], p. 5.)

Han empire and the consequent emergence of the old enemy of the steppes, the Hsiung-nu, for several decades of dominance before the second Han empire was firmly in control. The expansion of the steppe peoples threw all the other tribes in Mongolia, Manchuria, and Korea into restless activity and migration. In Korea, Lo-lang's capital, Wang-hsien, was in the hands of Koguryo for twelve years (A.D. 32–44), and three confederacies of Korean tribes—already loosely associated as political units that were to develop into the Three Kingdoms—grew bolder and stronger.*

The interlude of freedom did not last long, however, for the Han empire was restored in A.D. 25, and its control over outlying areas was very gradually reasserted. Lo-lang once more came under Chinese control, and its life of trade and commerce apparently continued without serious interruption during the rest of the first century and most of the second. The Chinese governors, in addition to the administration of their own territory, had the extra duty of keeping track of the activities of the surrounding tribes. This they did by granting titles to the chiefs, giving them gifts from time to time, regulating the trade, and arranging annual parleys.[2] The Korean confederacies, on their part, tried out their strength by wars with one another but seldom attacked Lo-lang. A few raids are recorded and a few kidnappings for the sake of ransom, but on the whole the Chinese policy of conciliation achieved results. There was comparative peace not only in Korea but also throughout the empire, while in the border areas the process of Sinification went steadily on.†

The third century brought a change. Toward the end of the second century, the Chinese house of Kung-sun gained control of the Hsuan-t'u commandery, then took Lo-lang, and in 204 set up a third colony south of Lo-lang between the Han and the Taedong rivers which they called Tai-fang (Taebang in Korean). The Kung-sun family remained in power for fifty years until, after the end of the Han empire, it was destroyed by the kingdom of Wei. Koguryo saw the possibilities, at this point, of playing off the three Chinese kingdoms of Wu, Wei, and Shu against each other. This was a dangerous game, however, and after initial success, Koguryo drew down upon itself an invasion from Wei in 244–45 and had its capital on the Yalu burned. After this event Lo-lang and Tai-fang were once more firmly incorporated under the Chinese control, first of Wei, then of West and East Chin. When East Chin in its turn fell, the governor of Liaotung attempted to assert his personal control over his commanderies, as Wei-man had done at the beginning of Han and Kung-sun had done at the end of Han, but this time the barbarian tribes were too strong. They took over the whole Korean peninsula themselves. In 311, then, the Hsiung-nu once more took north China. The Chinese governor in Liaotung failed in his attempt to protect his area from the Sienpi, and in Korea Lo-lang and Tai-fang soon fell to the Korean kingdoms of Koguryo and Paekche. Thus the long-lived colony of Lo-lang finally came to an end in A.D. 313.

We turn now to the material civilization of the colony, starting with its architecture. A

* Silla, 57 B.C.; Koguryo, 37 B.C.; Paekche, 18 B.C.

† During Wang Mang's regime, government schools were established in the commanderies as well as in China proper. Within one generation there was a body of educated men—all Confucianists—in all parts of the empire. As Confucianists, they were entitled to present memorials to the throne.

most important discovery was the site of the colony headquarters, which occupied an area some six hundred by eight hundred yards in extent—Government House, it might be termed, because a governor's seal was found on the site. Roof tiles indicated the location of a special ceremonial hall within the compound.[3] The wall, outlines of which remain, was made of rammed earth. The remains of what appears to have been a water reservoir were also discovered. The city wall was apparently irregularly shaped, unlike the typical rectangular form of the town walls of the Chinese plains. This irregular shape, in conformity with the terrain, became a feature of all later Korean walls and may best be seen in the remaining city wall of Seoul. It is interesting to note that this Korean variation in the city wall occurred so early.

From these finds we may deduce that official buildings were built of wood and brick, and roofed with tiles. They were apparently set upon fairly high platforms of pounded earth, faced with brick or stone, a feature of Chinese construction of the north China plains. The roofs were supported by pillars rather than walls and originally had straight, narrow eaves. Houses were often of more than one story, it also appears from the pottery replicas.

Building materials were, as seen from the shards and from tomb remains, brick, tile, stone, and wood. Chestnut was favored for light construction and the Mongolian oak for heavy timbers.[4] The bricks, small in size, unlike the large Chinese variety, and doubtless all the tile, were produced locally. Their production may well have been the first industry to grow up in Korea under Chinese tutelage. Certainly it developed ultimately into one of the most prominent of Korean industries, especially in the production of refined clay products of the ceramics type. Both bricks and tiles were decorated by means of stamping, incising, moulding, and carving. The designs were varied, and some were of a high artistic quality, over five hundred having been isolated and compared by Japanese scholars.[5] Some designs were geometric, some floral, some animal, and many bore characters giving dates and names of contractors or owners in a decorative use of the ideogram. Dates range from A.D. 40 to 404, the latter date confirming the continuance of Chinese styles in tile long after the end of the colony as a political entity. A brick bearing a date that corresponds to the year 288 was found among the debris of an ancient town site in Hwanghae Province that may well mark the site of the Tai-fang headquarters.[6]

Walls and doorways were simply constructed. Walls, not required to function as supports for the roof, could be treated as screens and constructed of lightweight materials. Some were plastered or whitewashed and some undoubtedly painted with scenes, especially in the women's apartments in wealthy homes, of pious subjects such as are found on the Painted Basket *(Plate 16)*. Doorways, as found in the tombs, were usually the simple post-and-lintel type, and the doors, composed of panels of wood, were flaps opening in the middle and swung on sockets in the upper and lower lintels. Some arched doorways occurred in tombs, and the arch principle was also employed in the construction of the concave walls and roofs of brick tombs to prevent cave-ins. This principle was early understood but later little employed except in the construction of bridges. Concave drainage ditches were also used.

Simple but effective methods of joinery used at this period may be studied in the construction of coffins—such as the cramp in hourglass shape, the tongue-and-groove jointure, and other varieties. Iron nails came into use in the later Han period. Some carpenter's tools, perhaps left by mistake in one tomb, such as mallets, wedges, and bolts, are all similar to types still present in the Korean carpenter's toolbox.[7]

Methods to prevent decay or insect destruction were apparently utilized. Pillars were placed aboveground on brick or stone supports, and no wooden part was put into contact with the earth except in the tombs. The pillars may also have been lacquered to preserve them.[8] Certainly coffins were lacquered and, although imported, were also sealed with lacquer, a testimony to the existence of local lacquering workshops.[9]

Houses were arranged to form courtyards, the commoners having one full court either surrounded by four narrow pavilions or partly surrounded by them in a U- or L-shaped plan; the nobles, on the other hand, having many courts in an axial arrangement. This plan has persisted to the present in Korean house planning. The southwest corner was considered the most honorable, the head of the family having his quarters there. The east was the vulgar side occupied by the kitchen and the servants' quarters or used for storage.[10]

Tomb construction during the Lo-lang period was of two general types: the wooden subsurface tomb and the shallow surface-level tomb.[11] The wooden type dates from the first two hundred years of the colony (ca. 100 B.C. to ca. A.D. 100), and the brick type from the second two hundred years (ca. 100 to 313). The wooden tomb, single-chambered and entered from the top, contained articles of use in real life, many of which were family treasures from the imperial workshops*; whereas the brick tombs, double-chambered and entered by a passageway, contained in general mortuary objects produced in quantity for burial with the dead but decidedly inferior in quality.

One tomb near Sogam-ni, labeled Tomb Number 9 yielded several spectacular finds, one a gold-inlaid buckle and another some gold sword fittings.[12] This tongued form of the buckle is interesting in that it is more like the harness buckle than the usual Chinese belt hook. Other buckles of the tongued type were found in Lo-lang tombs, as well as in later Three Kingdoms tombs, indicating perhaps a local preference for the type. The buckle from Tomb Number 9 (Plate 12) is about four inches long and about two and a half inches wide and is ornately decorated by means of a hammered gold ground on which are arranged seven dragons and a number of blue semiprecious-stone inlays. The one large dragon is easily identified, but the smaller ones are almost lost in the background of clouds and geometric borders. Two of the small dragons face each other to the left of the opening of the buckle; another is under the large dragon's chin, one between its legs, another above its back, and one above its curved tail. Gold granule beading outlines the spine of each dragon, and the rest of their forms are outlined by gold wire. Small teardrop shapes of gold wire formerly contained contrasting blue inlays, doubtless of turquoise, but only seven of these are still in place. The border of the buckle is bounded by a heavy twisted wire, and inside this there is another border of fine wire loops.

---

* Lacquer made in the imperial workshops and destined for court use was carefully inscribed with the names of all the craftsmen who worked on a given piece. The fact that inscribed lacquer pieces have been found in the tombs of border-area officials presupposes that the pieces were gifts made at the time of promotion or some other moment of triumph in the life of the official. See Otto Maenchen-Helfen, "Zur Geschichte der Lackkunst in China," *Wiener Beiträge zur Kunst- und Kultur-Geschichte Asiens*, Vol. XI (1937), p. 57.

The buckle, like so many of the best of the Korean finds, presents an enigma. There are few other pieces in all of Han art which show evidence of this filigree and granule technique that was known to the Greek silversmiths in a much earlier period. Mr. Griessmaier, in an exhaustive study, falls back upon attribution to non-Chinese sources for the inspiration of this piece:

"The appearance of the buckle in Chinese civilization is remarkable, since the hook in its different shapes was usual at that time. Both the material (gold) and the way it was used were unusual for the Chinese of that age. Gold was usually used only for inlay. . . . We are dealing in this buckle with a border region of the great Eurasian continent where local art mixes with other art fashions whose origins cannot be determined but have to be looked for in the interior of the continent. Rosenberg dedicated his wonderful work on granulation to Stryzygowski as an indication of a shift of emphasis from Asia Minor to Inner Eurasia as regards origin . . . and K. Hamada, in describing the Chinese myth of the golden bird from Hung-ming emitting nuggets of gold from Pi-kan for use in jewelry making, also points to a non-Chinese origin of the granulation technique. . . . The most significant picture of Chinese art may be had from a consideration of the technical aspects of this buckle, for it exhibits the full combination of goldsmith's techniques, hitherto unknown in this area. One can find parallels in the later art of the Korean kingdoms or, for contemporary or former times, in the art of the Scythians, Sarmatians, and later occupants of South Russia."[13]

The tomb of Wang Hsu may date from the second half of the first century. It contained largely furniture and household gear. Some of the designs which decorate the furniture should be noted because of their frequency on all tomb contents of the period; e.g., a dragon and a tiger depicted in action conveying an impression of great vitality, a decorative presentation of the Western Queen Mother with fairy attendants, a number of galloping animals done in yellow lacquer (to represent gold?), examples of many variations of the lozenge pattern—combined with coiled dragons, floral and geometric scrolls, and the double lozenge on silk gauze (still a popular pattern on the same kind of silk)—and the twisted rope design for borders, found most often on jewelry but easily imitated in painting on lacquer. A tortoise-shell box with a deft and delicate design of eight figures and four pert winged genii painted in black lacquer on the underside of the lid, and a handsome drinking cup of birch stitched at the sides—unique in being a lacquered object not of Chinese but probably of local origin—were two of the more unusual finds. The cup is "extremely simple but full of elegance, and is one of the most attractive pieces found in the tomb."[14] Among the odd pieces of jewelry found in the coffin of the tomb's female occupant were two beads, one of coral and the other of amber. Another object of interest was a lacquer tray that displayed the manufacturing technique used to prevent warping in such items of lacquer ware. Six pieces of wood were employed instead of one large piece; four of these were glued together in a line and held in place by a semilunar piece along each side (Figure 1).

The tomb of Wang Kuang dates from the time of Christ. About two hundred objects were recovered from this tomb, of which eighty-four were lacquered and thirty-four were inscribed, thus giving us a fairly accurate date for the tomb. The tomb and its contents

43

were in a good state of preservation. The coffins of Wang Kuang and his wife were finished
in glossy black lacquer. The tomb itself was
a simple rectangular chamber made of heavy
wooden timbers covered with a layer of
brick and then mud. In Wang's coffin were
found a hat, leather shoes, a sword, and a
lacquered sheath. It was unusual in the Chinese bureaucracy for a civil official to own a
sword, but life in the outposts in Han times
demanded it. The sheath was identical in
many ways with the sheath of a ceremonial
sword belonging to the end of the Huai
period, but the bronze *porte-epée* appears to be
unique. Hairpins, jewels, and rings were
found in the wife's coffin.

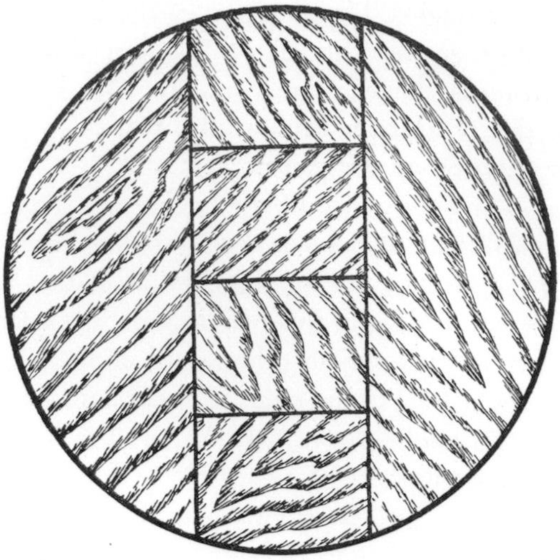

A number of *pei* cups were also found in
this tomb. The pei cups, oval in shape with

Fig. 1: Jointure technique to prevent warping of lacquer ware. Lo-lang period, 1st–3rd century.

flat ear-shaped handles, were the vessels "par excellence of the Han period," used widely among the poor and elegantly painted and supplied with silver-gilt or bronze rims and handles for the rich. A book that is still extant contains practical recommendations, dating from the sixth century, for preventing the red lacquer on the inside of such cups from being spoiled by salt and vinegar.[15] Other lacquer utensils in the tomb included spoons, ladles, and trays.

Of special interest are a cosmetic box, a chest, and a tray decorated with a medallion in which three dancing bears appear *(Plate 13)*. Two wooden seals give us information as to the identity of the man buried here. Some of Wang's dishes bear artistically placed characters reading: "Hail, Wang!" or "Long live Wang!" and so on. The tomb also con-tained five Han mirrors.

The Painted Basket Tomb dates from the turn of the first century. This tomb was built of logs laid alternately lengthwise and crosswise in a bricklike construction pattern. It is an example of the intermediate type between the earlier wooden and the later brick construction. Its contents also showed transition in that most of its furnishings were of the inferior mortuary variety, although some, including the Painted Basket itself, were of first-rate quality, intended for, and actually put into, a long life of daily use. The date of the tomb has been assigned to either the first century or the early second century, but the argument that two of the worthies depicted on the Painted Basket, Ting Lin and Li Shan, still lived during the latter half of the first century appears to settle the date, at the earliest, at the turn of the century.

The tomb had two chambers: the main room, containing three lacquered coffins, and an anteroom filled with objects, mostly of lacquer, floating in water. Among these was the Painted Basket, made of split bamboo. Its lid was close by, along with a number of chestnuts: an indication that the container had been used as a picnic basket. Baskets of this

44

size ($15\frac{3}{8}'' \times 7\frac{1}{8}'' \times 8\frac{3}{4}''$) and shape—two baskets of nearly equal size fitting one over the other—are still common in rural Korea for use as food containers. Some other plebeian objects similar to those still found for sale at country markets included a half-gourd, called a *pagaji,* a shallow willow basket in the shape of a large dustpan, and carpenter's tools.

A lacquer pot *(Plate 14)* whose worn-out bottom testifies to long use before its burial is a prime example of the good taste and utility of utensils intended for daily use. The pot is furnished with a lid which has a hole to permit its removal and is decorated with strips of gilt bronze which divide it into zones of black and red lacquer ornamented with flying animals and clouds. A case *(Plate 15),* similar in size, shape, and décor to present-day bride's boxes, is decorated in a lighthearted way with dragons and clouds and border zones of lozenges and clouds. A gorgeous red lacquer table, whose surface was elaborately ornamented with patterns in gold, silver, and other colors, displays the two general zones of decoration found on most of the objects: border areas in geometric design—a lozenge-and-cloud pattern—and a central area filled with unconfined moving clouds, animals, and imaginary beings.[16]

An item of special interest in the tomb was the presence of a number of wooden mortuary horses, for these provided evidence of the new practice of substituting images of horses for the real ones that had formerly been buried with important persons.[17] The mortuary horses had originally been supplied with manes and tails of fibrous materials and with bits and harnesses in lead and leather.

Small objects of value found in this tomb were the daggers and leather shoes in the man's coffin; the hairpins of tortoise shell, silver, and bamboo, the rings, and the bracelets in the coffins of the woman and the child; and the gold and silver buckles, remnants of yellow silk and hemp, and the rush mat found there also. A wall painting is also of interest as a link between Han mural painting and later tomb painting. Men on horseback can still be made out, though the mural is badly damaged. Better examples of the painting of the times are the figures found on the basket. To these we now turn.

Both basket and lid *(Plate 16)* are decorated with strips of lacquer on which are painted ninety-four figures framed in narrow bands of lozenge pattern. The center of the lid has a central sash of lacquer decorated with a long bronze ornament in double-lily form, whose tapering points at either end cut across three seated figures. The sides of both cover and basket are reinforced with lacquer bands decorated in lozenges and coils or triforms and by standing figures at each of the eight corners. Many of the ninety-four figures are named, a double precaution so that, though the characters depicted were familiar to all for their good deeds, they should be more readily recognized and emulated. Objects for the use of women and children were apt to be decorated with subjects inculcating good morals.

The rendering of these figures shows great mastery of medium *(Plate 17)*. Texture was indicated by breadth of stroke; hairlines were used to portray flesh; thicker lines, draperies. A light flesh tint was used for the faces of women and children, a darker hue for male faces. Patterns appear on some robes to create liveliness of design, and space is indicated by profile, three-quarter, and rear views of figures, as well as by hanging cords, looped curtains, and a screen that is placed on the diagonal.

The poses and gestures also show a close and shrewd observation of people, their ages, personalities, and other characteristics. The youthful Shan Ta-chia *(Plate 17, top, fifth from left)*, with his round face and heavy eyebrows, is expertly contrasted with the aged Po I *(Plate 17, middle, extreme left)*, whose thin hair and remaining teeth are skillfully suggested with a few casual strokes. Moreover, there is a sense of space and life and, most appropriate of all, a sense of design. Mr. Sickman has described these figures well:

"As in the Boston tiles, there is a strong impression of communion between the figures —their gestures are lively and natural; their poses, and even the folds of the garments demonstrate a close observation of reality. . . . Although the figures are posed on a baseline, they are not silhouetted against a flat surface. . . . Chinese figure-painting in the first two centuries of the Christian era had become an art of great capabilities."[18]

These figures are generally conceded to be the best examples of figure-painting that remain to us from Han times.

In the same tomb, a metal scroll holder *(Plates 18, 19)*, illustrating an entirely different type of scene, demands more than passing attention. Whereas the Painted Basket is decorous, with little movement, the scroll holder is characterized by exuberance of activity. Flying figures fit into a delightful landscape of sinuous mountains, slim bladelike trees, and curling cloud forms. Bears, peacocks, deer, birds, camels, tigers, and mounted huntsmen combine in a magnificent design of repeating and contrasting patterns—the tiger's stripes and the huntsman's sleeves, for example—and all appear to inhabit a world of speed and action.

The tomb of Wang Kun, near the site of the ancient government headquarters, was excavated in 1942. No complete description of it has been published because of lack of funds during the war.[19] The mound was about seventy feet in diameter, fifteen feet in height. A subterranean chamber, set inside a square pit, was constructed of wooden timber and reinforced with stone slabs. It was divided into rooms, each containing a lacquer coffin inside a wooden outer shell. In the coffin to the west were found a coronet headdress decorated with beads, a wooden pillow, a necklace, silver rings, combs, an iron sword with a lacquered sheath, silver ornaments for a sash, much silk stuff, and a silver seal with a tortoise-shaped knob. These objects indicated that a man had been entombed there. The name found on the seal was Wang Kun.

In the other coffin, the gilt-bronze headdress, necklace, earrings, rings, and a pair of bracelets indicated that a woman had been interred there, although the skeleton had entirely disappeared. The coffin also contained a seal with the name of the deceased on it, and a lacquer box containing glass beads.

Outside the coffin, mortuary objects such as weapons, harness, and parts of a chariot were found along the wall, bronze and lacquer objects along the north. The bronzes included several typical Han-style objects such as censers, sleeve weights in the shape of tigers, *chiao-tou* (dragon-head door handles), and a variety of other articles used in daily life. The lacquer ware included toilet sets, wine cups, and tableware. Among the weapons was found a crossbow, the wooden parts of which were in excellent condition. Also in good condition was the wooden shaft of a canopy on the chariot and its bronze rib tips. The animal style was apparent in the decoration of all the fixtures connected with horse equipment, chief of which was one horse mask.

The five above-mentioned tombs were all of wooden construction, and their contents

46

were of greater artistic merit than those of the brick tombs. All tombs, however, contained articles belonging to one of three categories: (1) furniture, clothing, and household gear; (2) weapons, chariots, and military gear; (3) symbols of religious significance.

Objects in the third category put us on more uncertain ground. Some authorities think that the great number of mirrors that were found indicate the presence of a mirror cult, the central idea of which was that spirits might reside in a mirror. Religious reasons for the presence of these mirrors in the tombs are to be considered, because the generally high-calibre articles were found in the early tombs and the poorer articles in the later tombs. The mirrors are generally superior in every way, but many appear to illustrate fashions current in later Han, not early Han. Their great number, preserved in good condition, has constituted a source of importance to our understanding of Han art in general. By 1930, about two hundred had been recovered; by 1945, the number had been very substantially increased. One design frequently found on the Korean mirrors was a band of saw-teeth projected inward.[20]

To what use were these elegantly decorated but humble objects of everyday life put? A consideration of their function is appropriate here. Furniture was sparingly used. What there was, was highly decorative and removable, permitting living space to be used twenty-four hours daily as dining room, bedroom, and living room, even in wealthier homes. During Han times, the Chinese did not use chairs, which came into fashion in the eighth century. Korean furniture still does not include chairs except for thrones and altars. Low tables of several types were found, some in gaily painted red lacquer for use during meals. Others were used for writing or study, or even as seats for exalted guests.[21] The table legs were carved and decorated, or rendered in a simple curved form, and joined to the table by tenons. Clothes and blankets were kept in chests, much as they are stored today. One gaily painted chest carried a decorative inscription with the popular good wish: "Long life, many sons and grandsons."[22] Woven mats were found on floors—one such was found in the Painted Basket Tomb—and were used to sleep upon in the summer. (Sheepskin was used in the winter.) Low platforms, protected by screens, were also used for sleeping. Screens were found around the coffins in a Sogam-ni tomb. Pillows were sometimes made of pottery, wood, or woven bamboo. Formal dinner services were made of lacquer and included the oval "soup" cup with handles, tureens, spoons and ladles, oblong flat-sided water bottles, and covered containers.[23] Basins, trays, and lacquer goblets were also popular forms. Among the bronze utensils were a nine-branched candlestick and a vessel for wine or oil.[24] Pottery jars of an unglazed thin-walled variety were numerous. Among the toilet articles and clothing found in the tombs, some of special interest have been selected for description below. Many tombs yielded fragments of silk, belt buckles of a tongued variety used for clothing as well as for horse gear, swords, combs, remnants of lacquered headgear that may have furnished one prototype of the present-day lacquered black hat, silk cords for tying socks, and leather shoes—all items of Korean apparel that can still be found in daily use.[25]

Hairpins, as well as other hair ornaments of gold, silver, and jade similar to those depicted on Han funerary stones, were found in most tombs. Women wore leather shoes with slender pointed toes quite like those worn for formal wear now. Earrings were also worn by

Chinese women of Han times, although it was considered a "barbaric custom." Their toilet articles were often kept in cases whose nests of little fitted boxes, repeatedly copied in later times, often in ceramics *(Plate 175)*, were a favorite form.[26]

These articles represent a small selection from the hundreds of objects that were found in the seventy tombs. The tombs, on the other hand, represent less than one percent of the number still to be excavated. It is obvious, therefore, that few conclusions should be drawn from such scanty evidence. Nevertheless, two statements may safely be made. One is that all the objects described above illustrate a Han art ideal of elegance and beauty so broad that it could include even humble objects intended for everyday use. The other is that all the objects and designs just discussed served as prototypes for articles and designs which later became familiar in Korean culture and remained long after the Chinese colony had disappeared from Korean soil.

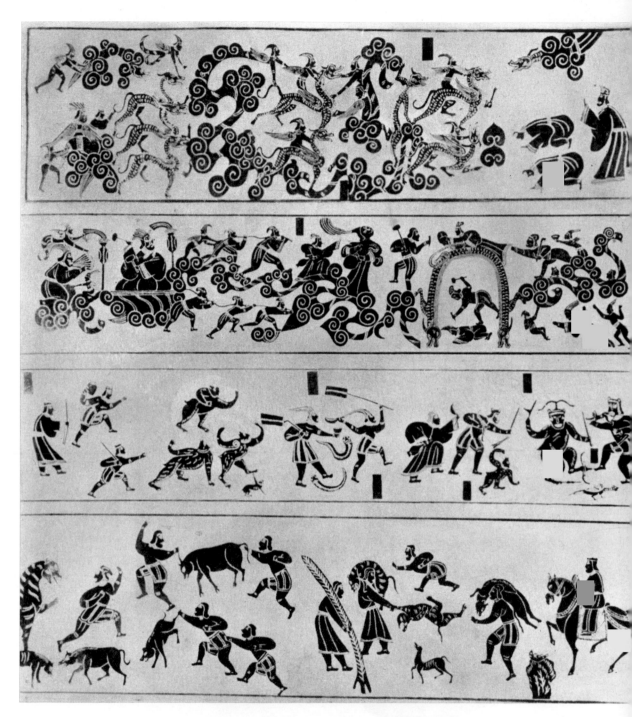

2: MORTUARY SLABS PORTRAYING TANGUN LEGEND (page 28). Tomb of Wu
Liang-tz'u, Shantung Province, China. Han dynasty, 206 B.C. to A.D. 220.
Height: 4 1/2'; length: 3 2/3'. After a drawing in the *Chin Shih So*.

3: NEOLITHIC ARTIFACTS (page 30). Excavated in North Hamgyong Province. A little less than half actual size. Prehistoric period, not earlier than 1000 B.C.

4: DOLMEN (page 32). Hwanghae Province. Length: about 20';
height: about 8'. Prehistoric period.

5: MIRUK (MAITREYA) (page 32). Vicinity of
Sunch'on, South Cholla Province. Height:
about 10'. Modern copy of an ancient style.

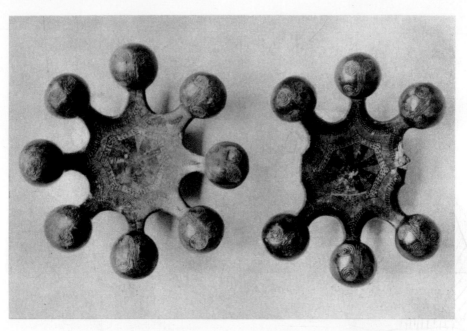

6: EIGHT-PRONGED ORNAMENTS (page 34). Copper. Excavated in Naktong River basin, South Korea. About two-thirds actual size. Transition period, 1st–3rd century B.C.

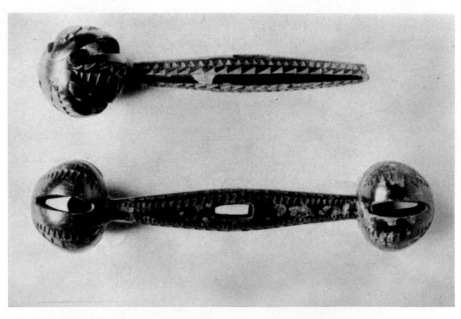

7: HORSE BITS (page 34). Copper. Excavated in Naktong River basin, South Korea. Length: about 7 1/4″. Transition period, 1st–3rd century B.C. Formerly in collection of Mr. Fusanoshin Ayugai, Tokyo; present location unknown.

8: DOTAKU AND OTHER RELICS SHOWING SCYTHO–SIBERIAN STYLES AND SHAPES (page 34). Copper. Excavated at Kyongju, North Kyongsang Province. Transition period, 1st–3rd century B.C. Kyongju Museum.

9: MIRROR (page 34). Bronze. Excavated in South Ch'ungch'ong Province. Diameter: about 4 1/2". Transition period, 1st–3rd century B.C. Formerly in the P'yongyang Museum.

10: MIRROR MOLD (page 34). Earthenware. Excavated in South P'yongan Province. Diameter: about 5". Transition period, 1st–3rd century B.C. Present location unknown.

11: BELT HOOKS (page 34). Bronze. Excavated in North Kyongsang Province. Length: horse, 6 1/2"; tiger, about 8". Transition period, 1st–3rd century B.C. Formerly in National Museum of Korea.

54

17: DETAILS FROM THE PAINTED BASKET (page 45). Lacquered bamboo. Excavated from Tomb of the Painted Basket, South P'yongan Province. Lo-lang period, 1st–2nd century. Formerly in the P'yongyang Museum.

18, 19: SCROLL HOLDER AND DETAILS OF DESIGN (page 46). Bronze. Excavated from Tomb of the Painted Basket, South P'yongan Province. Length: about 14″. Lo-lang period, 1st–2nd century. Tokyo National Museum.

60

PART TWO

# The Three Kingdoms and United Silla

WITH PLATES 20–116

FOLLOWING PAGE 101

Sienpi (Toba Tartars),
later Kingdom of Pohai

Mt. Paek-tu

Yalu R.

*Boundary of United Silla (715)*

LIAOTUNG

KOGURYO

P'yongyang

Taedong R.

Ullung

*Seoul*

SHANTUNG

Han R.

PAEKCHE

*Kongju*

*Puyo*

Kum R.

SILLA

*Kyongju*

Naktong R.

*Kimhae*

KARAK

Map III:
The Three Kingdoms
(*ca.* A.D. 300)

Cheju

KYUSHU

Yang-tze R.

# CHAPTER FOUR

# The Three Kingdoms:
# Paekche and Karak

GENERAL BACKGROUND    THE FIRST PHASE (57 B.C.–A.D. 313): Stimulated by the establishment, during the first century B.C., of the Chinese
colony in the northeastern part of the peninsula, Korean tribes, not quite a hundred
in number, consolidated into three confederations which gradually centralized in self-
defense. The dates of this consolidation are traditional and must be regarded as marking
a beginning only. No abrupt changes in tribal customs or tribal government apparently
took place. The bureaucratic organization of the Chinese colony under the *kun-myon*
(county-district) system provided an important model of centralized administration. Korean
chieftains who were within the colony were tutored by direct contact with it, and those
who were outside the area of direct control were within range of Chinese manipulation,
exploitation, or flattery as the case might demand. One of the methods used by the Chinese
officials to accomplish their objectives was to offer the Korean chiefs special annual gifts of
regalia: flattering symbols of rank such as swords, titles, and ceremonial hats. This last
type of presentation doubtless partially explains why Korean officials down to modern
times regarded their hats as the most important part of their official garb. This combination
of cultural and political penetration of Chinese government into Korean life caused Koreans
from that date on to regard foreign culture as exciting and desirable but politically dangerous.

Under the catalyzing effect of the Chinese colony, the cultural development of all three
kingdoms took place at about the same rate, although Koguryo was slightly ahead from
the start. As might be expected, the greatest advance was noted in the capitals of the three
areas, whereas the peoples living in the many isolated valleys remained at a neolithic level
long after the use of iron and bronze was well established in the towns. The chief cohesive
forces that brought about the slow cultural advance of the Korean peoples were a growing
similarity of modes of life (fishing and hunting, as well as farming, in the marine and
mountain areas; cereal and fruit.cultivation in the lowlands), a common language, the
necessity to unite in larger political units against common enemies, the retention of the
old shamanistic religious practices in all three kingdoms, and last, the gradual acceptance
of Chinese political and social institutions centering on the family and the state rather than
on the tribe or the clan. The Korean clan social structure, in contrast to the Chinese, had

63

operated democratically. Decisions were made by conclave, and leadership was in the hands of the able or the supposedly able, such as sorcerers and sorceresses. Women were often hailed as powerful leaders, as in early Japan. The gradual change favored the upper classes and was therefore favored by them, inasmuch as it took power away from the tribe and concentrated it in their hands.

The material culture of the early Three Kingdoms catered to two chief groups: those living in areas with simple rural demands and the more sophisticated court. Implements and utensils were made of metal, basketry, pottery, leather, wood, and gourds. The manufactures included wooden carts, boats, and furniture; hemp and silk textiles; leather belts, shoes, and harness; iron hoes, plows, and cooking pots; bronze and inlaid ceremonial objects like the dotaku bells, daggers, and mirrors.

The religious practices of this first phase of the Three Kingdoms era appeared to be of five general types. First, there was sun or sky worship, which emphasized Shang Ti in China or Hananim in Korea and included star worship (the Great Bear and other constellations, twenty-eight in all) and worship of the weather powers (thunder, rain, cloud, wind). Second, there was sacrifice to the earth and the spirits of mountains, rivers, and crops. Third, the ancestral spirits were thought to be a part of the family, not entirely separated by death. Fourth, divination was practiced to discover the will of Heaven. And fifth, the shaman was used as intermediary between the world of spirits (largely evil) and the world of men, especially in the attempt to control disease and similar calamities. Shrines were built, and sacrifices of eggs, fish, meat, and cereals were made at stated places and times, at graves and sacred groves. A belief in a life after death requiring the same sort of material comfort as was available in the mundane world persisted in Korea until well past the middle ages, resulting in the custom of burying much treasure with the dead. The tombs of royalty were supplied with worldly goods and chattels, including live servants and concubines, until at least the sixth century.* They were built with as great care as palaces and were located in the most beautiful scenic spots the country afforded. Even today the dead command better sites for their burials than the living for their homes.

The kingdom located in north Korea, Koguryo (Kao-chu-li in Chinese), began as a small tribal unit whose headquarters were near Paektu-san on the upper reaches of the Yalu River. It grew until it included half of Manchuria and, after the fall of Lo-lang in 313, all of north Korea. The traditional date of founding was 37 B.C., and the traditional founder was Chumong, younger son of the king of the Fuyu of north Manchuria. The three capitals were located on rivers, two on the Yalu and one on the Taedong. P'yongyang, on the Taedong, became the main capital after 427. The people were martial, engaging in annual warfare. There was little raiding upon Lo-lang, however, with which commercial ties were strong.

Paekche was traditionally founded in 18 B.C. by Onjo, a younger son of the king of

* This custom was practiced on a larger scale and for a longer period in Korea than it was in Japan, although in both countries the practice of burying living retainers about the tumuli of kings was associated with a material culture using iron which was derived from central Asian and Chinese sources. See Carl W. Bishop, "Historical Geography of Early Japan," *Report of the Smithsonian Institution*, Vol. LXVI (1925), p. 558.

Koguryo—a tradition which links up the ruling houses of people who occupied contiguous lands all the way from north Manchuria to Japan. Onjo, it appears, had little difficulty in establishing himself as ruler over the fifty-four Mahan tribes, whom he ruled from several headquarters, all near modern Seoul. The location of Paekche was on Korea's west coast from near the thirty-eighth parallel south to the tip of the peninsula.

Silla occupied the eastern half of the peninsula. Silla, or Kyerim (Forest of the Cock) as it was called at first, was founded by Pak Hyokkose, who was, according to tradition, elected by a confederation of Chinhan tribes who made up Silla in 57 B.C. There was one capital well to the south, at Kyongju, sixty miles from Pusan, which remained the capital for the thousand years of Silla's existence.

The art of contemporary Lo-lang and of the "transition period" extends throughout the first phase and has already been described. Moreover, no Korean tomb or tomb contents dating from the Three Kingdoms period can be dated with certainty before the fourth century. Therefore it will be necessary to move on into the next four centuries, the "second phase" of the Three Kingdoms, before we can find the Koreans producing a truly native art.

THE SECOND PHASE (313–668): Until Lo-lang fell, the Korean kingdoms grew very slowly under the watchful eye of the mighty Han dynasty. After the Han collapsed and China disintegrated into numerous petty kingdoms, the three Korean states entered upon their great period of independence. In both China and Korea the next four centuries saw much barbarian blood absorbed into the populations; many barbarian innovations adopted; much building of new palaces, fortresses, and shrines; and constant warfare among rival kingdoms. One of the greatest of the innovations, if not the greatest, was the adoption of the foreign religion, Buddhism. In China the Toba Tartars promoted Buddhism on a grand scale under the aegis of the Northern Wei dynasty. In Korea, Koguryo and Paekche adopted Buddhism officially in the late fourth century. Travelers went to central Asia and India and by means of such contact with contemporary civilizations greatly enriched the mixed Han Chinese and Scytho-Siberian inheritance already present in strong measure.

The first phase of the Three Kingdoms, then, was one of gradual acculturation under Chinese auspices and the second, of independent and rapidly accelerated development under the stimulus of the Indian religion, Buddhism. In art the surviving remains give us a fair glimpse of the painting of Koguryo, the ceramics of Paekche, and the goldsmith's art of Silla.

PAEKCHE: 350–663    The history of Paekche during the three hundred and fifty years between the fall of Lo-lang and its own fall in 663 was marked by fruitful foreign relations with south China on the one hand and with the emerging imperial clan in Japan on the other, and by intense rivalry with the other two Korean kingdoms. Paekche's relations were with south China, which was reached by sea, north China being cut off by Koguryo's occupation of all the land routes to the north. Numerous missions were exchanged between south China and Paekche as long as Buddhist powers were in control in Shantung and the Yangtze valley,[1] but after the T'ang dynasty was established, and before Buddhism came into favor at the T'ang court, strongly Buddhist Paekche was viewed with suspicion.

Japan's foothold on the Korean peninsula had at first centered in the small state of Karak, with its capital at Kimhae, but collapsed when Silla conquered Kimhae in 562. The Japanese next concentrated on friendly relations with Paekche, and during the whole of the next century (562–662) the ties between Paekche and Yamato were close and mutually stimulating. In 662–63, combined Paekchean and Japanese forces were defeated by T'ang and Silla armies converging on Paekche, and that country went down to a Carthaginian defeat. Over a hundred thousand Paekcheans were taken as captives to China, and probably as many fled to Japan, where they were welcomed as educated or skilled additions to the Japanese state. That many of these Korean refugees were of the upper class is attested to by the names in the Japanese list of nobility, about a third of which were Korean or Chinese.[2]

Important dates in Paekche's history are the following: 384, when Buddhism was officially adopted (Hinayana or the Lesser Vehicle, introduced by Marananda, an Indian or west Asian monk who was sent by the king of East Chin to the king of Paekche); 393, when the crown prince went to Japan on what appears to have been a good-will mission; 405, when two Korean scholars, Wani and Achiki (Wang In and A Chi-ki in Korean), were sent to Japan as tutors to the crown prince; and 552, when Buddhism was officially adopted in Japan. Paekche capitals, as Koguryo in the north grew stronger, were moved twice, farther south each time: from Namhansong on the Han River to Kongju on the Kumgang in 478 and to Puyo, near Kongju, in 538.

Thus we see that Paekche, situated in Korea's most fertile land and possibly the area in which Korea's most dominant culture, her language, and her arts first developed, became a "bridge of learning" for Japan. Paekche's prosperity and high culture found expression in the great Buddhist temple-cities and in the many-faceted Buddhist art that we know flourished there. Monks, students, books, and goods flowed between Paekche and China and again between Paekche and Japan. Japanese culture during the reign of the Empress Suiko (593–628), for example, was inspired and tutored by Koreans, and early Yamato institutions, both religious and administrative, were shaped by Paekche scholars, architects, artisans, priests, and courtiers.[3] Fenollosa, an American who had a unique opportunity to study Japanese art treasures at close hand, was one of the first to see Korea's role as a transmitter:

"Corea, in some real sense, was a link between the two; and for a moment, about the year 600, her art flared up into a splendour which fairly surpassed the achievements of her two chief rivals."[4] Further comments on the nature of the art that flowed into Japan from Korea at this time raise provocative questions. For example, "Some European writers have appeared to hold that Corean art in the sixth century must have been influenced quite specially by the art of Persia. This seems to be due to their assumption that Persian art in the sixth century was like what it became after contact with Mongolian races after the thirteenth century and onward."[5]

There was little left in Korea itself, however, to witness to the calibre of Paekchean culture after T'ang and Silla armies had razed the palaces, destroyed and looted the temples, and desecrated the tombs. The foundation stones of some of the temples do remain, nevertheless, to testify to the great size of these centers of learning and culture, and shards of brick and tiles that have been discovered at these sites also give us more than a glimpse of the taste and refinement which characterized the Buddhist art of the times. One must look to Japan, to the Horyuji, which is still functioning as a holy place, to see an example of what the Buddhist art of Paekche must have been like in its original environment.[6]

Among the extant remains in Korea, the tombs in the vicinity of the three capitals of Paekche offer the best clues as to construction methods and materials. The earliest tombs appear to have been of the cairn type and were located in the basin of the Han River within a day's journey of the first capital. The later tombs were tumuli, one type with a small, vertical pit admitting only one person, and the other with a large stone chamber entered through a lateral passage. The second type showed affinity with the Lo-lang tombs, whereas the first was of unknown derivation. A feature of interest in the stone-chambered tomb was the construction of a floor by means of a thick layer of small white river pebbles—a local resource of generous supply—which were laid on the ground. The ceiling also was made more sightly and less boxlike by a beveled edge between the top of the walls and the ceiling.

For a short time apparently tombs were built of brick. One such, called Number 6, of Songsan-ni (Kongju), had a feature unique in Korea though common enough in Indo-China: a vaulted ceiling. Both the use of bricks and the arch construction were Chinese importations. Moreover, the bricks were similar in size and shape to a south China variety, not the Lo-lang type, and were laid in alternate vertical and horizontal blocks. Subterranean channels, also made of bricks, were constructed to drain off the water, and small niches were let into the brick walls to accommodate Buddhist images. One tomb near Kyongju was built of blue bricks. The stone tombs were frequently composed of granite slabs of great size, highly polished and often decorated with paintings of the Four Spirits and other themes similar to those of the murals of Koguryo. The paintings, however, have nearly all disintegrated, although one, of an overall lotus and cloud pattern, is clear enough to be made out. Some bricks are decorated with the name of the Chinese dynasty Liang, thus reinforcing literary testimony as to the strong ties that Paekche enjoyed with Liang (502–57).

Little has been found in these tombs, but a few bits of jewelry, a *magatama* (curved jewel of the type found in Japanese neolithic sites), and a crownlike helmet appear to show that Paekchean nobles, like the nobles of the other two kingdoms, wore gold earrings, necklaces, and headdresses, as well as clothing woven with golden threads.

Other than tombs, little of the architecture remains. Several temple foundation sites near Puyo and ten or twelve pagodas are all that may now be seen. These, however, show that Paekchean architects had advanced ideas for the time and that they understood the use of a variety of materials: stone, brick and clay tiles, wood, plaster, and bronze. The temple plan was the same as that which characterized the temples of the Asuka period in Japan. The large rectangular enclosure was oriented on a north-south axis, and its entrance gate was directly in line with a large pagoda, the "golden" or main hall, and a lecture hall —all enclosed in a gallery. The eating and sleeping quarters appear to have been outside

67

the sanctum. At least six sites of Puyo temples were discovered in 1940. The pagoda of one of the largest of these, Chongyim-sa, has survived *(Plate 20)*. It is one of the oldest extant pagodas in Korea and is also, perhaps, one of the most beautiful.[7] It is often mistakenly called the "pagoda of the conquest of Paekche" because the T'ang general, Su Ting-fang, after his conquest of Paekche and the destruction of the temple itself, left on its pedestal an inscription describing the T'ang victory. This pagoda, still standing in simple dignity among the rice fields around Puyo, gives in its proportions an impression of massive strength very different in feeling from that conveyed by the delicate soaring spires of later pagodas. Each tier, with its slightly upturned eaves, is slightly smaller than the tier just below it, and the pagoda thus has a square and solid look. Characteristic of the Three Kingdoms pagodas are the four corner shafts of the lowest story. The temple to which the pagoda was attached may have served as a model for the Shitennoji in Osaka, which was built according to the same plan and measurements.[8]

Eight ornamental wall tiles discovered in 1938 at the site of one of the temples in Puyo constitute without doubt the most important Paekche discovery to date.[9] These tiles are each about a foot square. They are made of gray paste, and the design is rendered in relief by means of molds. There are four pairs, each pair illustrating a different subject. The first pair *(Plates 21, 22)* show landscape designs composed of stylized rounded mountains, rocks, and cliffs, along with the symbol for clouds which we saw in the Koguryo murals. Simplified trees appear on the mountain tops, and in the second tile the Firebird of the South, or phoenix, is seen astride the highest hill. In the center are seen three houses and a lantern or a stele. The first tile in the landscape pair has the interesting addition of a human figure near the bottom which appears to be that of a priest walking towards a building in the center. Decorative touches are the spraylike sprigs of grass that dot the whole landscape. The next pair of tiles *(Plates 23, 24)* are of fairly deep relief and bear the representations of two standing figures of monsters called *kwi–hyong* by the Koreans. These figures are conventionalized, recalling the ancient *t'ao–t'ieh* that appeared on early Chinese bronzes but recalling even more vividly the monster figures that were painted as caryatids on the walls of the Koguryo tombs. The first monster stands on a lotus pedestal, the second on rocks. The third pair of tiles display the reliefs of two of the Four Spirits of the cardinal points: the dragon and the phoenix *(Plates 25, 26)*. Both dragon and phoenix are shown in extremely stylized form within medallions that are encircled by roundels of beading. The four corners have been filled with sections of a four-petaled flower design. On the last pair of tiles *(Plates 27, 28)* the decorations are floral. They too are placed in roundels edged with beading and have ornamental sections of the four-petaled flower design in the corners. One has a ten-petaled lotus and the other a design of clouds and flames. The flame design is similar to the flame spiral found in a P'yongyang tomb. The tiles are superior in design and execution, and their chance discovery provided evidence of the widespread practice of an advanced art.

Excavated at another of the temple sites in or near Puyo were several Buddhist figurines of a type doubtless produced in quantity during the heyday of the capital in order to supply worshippers with sacred objects for home use. One of these figurines is a gilt-bronze Bodhisattva about four and a half inches in height *(Plate 29)*. In its archaic facial features

68

and its rigid stance, it exhibits all the characteristics of the Wei period in China. The figure is cast in a flat, two-dimensional form, not in the round, and may have been part of a group. There are traces of pigment on the hair and eyes. The crossed scarves, saw-tooth drapery, princely crown, and headdress in the Indian fashion were all "in style" during the Toba Wei period. The raised left hand with the downturned fourth and fifth fingers was a gesture frequently used in Korean Bodhisattvas of this period.[10] The arrangement of the hair in pigtail-like swatches must have been popular in the iconography of the period, especially in Korea and Japan. A Japanese example can be found in the Kannon of the triad at the Horyuji dating from 623. Another Paekche Bodhisattva, apparently from this period, is inscribed but not dated. It is a small Maitreya standing on an inverted lotus socle, its hands in the usual *abhaya-vara mudra*. The inscription tells us that it was donated by one Chong Chi-won in memory of his wife, Cho Sag-gyong, who "died too young. . . ."[11]

At this point a word should be said about the nature of the "bridge of culture" between Paekche and the young, centralizing Japanese kingdom of Yamato. Under the aegis of Shotoku Taishi, the foreign religion of Buddhism took deep root in Japan. However, foreign teachers and technicians were needed, and in 577 Paekche sent a number of specialists to Japan, including an ascetic, a teacher of meditation, a nun, a reciter of *dharanis* (magic formulas), makers of images, and temple architects. In 588, two more temple architects, a caster of pagoda spires, tilemakers, and painters were sent.[12] Korean temple architecture was transplanted to Japan, and so we must turn briefly to the Horyuji, near Nara, to see what Paekche temple art must have been like, and particularly what the great central images must have been like, since the small figurines of the period can scarcely show us this. The Kudara (Paekche) Kannon is one of these great images. Carved from a single block of wood, more than life size, with accentuated height and slimness and little modeling, this image is one of the outstanding examples of the so-called Six Dynasties style of religious sculpture remaining to us in all of east Asia. The crown and sidepieces, as well as other metal ornaments attached to the wooden image, were done in the openwork technique that was a highly developed and long-established art in Korea. A small gold crown ornament that Dr. Sekino excavated from a Paekche tomb is so similar to the openwork on the crown of the Kudara Kannon, as well as to the metal border on the Tamamushi Shrine, that he regarded it as the link between the art of Paekche and that of the Horyuji.[13]

Another Horyuji statue in the Korean style is the Yumedono Kannon, which in 1884 was unwrapped from its encasing five hundred yards of cloth by Ernest Fenollosa, the American who was commissioned by the Imperial government to list Japan's national treasures. The image so dramatically uncovered was listed in the temple's inventory of 761, but "till the present era it has been kept jealously concealed by monks."[14] Fenollosa considered this image and the Tamamushi Shrine to be the two outstanding examples of Korean art of the Asuka period. The metalwork on all these objects is the connecting link between them and with Korea. The Sekino ornament and the border designs of the Tamamushi shrine; the Kudara Kannon's crown, the flame-shaped halo of the Yumedono Kannon, the stylized foliage and the flame designs on Paekche tiles are all of a kind, exhibiting

69

the vital "dragon line" first seen in Korea in the work of the Han lacquerer centuries before and appearing in all the major media of the work of the Three Kingdoms period thereafter —in the curling, curving, blossoming cloud, vine, and flame shapes that so handsomely characterized the art of the entire period.

There are other isolated evidences of links that may be noted in passing. The bamboo-like support of the Kudara Kannon, for example, is carved in the same fashion as the stone pillars of one story of the *tabo-t'ap* pagoda at Pulguk-sa. The *mitsuda* painting on the Tamamushi Shrine was done with a mixture of white lacquer and oil—a technique which, though introduced to Japan through Korea, was ascribed by Chinese scientists to Persian sources. This ascription, however, suggests a later date than that of the shrine, thus posing a question as to the source of Paekche's knowledge of the technique. An almost identical technique of painting, though in colored lacquer, was well known in Korea. "The style is that of the Chinese Six Dynasties transmitted through the medium of Corea."[15] The rock formations appearing in the Tamamushi paintings, which are described by Stryzygowski as appearing around the year 550 in the landscape backgrounds of the art of Ravenna and Ajanta,[16] occur in the Paekche tiles described above, in an eighth-century sculpture of a horse-headed guardian at a Silla tomb, and under the Bishamonten at the Horyuji. All, perhaps, stemmed from a Hvarneh landscape of Iranian origin.

Paekche thus appears to have been the recipient of continental art influences from central Asia, north China, and more importantly still, south China from the period of Liang Wu-ti on, when Indian influences entered directly into Chinese Buddhism. Paekche assimilated these diverse art styles, receiving its inspiration and guidance through the contiguous Chinese and Korean kingdoms in sporadic waves contingent upon the fall of some local dynasty and the institution of a new ruling family—a process that required a hurried adjustment between the courts through diplomatic missions. Buddhism was the means of communication between the courts of many petty kingdoms of sixth-century east Asia, and Buddhist art travelled with the envoys.*

Paeckche in the sixth century had time to develop under benign influences, and it was the result of this high achievement that was passed on to a discerning and awakening Japan. Paekchean art, even when examined in scattered remnants, shows its derivation from Chinese models. It also shows its independence. A prototype may be found in Chinese art for each of the features of Paekche art that we have noted above. But the manner in which such features were combined, the exaggeration of certain characteristics—the height, for example, or the feminine quality of a Bodhisattva—the partiality for the nude figure so unacceptable to the Chinese, the innovation of adding openwork metal ornaments to figures of wood or clay or of leaving off all such ornamentation for the sake of startling simplicity—these aspects appear to have constituted the important elements of the Paekchean style that was transferred, for a short period of tutelage, to Japan.

* Osvald Sirén, "Indian and Other Influences in Chinese Sculpture," in *Studies in Chinese Art and Some Indian Influences* (London, 1936), pp. 31–34. Sirén suggests that Gupta styles may have inspired the North Ch'i sculptures of Shantung via south China and Cambodia. Comparisons between some Pnom Penh and Korean figures of the period show interesting similarities: the smooth nude torso and the treatment of the upper lip, lower lip, eyebrows, and cleft in the chin. The cleft appears in the Horyuji Shaka and Amida but disappears from Japanese art after the Asuka period, although it persists in Korea.

KARAK: 42–562:     Karak was a tiny principality located on a beautiful stretch of the south
Korean coast with its capital at the site of the modern naval base of
Kimhae. Its history in Korean records extends from A.D. 42 to 562. Karak was largely
dominated by some sort of Japanese control, especially between the years 350 and 562.
It is not usually counted as one of the kingdoms of Korea but as an appendage of Silla,
which is what it became after 562. Some excavation has been done in the royal tombs
around Kimhae, and some effort has been made to determine the characteristics of Karak's
culture. Apparently there was little if any difference between the culture of this kingdom
and that of the surrounding area. Two examples of Karak art have been selected for inclusion here: a pagoda *(Plate 30)* from Koryang, in South Kyongsang Province, with the
characteristic corner shafts and stepped supports for the cornices that are seen in the Paekche
pagoda *(Plate 20),* and a group of ceramics *(Plate 31)* illustrating common shapes and
designs of the pottery and metal utensils of the times.

# CHAPTER FIVE

# The Three Kingdoms: Koguryo

THE TERM "tumulus builders" is most appropriate for the Koguryans, for they left well over ten thousand tombs in one area alone: the Yalu capital of the T'ung-kou plain. The tombs have been opened and looted long since, probably by the T'ang dynasty soldiery at the time of the destruction of Koguryo, but the murals have survived to furnish us with one of the most valuable sources in Asia for a knowledge of the painting of the fourth, fifth, and sixth centuries.[1]

Koguryo moved its capital south in 427 but maintained its strong position in Manchuria and north Korea by virtue of an alliance with Northern Wei (439–535). As long as this alliance was operating, Koguryo flourished, but when a Chinese dynasty, the Sui (598–618), regained control of north China, the position of Koguryo was radically altered. The Sui could not afford to leave a former ally of the Wei—a power, moreover, which was non-Chinese—in control of south Manchuria and north Korea, so they launched three costly and unsuccessful campaigns against Koguryo in 598, 612, and 614. The failure of all three campaigns contributed substantially to the downfall of Sui and left Koguryo weakened but still independent. T'ang T'ai-tsung also tried his hand against Koguryo in 645, but he failed to crush the kingdom—his only major defeat in a long life of victories. He did, however, acquire control of the Manchurian possessions of Koguryo, and the loss of these proved fatal to it. Eighteen years later, Koguryo fell under the combined attack of T'ang and Silla.

Koguryo's power and prestige were at their height from the middle of the sixth to the early seventh century, during the period of the Sui dynasty. Important dates in Koguryo's history are the following: 372, the introduction of Buddhism and Buddhist learning; 414, the erection on the Yalu of a monument whose 1,800 characters recite Koguryo's history to that date, as well as the achievements, wars, and glory of King Kwanggae Toji, in whose honor it was raised; 427, the removal of the capital to P'yongyang; 598–614, the Sui invasions; 645, T'ang T'ai-tsung's invasions; and 668, the destruction of Koguryo.

The architectural achievement of the Koguryan builders must have been impressive in its day. Some of the step-pyramid tombs measured two hundred feet square at the base, or roughly half the size of the Egyptian pyramid. Tremendous stones, fifteen by nine feet, were found rolled into position at the bases of the Koguryan tombs. The monolith of King Kwanggae (Plates 32, 33) also gives evidence of considerable engineering skill in mounting and erecting and of knowledge of stone masonry in the carving of some 1,800 Chinese characters that compose the inscription on its four faces. A part of this inscription, incidentally, is an instruction on how to preserve the monument itself for posterity.

Walled fortresses were built in commanding sites overlooking the plains and lowland farms. One such castle was built behind the T'ung-kou plain on a cliff overlooking a Yalu tributary stream.[2] The mountain peaks behind were used as part of the castle's defensive fortifications, which were, in all, five miles in circumference. A stream was planned to run through the castle enclosure and to merge at right angles to the castle gate in order to provide cover for this open spot in the overall defense. There appears to have been a reservoir within the fortress enclosure, as well as a palace where many artistically decorated tiles were found. Other similar castles were built on the T'ung-kou plain and at P'yongyang. These castles are nothing but rubble now. The tombs, on the other hand, have survived fairly well—well enough, at least, to show us construction types, methods, and materials. There were three types of tombs: the step pyramids, the great tumuli, and the cairns. The step pyramids are to be found only on the Yalu; they are older, and contain no murals. The mounds, on the other hand, are of later construction and may be found both on the Yalu and to the south, and they usually contain murals. The P'yongyang mounds, having been built last of all, contain murals that are in every way superior to the ones found in the Yalu tombs.

The tumuli were square, not round, and thus showed that Chinese ideas of round mound building had not yet penetrated to this remote spot. They were oriented to the four points of the compass. Their chamber walls leaned slightly inward, and the vaulted construction of the ceiling was topped by a single slab. These domed ceilings were generally made up of eight corbels, three of which were parallel to the walls and five of which were across them. As for the treatment of the walls, all were stone, some were plastered, and others were smoothed, polished, and painted. The stone masonry in all the tombs showed a high order of skill in the cutting, fitting, and finishing of large blocks of hard stone like granite and buff breccia. It is the mural decoration of these tombs, however, that constitutes their chief claim to glory.

Allowance must be made for the fact that the art of the murals was provincial in style and was rendered by lower-class craftsmen on order, as was the rule in ancient China.[3] The colors of the wall paintings have dimmed or become smoke-begrimed and have often been partially or entirely obliterated by water stains. The paintings that have survived, however, show a wide range of rendition from coarse and naive designs to refined, delicate, and masterly creations that are among the best we have from the ancient Orient, furnishing a connecting link in the history of painting from Han times to the mature, fully developed Buddhist painting of the eighth century.

One important Han feature to be seen in the Koguryo tomb art is the portrayal of movement. The flying wisps of cloud, the flying angels, the winged sprites, and the galloping animals that constituted such an attractive part of the Han lacquers may also be seen in the tombs. Another characteristic of Han lacquer decoration, the broad floral or geometric border, is also a conspicuous feature of the tomb murals. Further developed than it was in the Han lacquers is another characteristic: the attempt to show three dimensions in landscapes in combinations of mountains, trees, and figures *(Plate 1)*. A special feature of the

Koguryo murals which was also characteristic of Han mural art is the effect achieved by the lavish covering of all available surfaces, a style ultimately associated with the religious ideas of the times, which undertook to illustrate the afterlife of the dead and to depict in exaggerated but nonetheless vivid detail the supramundane world in which the dead were thought to live. This new world was indicated by a new treatment: a reproduction of the terrestrial and celestial world within the tomb itself. The lower part was painted to represent the terrestrial world. The four corners were painted to represent pillars and brackets in order to suggest that the tomb was the interior of a house, and scenes of daily life, together with depictions of flowers, trees, human beings, and animals, covered the four walls. Sometimes a man and his wife—the occupants of the tomb—or even a man and two wives are seated in state on the wall opposite the entrance, while on both sides are depicted household activities to comfort them or bands of dancers or wrestlers to amuse them, and on the wall directly facing them is painted the outdoor scene they are supposed to be viewing: hills, trees growing in a field, flowers.

The upper part of the tomb, the corbeled dome, on the other hand, was painted to represent the celestial regions, one merging imperceptibly and by stages into the other. On upper corbels were clouds, stars, the sun and the moon, and flying figures of many kinds. The subjects used for the tomb decoration, therefore, while appearing at first glance to be scattered, disconnected, and confusing, all serve to portray the future life and all fall into one of three general groups which constituted the stock in trade of the tomb artists. While the subjects were conventional, depicting the general religious ideas current in northeast Asia at the time, the details of costume and accoutrement were local and original, as were the widely varying ways of rendering the same cut-and-dried theme. (Compare, for example, the different treatment of the "Dark Warriors of the North" in Plates 42 and 51.)

The subjects used in the murals, then, may be classified as (1) the whole group of heavenly spirits, (2) the genre scenes, and (3) the stylized floral and geometrical decorations. The first category includes the Four Spirits of the cardinal points of the compass, the three-legged crow, the toad in the sun and the rabbit in the moon, which we are told were "characteristic of Koguryo worship,"[4] constellations of stars, demigods, and all sorts of delightful angels and spirits. The genre scenes of the second category are valuable in furnishing us with historical data about the customs and dress of the times but as a general rule are artistically somewhat insipid and naive. They include the personages for whom the tomb was built (always presented in larger size than the less important persons), courtiers, knights in armor, hunters, priests, musicians, dancers, and the like; and the scenes that are depicted are calculated to amuse and divert the important ones: scenes of dancing, wrestling, hunting, and so on. Certain details of dress, such as the pleated skirt, the upturned toes of the shoes, the baggy trousers, and the white headcloth, are significant in that they appear in the national dress of present-day Koreans. Such features of the warrior's equipment as his plumed, helmet-like cap and the "buzzing" arrow went out of style with the dynasty,[5] although the stirrups, the short bows adapted for use on horseback, and the sword with the ring-shaped pommel were certainly used much longer.[6]

Without doubt some of the most perfect paintings of the whole class of mural art are to be found in the third category, the floral and cloud designs. Appearing in single designs

*(Plate 35)*, in medallions *(Plates 37, 38)*, in borders *(Plates 34, 36)*, and in overall designs, these paintings show in large measure a deftness of brushwork, a liveliness, and a sure sense of design that continue to capture the interest and admiration of artists of the present day. To permit understanding and appreciation of the paintings in their settings, five of the more important Yalu tombs and four of the P'yongyang tombs will be briefly described below.

Tomb of the Dancers: There are two chambers in this tomb: a main room, which is square, and an antechamber, which is rectangular. As noted earlier, the tomb mound is square; the chambers are generally rectangular; and the walls, slanting slightly inward, are plastered and are topped by a corbeled ceiling. The customary painted pillars and brackets appear in the corners, and the lavish decorations covering every inch of the surfaces are unusually well preserved. The three lower stories of the corbeled dome are parallel with the walls. There are odd-looking triangular designs in a row along the first stage *(Plate 39)*, floral scrolls along the second, lotus blossoms alternating with buds on the third, and signs of the firmament (circles joined by three parallel lines to indicate constellations, all in their proper astronomical positions)[7] amid flying clouds and celestial beings on the fourth to eighth stages.

On the back wall are the two main human figures seated on stools. They are enjoying a number of activities that appear to be going on simultaneously both outside and inside the house. On the right are musicians and dancing figures, and on the left a hunt is in full swing, while on the wall facing them are two trees in a field with clouds above: a scene suggestive of the outdoor view visible to the two chief figures. The five dancers *(Plate 40)* are of both sexes. They are depicted with arms outstretched and with long, narrow sleeves covering the hands, flung backwards. Below the dancers is a row of seven men and women singers. Pleated skirts, long overlapping tunics, baggy trousers, and pointed shoes complete the costumes. It is interesting to note that the present-day Korean dancer's costume still retains the long sleeves, pleated skirts, and trousers.

The hunting scene on the left wall *(Plate 1)* captures the movement and mood of the chase. Hunters are shown riding at full gallop in two valleys separated by a range of mountains. One of the hunters is shooting backwards at two deer, while another is chasing a tiger whose yellow and black stripes are pleasingly repeated by the artist in the depiction of the range of hills. The conventional cloud design at the top of the painting is also found in a number of other places on the domed ceiling and is intended to convey the idea of blue sky over hunting grounds.[8] Though the scene in general is carelessly and somewhat roughly painted, details such as the feathered hunting cap, the buzzing arrows, and the short bow are painstakingly rendered.

Three-chambered Tomb: This tomb was first studied by a Japanese architect, Tadashi Sekino, in 1913. The murals were found to be smoke-begrimed because local brigands used the tomb regularly as a refuge. The paintings that Sekino thought were of particular interest were the human figures depicted as caryatids to support the beams in place of pillars *(Plate 41)*. Their faces were rendered very like those of later Buddhist images, but the scarves, the flames shooting from the bodies, the flying clouds, and the snakes twined about the legs certainly hark back to pre-Buddhist symbolization. The rendering of these lithe

*75*

caryatids is sure and pleasing but does not at once convey to the Western eye the impression of weight-bearing. To the Oriental accustomed to seeing weights lifted from a squatting position, however, it does not seem awkward. The figures are dressed in tight-fitting short coats and trousers and wear sashes. The collars show two different styles: one a round neck and the other a long neckband. The cuffs of the short sleeves are decorated with an odd lotus-petal band.

Tomb of the Four Spirits: The walls of this tomb are painstakingly prepared stone surfaces on which the painting has been applied directly.[9] On them are seen the Four Spirits symbolizing the four cardinal points of the compass. A handsome honeysuckle scroll in gaudy colors encircles the chamber along the top of the walls. On the north wall are pictured the entwined tortoise and snake, possibly symbolizing the creation of the world (Plate 42). The body of the snake is enlivened by bands of color. It arches against a blue sky filled with bits of scudding cloud and then twists into an intricate and eye-pleasing knot. The heads of the snake and the tortoise confront each other in a heraldic design.

The other three spirits are represented as lithe reptilian creatures hurtling through space, this sensation being produced in the beholder by the flying clouds that seem to separate in all directions away from the figures. A close look at the background reveals a number of small heavenly beings scouring through the air on odd-looking steeds: unicorns, cranes, tigers, horses, mice. In the northeast and southeast these small beings are shown wearing mortarboard hats and cloaks, like professors at a graduation ceremony (Plate 43). In the northwest and southwest the beings wear high headgear, riding jackets, and trousers (Plate 44).

The Tomb of the Lotus, the Tomb of the Concentric Circles, and Tomb Number 17 at Wukuaifen are interesting for the allover designs that decorate them. In the Tomb of the Lotus the dome is polka-dotted with half-open blossoms and the wall with fully opened flowers. The Tomb of the Concentric Circles, on the other hand, is dotted with geometric figures: brown, blue, and yellow concentric circles, the outside circle in each case being about seven inches in diameter. In this tomb the customary paintings of pillars are decorated with an unusual scroll pattern whose repetitive design breaks into blue heart-shaped figures at intervals down the length of the pillar (Plate 45). Tomb Number 17 at Wukuai-fen was constructed on a gigantic plan, originally a pyramid some 160 feet square. The paintings of the Four Spirits that decorate the inner walls are fresh and in good condition. A border of interlocking snakes along the top of the walls is a striking feature. Fairies riding on dragons and illustrations of folk tales appear on the corbels (Plate 46). Thin gilt metal cutouts formerly embellished the scenes at intervals, and jewels were inserted into the eyes of the dragon and the tiger.[10]

Out of the scores of tombs in the vicinity of Koguryo's southern capital at P'yongyang, four have been selected for comment here.[11] Their murals show the tomb art at its height —fully developed, refined, and sure of itself. Most of the murals of the southern tombs are fifth- or sixth-century paintings done after 427. The Twin Pillar Tomb, the Great Tomb, and the Shinba-ri Tomb Number 1 constitute the climax of Koguryo art.

Twin Pillar Tomb: The two pillars (Plate 47) between the main chamber and the ante-room are, in the case of this tomb, real and not painted on the wall. They are most unusual, the only similar pair in Korea being found at the entrance of the Sokkuram cave temple, which was built about two hundred years later. The pillars are painted with dragon designs that are reminiscent of ancient Cretan decorative styles. Minor figures in this tomb are of very great interest to us, since they are much more skillfully rendered than the figures found in the northern tombs. A mounted warrior *(Plate 49)*, an ox-drawn cart and an outrider on his skittish horse, and three ladies with headbands and pleated skirts *(Plate 48)* are examples of the careful drawing and lifelike movement found in the decoration of this tomb.

The Great Tomb: This tomb (called T'ae-myo by the Koreans) and two that are close to it have been dated from the reign of King Yangwon (545–59) by Mr. Eckhardt and from the late sixth or the early seventh century by Messrs. Ikeuchi and Umehara. There is no human figure in the tomb. Its chief claim to notice is its foursome of magnificent fantastic animals symbolizing the points of the compass. The so-called creation symbol of the north, the tortoise and snake entwined *(Plate 51)*, is perhaps the most interesting of the group, if not the most esthetically pleasing. In this representation of a hackneyed theme, the artist has rendered a fresh and vital depiction. It is more idealized than the rendering found in the Tomb of the Four Spirits on the Yalu *(Plate 42)*, more refined, and more elegantly and subtly powerful. It is also more simply rendered. The oval sweep of the snake's body appears to have the hidden strength of a coiled spring, and the two heads confronting one another are still heraldic but with a vastly improved sense of dramatic pose and design. The Azure Dragon of the East *(Plate 52)* and the White Tiger of the West *(Plate 53)* are also unsurpassed in strength and dexterity of brushwork and high artistic quality.

Several new tombs excavated in 1941 were found to have murals that were equal to, or possibly superior to, the best found in the tombs just described. Certainly the paintings were found to be the best preserved up to that date.

Shinba-ri Tombs Number 1 and Number 2: These tombs are located about ten miles southeast of P'yongyang. The chamber in the first tomb in this group was built of hewn stones in rectangular plan, measuring eleven feet in length by eight in width, and constructed in the typical vaulted style of the Koguryo tomb with corbeled walls. The inside was plastered with white stucco, and the paintings were done on this surface. These paintings were of the four animals mentioned above, which were popular motifs in the Koguryo tombs. The decorative bands below and above these paintings, on the lintels, and on the ceiling stones contained designs of lotus flowers, clouds, stars, and the sun and the moon. Especially remarkable were the paintings of the dragon, the tiger, a pair of fir trees[12] on the north wall; the sun and moon designs; and two representations of armed guardians flanking the entrance. All of these paintings were done in a more fluid style than the ones previously discovered. This tomb may date anywhere from the fifth to the seventh century.

Mention should be made of the decoration of the ceiling and the corridor walls of the fourth tomb in this group.[13] The ceiling was adorned with stars of gold foil. On the east wall of the corridor was a dragon with a man riding on it; on the west wall, a flying bird with a woman rider. We may conclude that these are the finest examples of Koguryo painting in Korea and that they exhibit at a new high level all the characteristic features of the provincial art of northeast Asia at that time.

Of the minor arts of the period, we have little knowledge, since looting of the tombs has left us nothing but tile remnants and a few bits of jewelry, bronze, and pottery. These few bits, however, show that personal adornments—earrings, bracelets, and the like—were similar to those of current styles in Silla and Paekche.

A bronze vessel, found in a Silla grave and dated 415, is a rare example of Koguryo bronze casting *(Plates 54, 55)*. It was excavated in 1946 by Kim Che-won, curator of the National Museum of Korea. According to the inscription on the bottom of the vessel, it was cast as a washbowl *(ho–u)*. The inscription reads: Ul myo-nyon (the year name corresponding with 415), Kuk-kang-sang (place name), Kwanggae Tojiko Taewang (great King Kwang-gae Toji), ho–u (vessel for washing), sip (ten).[14] The word "ten" here has no meaning that anyone can decipher but is thought to be a space filler or an inventory number. The characters of the inscription are in a superior style, like those of the 414 monument, and are much admired by calligraphers. The shape of the bowl and its lid has remained popular in the repertory of the modern Korean brassmaker.

In pottery-making, Koguryo was apparently more advanced than its southern neighbors, since remnants of a hard green-glazed ware have been discovered. An unglazed, hand-painted pottery was also made, as well as innumerable ornamental tiles and bricks.[15]

Very little of value from the early Buddhist sculpture of Koguryo is extant. One terra-cotta figurine, about nine inches in height, was found near P'yongyang *(Plate 56)*. It appears to be an image of Sakyamuni seated on a lotus pedestal with his hands in an archaic type of *dhyani mudra* (meditation gesture). The head, large in proportion to the body, the lotus throne, and the pose are all common features of the North Ch'i style of China, but the drapery and the gesture are similar to those of a dated image of Southern Sung.[16] The face, the shape of the head, and the unclothed torso, on the other hand, are unlike the sharp features, narrow heads, and heavily draped bodies of the common Chinese renditions of the Buddha figure of the period. This Korean figure shows a rounded and full style that was becoming popular, even dominant, at the end of the sixth century in Paekche and was transmitted at that time to Japan. The mellifluous blending of features and the rounded and undraped or lightly draped torso were characteristics similar to those of a style currently popular in Cambodia.[17] A mold for the casting of terra-cotta images of this type was also found near P'yongyang *(Plate 57)*. Both figurine and mold were made of excellent refined porcelaneous clay which became very hard when baked.

Unlike the terra-cotta figure, a small gilt-bronze standing figure, which may be either a Sakyamuni or a Bodhisattva *(Plate 58)*, shows all the conventional characteristics of the old-fashioned Wei style in its "fish fin" drapery, crossed scarves, and pose. Its right hand is raised in the *abhaya* (protection) mudra; its left is lowered in the *vara* (charity) mudra, the last two fingers being folded against the palm in a variation that occurs frequently in Korean images and in those produced in the Korean tradition.[18] The abhaya-vara mudra in Korean iconography was of the kind used for standing figures of Maitreya (Miruk) but sometimes also for Sakyamuni (Sokkamoni in Korean).

A Buddhist figure similar to this one in general appearance and style is to be seen in a Chinese piece dated 571.[19] It stands on a simple pedestal, its hands in the abhaya-vara mudra, its fingers in the same variation. The image is probably the Maitreya. Attendant

78

figures show the same mudra, a rare gesture for Bodhisattvas in Chinese iconography of the period. The full-length *mandorla* (which went out of fashion in China with the downfall of the Wei) is decorated in fifth-century style with flames and the Three Buddhas of the Past. The halo, which is similar to that of the Shaka at the Horyuji, contains a design of stylized acanthus and, at the top, a flaming pearl. The *ushnisha* is high, and the hairline dips in a peak that is infrequently found in Chinese iconography. The headgear of one of the Bodhisattvas is similar to the mortarboard headgear of the Korean Miruk.

In conclusion, the outstanding survival of Koguryo culture is the painting found in the tombs. The style and subject matter reflect religious and artistic themes of the Han and Six Dynasties periods that were currently popular in the area, but the rendering shows originality and skill in that no two designs are alike in execution, and they depict local custom with *élan* and verve.

# CHAPTER SIX

# The Three Kingdoms: Silla

THE EARLY history of Silla was colored by the fact of its geographical isolation, which delayed the cultural growth of the kingdom but also saved it from mighty China's predatory advances. Though hard to reach from China, Silla was vulnerable to attack by sea from Japan and by land from the two other Korean kingdoms. However, Silla's warrior nobles were equal to the task of military defense and knew the advantages of strategic alliances. After eliminating the Japanese from the peninsula in 562, Silla turned next to defeating the Korean kingdoms. This was accomplished in a coalition with T'ang against Paekche in 660–63 and against Koguryo in 668. After that event Chinese continued direct control of the Manchurian portions of Koguryo and eventually left the territory south of the Yalu to Silla.

Silla's capital at Kyongju, like Koguryo's capital at P'yongyang, is one of the few ancient capitals of the world that continue to flourish in modern times. Situated in a wide and fertile valley, watered by several rivers, surrounded by a circle of mountains, and tucked into the southeast corner of the peninsula, where it escaped much of the brunt of Korea's numerous invasions, Kyongju enjoyed many centuries of tranquillity and prosperity. During the two centuries of its apogee (600–800), the city boasted a million inhabitants, many flourishing industries (of which brocade making was the chief), wide streets, a brisk foreign trade, and strong rulers. Four forts, the remains of which can still be seen, protected the city—one on each side.

From 514 to 660, a succession of able rulers set Silla upon its political feet. Before the unification, Silla kings were first elected, then became semihereditary, being chosen from the three royal families of Pak, Sok, and Kim. After unification, the Kim family alone became the royal family.

Important dates in Silla's history are noted in the following summary. In 424, Buddhism was informally and not very successfully introduced by the "black monk" Mukhoja. It was introduced again a hundred years later, in 524, when it was adopted by the court, and after that it prospered. In 503, according to the record, Confucianism was introduced, and at the same time certain practices, such as the live burial of attendants with deceased members of the royal families, were discontinued by edict. One of the strong kings, Chinghung (540–76), expanded Silla's holdings and set up boundary stones which still stand—one on the peaks behind modern Seoul, two near Wonsan, and one on the southwest frontier—and sent frequent missions to south China, sometimes two or three a year. From 634 to 653, two queens inherited the throne in their own right—an indication of a significant difference between ancient Silla practices and the strictly male-line hierarchy of China. The queens established good relations with the founder of the T'ang dynasty and introduced many foreign customs. Queen Songdok, in particular, introduced Chinese fashions in court dress and many other innovations in cultural and technological fields in vogue at that time in T'ang China. She sent students to Chinese universities, built temples and schools in her own kingdom, and astutely patronized Confucianism and shamanism as well as the state religion, Buddhism. One of her great interests was astronomy (astrology, as it was then known and practiced), and she built herself a "star-gazing tower" near Kyong-ju. She sponsored a military-religious school for selected young noblemen who were trained at her expense from their fifteenth to their twenty-fifth years in a semichivalric code called *hwarangdo*, in which swordsmanship was stressed. The queen thus built up a loyal core of able officials who conducted the final showdown campaigns in coalition with China against the other two kingdoms. Had it not been for these accomplished men, the ablest of whom was General Kim Yu-sin, Silla itself might have been conquered by China in 663–68. Instead, Silla was invested with title to Paekche by China in 668. In 676, the king was able to force T'ang troops out of Korea, and in 715 Silla was invested with title to Koguryan territories up to the Taedong. This title was finally confirmed in 735.

Silla came to a peaceful end in the tenth century, so that scores of aboveground monuments, such as stone pagodas, lanterns, temple foundations, and the like, escaped destruction and have survived to the present, supplying us with much valuable material for study.

We are also fortunate in having available a superb collection of underground remains that were preserved because of Silla's unique method of tomb construction. Unlike the tumuli of Paekche and Koguryo, Silla tombs could not be entered after burial. The subterranean chambers of the tombs were entirely below ground level; above them were heaped mounds of river boulders and above these a great mound of earth. As time went on, the mound settled, and the boulders sank into the tombs, destroying much of the pottery but not the jewelry, and sealing everything off from would-be looters. In the present century a number of excavations have uncovered rich remains that are valuable not only as antiques but have intrinsic value as well. The best known of the tombs are the Gold Crown Tomb, the Golden Bell Tomb, the Ornamental Shoe Tomb, the Lucky Phoenix Tomb, the Washing Vessel Tomb, and the Silver Bell Tomb.[1] Few of the finds show any sign of Buddhist influence and are thus in marked contrast with the advanced Buddhist culture of contemporary Paekche.

Most of the Silla monuments lie in the Kyongju valley. Some, however, are near two other Sillan centers of importance, Yangsan and Ch'angyong, near Taegu. The tombs near Kyongju are the largest, and though most of these cannot now be identified, they appear to have been the tombs of kings. The largest have a diameter of between two hundred and fifty and three hundred feet and are about sixty feet in height.

At first, Japanese archeologists thought that their most brilliant finds were the Han remains of the Lo-lang period centered near P'yongyang in the northern part of Korea.

However, the accidental discovery in south Korea in 1921 of the tomb of a Silla noble, possibly of royal descent, convinced them that native Korean remains dating from the period A.D. 350–650 were equally valuable, not only in objects of cultural significance like the gold crown itself (which will be described below) but also in terms of precious metals, jade, and finished jewelry. Umehara even claimed that these Japanese finds in Korea equaled in importance Schliemann's discoveries in the Near East.[2]

Recovered from the tombs were weapons, horse equipment, furnishings for palace and temple (urns, cauldrons, pottery, dishes), religious and ceremonial objects (e.g., a shamanistic mask), and, most spectacular of all, personal ornaments of gold or gilt bronze ranging from crowns to shoes. Apparently worn by both sexes, this jewelry was of the most exquisite finish and was for the most part made of soft gold. Necklaces were made up with magatama (comma-shaped beads or jewels) in the center. Both the magatama and other beads of various shapes—cylindrical, round, faceted—were often made of jade or glass imported from abroad.

The most spectacular tomb finds were the crowns, three of which have been recovered so far. Of these, the one from the Gold Crown Tomb *(Plate 59)* is the most interesting because of its pointed inner cap, to which are attached two beautiful pierced gold wings reminiscent of a Viking helmet. Suspended from the crown are two gold pendants ending in comma-shaped jewels of green jade. In all, from the tip of the pendant to the tip of the wing, the crown extends two feet and three inches: an impressive headgear in proportion, shape, detail, and intrinsic value. The crown itself is a circlet of cut sheet gold decorated with a punched pattern in the familiar saw-tooth design. On the front of the circlet are three tree-shaped uprights of equal height; in the back, two slightly smaller antler-shaped projections. All projections, both front and back, end in leaf-shaped finials and are edged with a punched-dot decoration. They are ornamented, in addition, with fifty-seven green jade comma-shaped jewels and one hundred and thirty-three sequin-like spangles attached by means of small twisted gold wires. The inner cap mentioned above is made of cut sheet gold, and the wings are held in a five-cusped clasp attached to the front. The pierced decoration of cap and wings shows four designs: a fish-scale design in the front on the headband, a pattern of T shapes placed between diamond patterns in the center, a comma design at the top of the cap, and a design of floral scrollwork in the wings. The wings are also covered with a great number of fluttering spangles on their gold wires. The pendants are attached to the crown by two narrow gold rings from each of which hang two pendants: one short, with a gold filigree bauble, and the other a long chain of gold wire carrying ten equally spaced gold rings, each edged with six freely hanging leaves.

Two other crowns, one from the Golden Bell Tomb and one from the Lucky Phoenix Tomb *(Plate 60)*, are similar in main features but differ in details. The Golden Bell crown has no inner cap but is embellished with elaborate pendants featuring hollow gold balls, each decorated with ten blue glass beads. The Lucky Phoenix crown has an inner cap of arching bands topped by a finial of three Firebirds of the South in flames, cut out of sheet gold.

Specialists have advanced many theories about the meaning of the tree and antler shapes of these crowns. Some even see a southern element in the coral-shaped uprights at the back of the crowns, and some have claimed an ancient tradition of reindeer-hunting peoples of the north Asian forests to account for the antler-like shapes of the same uprights, but no one has as yet been able to explain the total crown, which has no counterpart anywhere. Japanese archeologists without exception feel that the jade magatama are significant in relating south Korean culture of the pre-Buddhist period with Japanese culture of the same period, as magatama are found in quantity in the south both in Japan and Korea but are not found in north Korea or China. Others have seen in the crown an attempt to symbolize sun worship. "The King who wore it," writes Helen Chapin, "must have dazzled the onlookers like the Sun itself, as whose representative on earth he may well have been regarded."[3]

Whatever the significance of the crown or the religious belief behind it, which must have been intense to induce the authorities of the time to bury the genuine objects rather than mortuary substitutes, the total effect in life must have been impressive. The light reflecting from the five hundred odd spangles and pendent jewels, which the slightest movement of the head would set in motion, must have created a genuinely majestic and startling effect during the ceremonies in which it was worn, and now constitutes a source of esthetic pleasure of a very high order.

Almost as spectacular as the crowns are the numerous sets of gold earrings which came from the tombs. Both sexes wore them, and all three kingdoms, as well as some clans in Japan, shared the custom. Chinese literature also confirms that earrings were characteristic ornaments of the Koguryans.[4] Four pairs of earrings from the tombs have been selected for mention here. All have three elements: a hollow gold ring, another ring thrust through this one, and a pendant from the second. The major rings of a pair found at Pomun-ni (Plate 61) are fat and heavy-looking, although in actuality they are very light in weight because they are hollow. The minor rings linked to the first are also hollow. The pendant is composed of two circular tiers of small leaves and a large leaf-shaped finial. The major ring is decorated with a tortoise-shell design of hexagons inside of which are groups of circles, all outlined by means of gold beading in the famous goldsmith technique of granulation—now a lost art. The minor ring is decorated in granulation in a leaf pattern.

Another pair of earrings found at Pomun-ni also have two fat rings linked by two oval-shaped rings, both hollow but plain and undecorated, thus allowing the gold sheen full play. The pendants have two tiers of leaf shapes and a major finial, but in these earrings the finials are heart-shaped and are edged by granulated beading. The finials of a third pair of earrings found at Huan'go-ri Tomb Number 52 are heart-shaped and are decorated with granulation and extra free-hanging spangles on either side (Plate 62). The two main rings in this pair are small, and the pendant is elongated into granule-decorated cylinders which probably also had jewels set in the empty circles at one time. Another pair of earrings from the same tomb have similar major and minor rings and similar side spangles on the finials but, in place of cylindrical pendants, filigree baubles pinched in at the center. The finials are leaf-shaped.[5]

In the same casket with the gold crown were the gold belt and buckle.[6] Fortunately, the belt was found in situ halfway between the crown and the shoes, and the pendants were found in a position which established their use as accessories to the belt. The position of

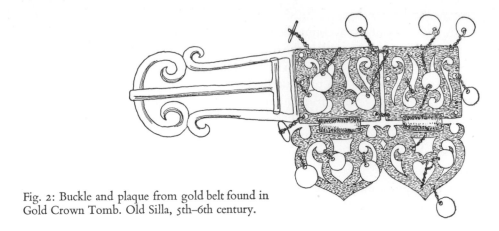

Fig. 2: Buckle and plaque from gold belt found in
Gold Crown Tomb. Old Silla, 5th–6th century.

the girdle also established the fact that this particular belt, with its buckle and plaques, was
used for human apparel and not for horse trappings, which they closely resemble. There
are forty-one pieces in all, counting the buckle and the end plate or tang. Each plaque has
two sections hinged together, one rectangular and the other heart-shaped. Both sections
are ornamented with an openwork design in what appears to be a floral pattern—possibly
honeysuckle. The sections also have small sequin-like spangles attached to the ends of little
twigs of gold wire—a form of decoration extremely rare in China and nonexistent in
Japan. The end plate is decorated with a simple punched border design. There are still bits
of cloth attached to the plaques, so it would seem that the gold bits were sewn to a textile
base. The end piece was probably attached to a protruding section of cloth in which there
were embroidered eyelets to receive the tongue of the buckle. An illustration of the way
the belt may have been worn may be seen in a wall painting of the Uigurs of the T'ang
period.[7] Because the end piece is larger than the buckle, it has been argued by Japanese
archeologists that the belt was fastened by the above-mentioned method, the initial step
being to turn the end piece sidewise in order to get it through the buckle.[8]

Another unusual feature of the belt is its length, which is sixty-four inches. It is the most
ornate belt yet unearthed in either Korea or Japan, or for that matter in China, where even
the emperor's girdle employed only nine to thirteen bosses. Belts were part of the Chinese
official costume during the Six Dynasties and T'ang eras.

It is the opinion of Japanese archeologists that these Korean belts were more closely
related to barbarian girdles than to those used in China, inasmuch as the belts of many
nomads were provided with rings of a utilitarian nature to support objects needed by the
horseman. The elaborate nature of the belt under discussion, with its many rings and pendants—although they are obviously of a ceremonial and not a practical nature—seems to
the Japanese to show that it was made in a non-Chinese tradition.*

* Kosaku Hamada and Sueji Umehara, *Keishu Kinkan-zuka to Sono Iho* (The Gold Crown Tomb at Kyongju
and Its Treasures) (Seoul, 1924–27), Vol. III, Part 1, p. 25. "In fact, they are overdecorated in a confusing
manner, showing a barbarous taste and a decadent tendency of style. We think also that such girdles were
perhaps introduced by the Turkish people into China. . . . The buckles naturally came from the same source
as the girdle."

In the same tomb were found scattered parts of at least fourteen other belts, belt pendants in gold and silver, and about thirty buckles which were similar in form and function to the buckles used for personal adornment. The material used, however, was different, for it was the bronze or gilt bronze commonly used for horse equipment.

In contrast with the lavishness of the belt and the pendants, the buckle itself *(Figure 2)* is quite simple in design. Yet it is an integral part of the whole and, as such, is in good taste. The simplicity contrasts with the elaborateness of the plaques and yet remains in relation to it, since the heart-shaped point of the buckle—an excellent functional design—repeats the shape of the ring section of each plaque and also repeats the openwork pattern of the cutout. This curving and graceful shape is in marked contrast to the plain, squarish, and functional design of the horse-trapping buckle with which it is so closely related. The closest parallel to this buckle appears to be another buckle from a Silla tomb found twenty-five years later.[9] The closest parallel in technique and general treatment seems to be a small ornament from Minussinsk,[10] but for the form of the buckle it is necessary to look to Europe: Hungary, Albania, and farther west,[11] since the hook, and not the buckle, was the usual Asiatic fastener, even in the Six Dynasties period.

Nothing could be simpler than the buckle under discussion. There is no design on it, no granulation, no filigree, no inlay or enamel. It is nothing but a functional piece of equipment, and yet its presence in a Korean tomb of the fifth (or sixth) century presents a most intriguing problem. Where did its prototype come from? Other objects in the tomb, particularly the crown, have been much studied, and the general opinion is that accumulated evidence points to a Western origin for much that is found in the Korean tombs of this period, indicating that both cultural and commercial ties with the "barbarians" were of great importance. Whether the contact was direct, or via the Toba Wei of China, is the next question, since no links of provable Chinese origin in the chain are yet available. Some scholars believe the presence of the granulation technique to be an indication that parallels may be found only in the "art of the Scythians, Sarmatians, and later occupants of South Russia."[12]

The seventeen pendants *(Plate 63)* found in the tomb offer a study in themselves. Two of these pendants are especially interesting because of the implications of Western or Northern origins of the materials used: glass and jade. The pendant of dark-blue glass was encased in a gold net and suspended by a complex chain decorated with five ball-like ornaments similar to pieces of jewelry found in south Russia.[13] The comma-shaped jade pendant was a piece of expensive imported jewel jade.[14] There were, in fact, about thirty thousand pieces of jade in the tomb. All this points to a strong and sustained contact with central Asia.

Near the gold belt in the Gold Crown Tomb were found twelve gold bracelets *(Plate 64)* and twelve hammered gold finger rings *(Plate 65)*. Each bracelet is a tube of gold that has been notched on the outer edge and bent into a circle. The rings, cut from sheet gold, are decorated in three ways: plain bands widened in front, others with crosshatching, and still others with a narrow central ridge notched with vertical file-made depressions. No finger rings have been found in Japanese tombs, although some were excavated in the Lo-lang tombs.

Figs. 3, 4: Incised designs on tiles.
Old Silla, 5th–6th century.

Fig. 5: Decorative design on pottery
bowl. Old Silla, 5th–6th century.

Also in the Gold Crown Tomb were five bowls, doubtless originally designed for the king's household. Each was made of hammered gold with a flat base and a rounded rim *(Plate 66)*.

In the recent excavation of a tomb called the Washing Vessel (Ho-u) Tomb by Professor Kim Che-won, there was discovered an important lacquered wooden mask. Oddly enough, the eyes were blue. They were made of glass and were set in rings of pure gold. It may have been a funeral mask.[15]

Among the thousands of shards of pottery that remain from Silla times, two of the most interesting items are a pair of vessels in the form of mounted horsemen. These were taken from the Golden Bell Tomb. They are fairly large pieces of partially hollow stoneware, nearly a foot long and almost as tall, and are furnished with a spout on the breast and a funnel on the croup of the horse *(Plate 67)*. The riders were made separately. The horseman in the piece described here wears a pointed cap and a military costume suggesting leather-plated armor. He carries a sword and wears the pointed Korean shoe. Both cap and shoes are similar to those depicted in the Koguryo murals. The saddle is similar to the type still in use on the stocky Korean pony. These pieces were doubtless ceremonial copies of vessels actually used to hold liquids. They themselves could not be used for this purpose. The pottery used in everyday life was also buried in the tombs. It was of two general kinds: one a hard gray type that was usually decorated with lattice or geometric patterns *(Figures 3, 4)* and recalled the Scythian-type decorations on early mirrors and horse equipment; the other, a soft reddish-brown earthenware that some experts consider to be a continuation of the red type of neolithic pottery.

Designs were incised or stamped on the finished vessels, often almost as an afterthought. One such piece *(Figure 5)* is appealing because of its carefree decorativeness. Pottery shards of both types were plentiful in all the tombs, but few unbroken items have been found. There were also glass cups (known as *po-li* cups in China and *p'ari* cups in Korea) of a light blue and of goblet shape. These have been reconstructed out of the shards and are very rare relics indeed.*

The Silla remains so far presented have been almost devoid of Buddhist influence. Yet the Silla aristocrats in the sixth century took to Buddhism with relish when they finally adopted it. It was not until Silla had united Korea under one rule in the seventh century that Buddhist art reached its height. During the Old Silla period it also reached a most impressive level of achievement, showing in general an affinity with the Wei style of Buddhist art in China. Fortunately, a good idea of what the art was like may be attained from a review of the gilt-bronze images that remain.

The most popular deity in Korea in the sixth century was the Bodhisattva Maitreya (Miruk). Dozens of representations of it are extant, varying in size and media from giant rock-cut images to tiny metal figurines. The Maitreya of this period was usually represented standing, often as a giant figure. It also appeared in the pose of the Bodhisattva of Meditation, rendered as a seated figure whose right leg was crossed over the left knee and whose right hand supported the cheek in a pose of profound thought. The seat was a draped stool or "bundle of grass," which was associated with the Bodhi tree in stele representations.† The figure was rendered bare to the waist, adorned with jewelry and wearing a crown or turban. Sometimes the crown carried an image of Amitabha on it, and sometimes curls or braids of hair were shown, these two attributes indicating the iconography of Avalokitesvara rather than Maitreya. In Japan this representation is considered to be an Avalokitesvara and is labeled the Nyoirin Kannon. The pose is believed by Getty and Munsterberg to represent Prince Siddhartha, by Wegner and others to be Maitreya. The correct interpretation depends upon the sutra involved and the sect which dedicated the figure.

Two small Silla figures are rendered in this meditation pose. One of these *(Plate 68)* supports his entire cheek in his hand and wears a crown of the ordinary three-cusped type. The other *(Plate 69)* barely touches his cheek with his fingertips and wears a pointed crown decorated with incised designs. The drapery of the latter, with its double-line pleat, shows more archaic features than that of the former.

Two other Silla figures, each nearly a yard in height, are the largest surviving bronze images of the period in this pose. On one of these *(Plate 71)* the gilding is in excellent condition. The diadem has unusual crescent-shaped finials, and the foot is placed on a lotus support of its own. Here the nude torso prescribed by the iconography, not so elongated as in the small figurine, is covered by a scarf that flares outward over the upper arms: an embellishment that seems to have been inspired by a Chinese tradition that eschewed nudity in any form. The second image *(Plate 70)* reverts to the simplicity of the small Maitreya with his chin in his hand as described above. The crown is simplified and is lower

* Tadashi Sekino, *Chosen Bijutsu Shi* (History of Korean Art) (Kyoto, 1932), p. 83. These cups were considered by Umehara to be Roman wine glasses, but later research shows that similar glass was made in China.

† Alice Getty, *The Gods of Northern Buddhism* (Oxford, 1928), pp. 90–91. There is a legend to the effect that the king of Silla sent an envoy to Empress Suiko with a gift of a gold-copper Avalokitesvara and that, from then on, this deity was known and greatly loved in Japan *(Ibid.,* p. 58). The Nyoirin Kannon is likely to show the hair in different style. It is a non-Tantric form *(Ibid.,* p. 96).

87

than those of the small figures. The torso is entirely uncovered, is more attenuated, and shows a slight swelling in the upper chest, a pinching in at the waist, and a general air of suppleness and grace lacking in the other figures. The drapery falls in a less rigid, more natural, and softer line and spreads out in graceful folds about the base. Both of the large figures reach the heights of genuinely great religious art.

The nude Bodhisattva, a possession of the Yi household, is so much like the Hokan Nyoirin of the Horyuji in Japan that some Japanese experts regard the latter to be "in expression and workmanship more suggestive of Corean influence than any of the other Maitreyas that have come down to us."[16] The Horyuji figure lacks the neck ring; its hand does not actually touch its cheek; and the lotus-bud support for the foot has merged with the base to form one pedestal. The Korean figure adheres more closely to Chinese models in these details, but in major characteristics it is strikingly like the Horyuji image. It is even closer in style and feeling to the wooden Maitreya of the Koryuji at Uzumasa in Kyoto—an image which is similar enough to be a "product of the same workshop in spite of the difference in medium."[17] Still another Japanese Bodhisattva in the meditation pose is the Chuguji Siddhartha, long called the Chuguji Kannon, which resembles the other two Japanese figures mentioned above in its simplicity and lack of ornament, but is like Korean prototypes in its separate footrest and the two knobs on the head, which recall those of a Bodhisattva in the National Museum of Korea.

Chinese representations of the Bodhisattva of Meditation are many, especially at Yun-kang and Lungmen, but the similarity is one of iconography and little else. In order to discover images akin to the Korean figures in style and feeling, one must turn to the white marble steles of North Ch'i. The central deity of many of these steles was the Bodhisattva of Meditation, who was represented in an assemblage of trees, Nagas, Apsarases, attendant deities, monks, stupas, *yakshas,* lions, and other symbols of syncretic Indian Buddhism. Even more Indian than the composition of such crowded plaques was the plasticity and feeling for form in the round rather than strictly linear form, in the handling of which the Chinese had excelled for centuries. Korean artists and those of Asuka Japan generally represented the Bodhisattva of Meditation by himself without a background—although the Tachibana Shrine assemblage is a notable exception—at first in the stiff and archaic poses of the Kudara and Yumedono Kannons and later in the more plastic images represented by the Koryuji and Yi household figures. The problem of influences and connecting links is a primary one in the attempt to evaluate Korean Buddhist sculpture of the Three Kingdoms period, and it has hitherto been only slightly, though brilliantly, touched upon by such scholars as Sirén, Stryzygowski, Sekino, and Soper. Although we lack a definitive study in this field, it might be useful to summarize here some of the elements present in Korean religious sculpture of the period under discussion.

Buddhist iconography in Korean hands has its own story to tell as it shows departures from Indian and Chinese models. The *vitarka* mudra, for example, is often represented by the contact of the second finger with the thumb instead of the index finger. The *vara* and *abhaya* mudras often show the last two fingers folded against the palm. The *bhumisparsa* mudra, relatively rare in China, was very popular in Korea. The drapery arrangements also show some peculiarities. The neckline of garments frequently stands up behind the neck and is symmetrical, and the favorite fold is the hanging loop, with the fleur-de-lis fold next in popularity. Ornament was introduced on borders and in jeweled metal cutouts, as in contemporary Koguryo tombs. It was likely to be intricate, elegant, and lacelike regardless of the medium, and superb examples in stone, wood, metal, and tile are extant to testify to this. Halos were rendered in the archaic mandorla shape or in shoulder-length round or flame shapes, and these gave the artist room for the display of his talent for the type of decoration just mentioned. Pedestals produced in Korean workshops were unlike Chinese pedestals in the high preference for polygonal shapes. In conclusion, we may say that although prototypes for every element in Korean Buddhist art may be found somewhere in China or central Asia, the resulting Korean production showed the highly developed native art traditions of the non-Buddhist past and, more importantly still, showed that Korean workshops benefited remarkably quickly from the increased maritime exchanges that were taking place among Far Eastern kingdoms in the sixth and early seventh centuries.

That the architecture of the period was well developed is evidenced in the foundations of such temple sites as that of the Hwangnyong-sa (Temple of the Imperial Dragon), which was first built in the sixth century as a national temple.* Destroyed in 1229 by the Mongols in one of the two invasions that actually touched the Kyongju area, it was never rebuilt. This temple, had it been preserved with its original treasures, would have furnished for the study of the civilization of Old Silla the same excellent total effect that the Horyuji, near Nara, presents for the study of the Asuka era in Japan.

Two buildings remain in the Kyongju area dating from the period of Queen Songdok. One is a stone observatory *(Plate 72)*, and the other is the oldest datable pagoda (634) in Korea *(Plate 73)*. The pagoda of Punhwang-sa, a brick structure originally nine stories in height, retains only three of its stories. When it was restored, there was found inside, between the second and third stories, a relic box which was a valuable repository of *sarira* (Buddhist relics) and of gold and precious-stone ornaments, coins, scissors, belts, and even a needle case and needles: appropriate relics of a queen.[18] On the sides of the pagoda are four blind doors decorated with figures of guardians carved in relief in a vigorous Wei dynasty style. The four corners of the terrace on which the pagoda stands are guarded by stone lions.

* Alexander Soper, *The Evolution of Buddhist Architecture in Japan* (Princeton, 1942), chap. i. Robert Paine and Alexander Soper, *The Art and Architecture of Japan* (Edinburgh and London, 1955), pp. 170 ff. See also Ludwig Bachhofer's review of the former book in *Art Bulletin,* Vol. XXV (March, 1944), for an important comment on why Chinese Buddhism retained foreign art traditions and techniques in everything but architecture. Korean Buddhism appears to have retained many central Asian elements, even in architecture, where the corbeled roof survived, perhaps as a legacy of central Asian tradition, and was much used in the thousands of non-Buddhist Koguryo tombs. Other central Asian legacies were the "fluttering ribbon" of Bamian, the Turfan stupas that are reflected in the Silla pagodas, and the Tokharian military trappings on the Guardian (Deva) Kings.

# CHAPTER SEVEN

# United Silla

HISTORICAL BACKGROUND    The unification of the Korean peninsula into one kingdom in the late seventh century brought about the end of the three ancient regimes and heralded the establishment of a new type of government which was hierarchical, patrilinear, and hereditary on the Chinese pattern. The kingship of ancient Silla, which had formerly rotated among the three royal families of Pak, Sok, and Kim,* at this time became hereditary for the Kim alone. The two and a half centuries of the new dynasty became known as the period of United Silla. It was marked by peace and by great cultural advances in all the arts. Freed from both local and foreign wars, and heir to the assets of the other two kingdoms, Silla entered upon a period of hitherto unknown peace and prosperity. Foreign visitors, including Arabian merchants, appeared in Korea, attracted by Silla's far-flung reputation.[1]

During this period Korean institutions were radically transformed. New Buddhist sects were introduced from T'ang China and quickly took root. Buddhist learning and Buddhist art flourished not only in the capital but also in the provinces. Confucian political ideas were put into practice; Chinese family names became common, at least among the lettered classes; and Confucian literature stimulated the production by Korean scholars of the first national literature, which consisted of a body of poetry, memoirs, and history. This literary development was made possible by the adoption of a system of reducing the native language to writing. This invention, called *idu,* was perfected and put into practice by the scholar Solch'ong at the end of the seventh century.[2] It comprised a system of terminal syllables designed to act as connectives between ideograms in order to adapt Chinese writing to the Korean language. By the end of the ninth century, Korea was able to produce out-standing scholars, of whom Ch'oe Ch'i-won (858–910), sometimes called the "father of Korean literature," was one. Ch'oe took the *hanlin* (the highest literary degree of the Con-fucian system) at the T'ang court and entered the service of the Chinese emperor for ten years. His writings are extant in a little book called *Pen Scratchings in a Cinnamon Garden.*

Once again, as in Han times, political ties with the Chinese empire were strong. Silla was carefully watched by the T'ang administration, which was interested in keeping the

* Until 654, the kings came from the *songol* or main line. After the reigns of two virgin queens, the kingship reverted to a *chingol* or secondary line. See Chosen Shi Gakukai (Society for the Study of Korean History), *Chosen Shi Taikei* (Outline History of Korea) (Seoul, 1925), Vol. I, pp. 133–35.

peninsula a model border area out of the orbit of the nomadic tribes to the north. Economically, also, ties with China were numerous and increasingly important. As in Lo-lang days, there was much traffic between Shantung and Hwanghae provinces. The Koreans were apparently in control of the carrying trade of the Yellow Sea, and even Japanese travelers often contracted for passage on Korean ships.[3] Commodities of export were silks, horses, furs, and Korean paper, which was even then highly prized in China for documents, for fine calligraphy, and for painting.[4]

The increase in trade and travel naturally stimulated the Sillans to broader intellectual achievements of their own. On the one hand they had to absorb the fully matured culture of T'ang into their own more primitive culture, and on the other, to nurture and develop a racial individuality of their own. Their success in achieving this balance may be gauged in part by their art, enough of which remains to show that Silla at its best closely rivaled some of the brilliance of T'ang. The chief channel through which foreign importations reached the Koreans was the Buddhist church, and the first important native institution to grow up under its tutelage was the semichivalric, semireligious, semimilitary organization called hwarangdo, the way of the knight. This "way" included a philosophy, a code of personal conduct, a school, and an elite corps of public officials who were recruited, trained, and in mature life employed by the state. The training, which covered a period of ten years, was carried out at the expense of the state. Military arts, especially swordsmanship, were stressed, and Buddhist religious ideals of self-sacrifice and compassion for the weak were inculcated. The corps led the fighting forces of the king and owed personal loyalty to him. It was largely owing to the system of hwarangdo that Silla weathered many crises, both domestic and foreign, and it was through hwarangdo that foreign culture was absorbed and made native.[5] Started in the fifth century, it reached a climax in the eighth.

Through Buddhist initiative and skill at organization and financing, a great spurt of building took place as soon as the peninsula was unified in the late seventh century. Subsidiary arts and crafts were developed to embellish and furnish the various palaces and temples. Dozens of great temples were built, many of them similar to those of the popular Buddhist sects of T'ang China. These temples were actually small cities comprising many hundreds of acres of land, usually mountainous and wooded, with adjuncts of valley rice lands. Besides performing their religious functions, nearly all temples maintained schools which boasted of learned monks who could read Chinese and Sanskrit and had traveled abroad.* Those temples devoted to Bhaisajyaguru, the Great Physician (Yaksa Yorae in Korean), also maintained clinics and hospitals where the sick were treated. Many operated workshops which manufactured a great variety of bronze ware, clay products, textiles, and other goods. To demonstrate the religious messages that could be taught by the beauty of nature, monk gardeners kept up the temple grounds with rare flowering trees, nut trees, pines, and cryptomerias. The monks also undertook to organize festivals on Buddhist holidays, which were gay with banners, flags, colorful lanterns, mystery plays, and religious dances. The festivals followed the seasons and fitted into the agricultural life of the kingdom, accommodating all and permeating the life and thought of the people.

* Haejo, a Korean monk, traveled to India in the seventh century.

Certain favored foundations such as the Hwaom even functioned as a sort of department of state by providing educated monks to compose or carry official documents to foreign lands and to bring back replies.[6] Such special sects and their temple headquarters—Pulguk-sa, for example—often functioned also as havens for retired princes, dowager queens, and other nobles temporarily in disgrace, danger, or ill health. Clues to what these temples were like are to be found in the present-day temples in the Kyongju area.

In the middle of the eighth century, during the reign of King Kyongdok, Pulguk-sa (Temple of the Buddha Land) and the shrine of Sokkuram were built by the Hwaom sect of Buddhism. The rise of this sect marked an important stage in the centralization that was taking place in the Korean political system. The Hwaom Sutra was an important group of religious writings first brought to Korea from China in the mid-seventh century.[7] These scriptures honored a new Buddha, the Vairocana or Creating Buddha, from whom all others were thought to emanate.* The sect was particularly rich in elaborate ritual. The sutra, known also as Avatansaka or Wreath of Buddha, teaches that Sakyamuni, the historical Buddha, was only a manifestation of Vairocana. It represents the hierarchy of Buddhas by means of a pattern of the universe symbolized by the lotus. Vairocana was often represented as dwelling upon a lotus flower of a thousand petals, in each of which another Buddha was pictured as presiding over his own smaller universe. A thousand such universes were imagined to contain a thousand worlds apiece, and so on down to the smallest unit of existing creation. Vairocana may signify the sun at midday or even the sun which never rises or sets. His gesture, or mudra, is that of one hand clasping the raised fore-finger of the other hand, symbolizing the union of spirit and matter, or infinite and finite.

The ruling caste, first in Korea and then in Japan, saw an analogy between such a religious concept and a governmental system, the king being equated with the Vairocana and his officials with the minor Buddhist deities. In Japan, at the time that Pulguk-sa was going up, the emperor built the great temple of Todaiji and housed within it the Vairocana Daibutsu, which is still there in spite of several fires and numerous earthquakes. In 748 he decreed that the Avatansaka Sutra was to be the state scripture. In Korea, King Kyongdok made a similar effort to glorify his own position through patronage of the Hwaom sect. Both countries and their rulers were drawn into close connection through this sect by means of the tie of international Buddhism.[8] Hwaom (Kegon in Japanese) Buddhism became so important in these countries that the royal courts took from it many of their ceremonials, their new art forms, their literature, and their music.

PULGUK-SA: Built in a series of stone platforms on the foothills of Toham-san, eight miles to the east of Kyongju, Pulguk-sa is the oldest surviving shrine in Korea (Plate 74). First founded early in the sixth century (about 535) and later repaired under King Munmu (661–80), it was entirely rebuilt and enlarged by King Kyongdok in the period ending in 752. This king reportedly brought together the most skillful workmen he could collect,

---

* Vairocana has many positions in the pantheon of great Dhyani Buddhas, depending upon the sect of Mahayana Buddhism which is honoring him. He is first and all-powerful in the Chinese and Japanese schools based upon yoga (Hosso, Kegon, Tendai, and Shingon in Japan). To these sects, Vairocana is the central figure with four emanations, forming a group of five primary Buddhas. His name in Chinese is P'a-lu-che-na; in Korean, Pirosa-pul or T'ae-il Yorae; and in Japanese, Roshana or Dainichi Nyorai. Getty, op. cit., pp. 31 ff. See also Robert Paine and Alexander Soper, The Art and Architecture of Japan (Princeton, 1942), chap. v.

including Chinese artisans.* The original foundations of Pulguk-sa have survived to the present. They were realigned and repaired by the Japanese government early in the present century. The wooden buildings now standing are all of Yi dynasty construction and are believed to be smaller than the original buildings.

At the foot of the retaining wall of the first terrace there was originally located a lotus pond which was bridged by the first flight of steps. As the pilgrim mounts the steps, crosses the bridge, and passes through the entrance gate, he symbolically leaves the world behind him and enters the "Buddha Land." On the high platform before the worshipper stands the principal temple. Placed in front of it are two great pagodas, one simple in construction and the other complex, the two complementing one another. The simple pagoda represents the Buddha absorbed in transcendent calm; the complex one symbolizes his manifestation in a diversified universe. This helps the worshipper to realize that as he leaves behind the *samsara* of everyday existence, he enters the Gate of Deliverance, proceeds past the pairs of opposites that are characteristic of creation, and enters Nirvana, which is the last stage of his journey.

The simpler pagoda *(Plate 75)* is located to the left of the entrance. It is called "the pagoda that casts no shadow." There are five units all together: a pedestal, three main stories, and a tiny final story. The total height is about twenty-seven feet. The pedestal, with its simple, undecorated supporting slabs—thought by some to be a continuation of the dolmen style—and the truncated construction of eaves and projecting roofs constitute the basic formulas for Korean pagodas of all time.

The pagoda to the right, of the class called the tabo-t'ap or pagoda of many treasures *(Plate 76),* is unique in Korea and, for that matter, in north Asia. It may have been built when the temple was founded. It still stands on its original foundation and rises to a height of about thirty-four feet. The first story is a platform provided with four stone stair-cases leading up to an enclosed area which is thought to have accommodated a Buddhist image at one time. Four heavy corner pillars support the next stage, which is composed of a simple cornice of rounded, beamlike blocks of granite. Above this are three tiers of eight-sided units, each supported by a paling of stone spokes. The second paling is patterned after bamboo stalks, complete with nodes carved realistically in the stone. This central unit is crowned by a circular cornice of egg-and-dart molding recalling that of a Greek temple. The palings of the top story flare out to carry a morning-glory-shaped roof formed of a single slab of stone, from the center of which rises a finial in a crown-ball-and-plate sequence.

No mortar was used in the construction of the tabo-t'ap. Loosely flung together, "rather like a box of toy bricks,"[9] this delightful—one might almost say exuberant—pagoda was the result of many ages of stone-pile building by peoples who had dotted their peninsula with such monuments, thus giving expression to their religious feelings by simply laying one stone upon another.

Within the main halls of Pulguk-sa are two treasures of Silla: a bronze Amitabha, he who presides over the Western Heaven and is symbolized by the setting sun *(Plate 77),*

* A large seated Buddha located in an open field near a pond called Yongji (Shadow Pond) is the subject of a legend that tells the sad story of a Chinese workman who spent his life working on Pulguk-sa.

and a Vairocana whose mudra is the "creating gesture" and who is symbolized by the sun at midday.

In both design and construction, the total effect of Pulguk-sa was, and still is, one of restrained dignity and quiet peace. There is balance and symmetry in the relation of foundation walls, steps, bridges, pillars, pagodas, crowning pavilions, and the mountain setting in which the whole is located. Somewhat casually put together (the foundations are without mortar of any kind) and yet outlasting the earthquakes, tempests, and wars of twelve hundred years, this Buddhist temple remains one of the most remarkable achievements of the ancient Far East.

SOKKURAM: About a mile away from Pulguk-sa, on the crest of Toham-san, stands the rock chapel of Sokkuram, built at the same time and by the same master architect. A path winding in hairpin turns leads from Pulguk-sa up the hillside. At the summit the pilgrim is greeted by a magnificent view of the Sea of Japan, spread out like a floor below him and supposed to signify to him the "sea of crossing over from life to death." It also recalls the Buddhist text which states that as the sea has one salty taste throughout, so Buddhism has one function: that of delivering man from the fires of lust, anger, and ignorance that consume him.[10]

Somewhat farther along the ridge, reached by a long flight of stone steps, is the shrine, oriented to the east. Within it sits a Sakya Buddha eternally on watch over the eastern sea. The cave is round in shape, and the ceiling is domed (Plate 78). Originally cut from living rock, it was completed by a number of additions, as were many of the Indian cave temples. The open entrance, about four feet wide, is interrupted by two octagonal pillars that support stone arches flattened in the middle (Plate 79). The plan of the cave (Plates 80–82) differs radically from those of other cave temples found in the Far East in that it provides space for the worshipper to walk around the Buddha, which sits in the center. This feature is thought by some to be a throwback to the temples of primitive Buddhism in India; yet in structure the cave can also claim native descent from the tombs of Koguryo, which were vaulted and had entrance passageways sometimes flanked by pillars.[11]

The entrance passage at Sokkuram is lined with stone slabs on which are carved larger-than-life figures. The first six representations (three on each side) are those of the protectors of Buddhism in their warrior garb, paying homage to Buddha on behalf of the host of beings which each one commands.[12] Their postures are stiff, and they are somewhat forbidding. On the sides of the entrance proper are two powerful guards who stand in threatening attitudes (Plate 83). They are scowling, and their fists are raised as if to strike the intruder. They are represented as muscular and violent beings like the grotesque Japanese guardian figures found at many temple gates. These early Korean representations, however, are quite without the quality of caricature. They seem unself-conscious, vigorous, and active, and the hanging folds of their garments swing to one side as if caught in mid-movement. The upper parts of the bodies are carved with great anatomical skill.

A short vestibule, in which stand two octagonal pillars supported by lotus bases and encircled halfway up by lotus wreaths, leads from the lobby into the cave itself (Plate 79). On the vestibule walls are found the customary Four Deva Kings (Heavenly Kings or Guardians of the Four Quarters), two on each side, standing upon demons. The sandals and garters of the kings are, interestingly enough, Roman in style, except for the thong passing between the big toe and the second toe—once a feature of footwear in vogue on the Asiatic mainland but now to be found only in Japan.

Inside the cave itself are four Bodhisattvas, ten disciples, and, in the center of the back, a beautiful figure of the Bodhisattva of Mercy. Above the panel of these chief figures (each about seven feet in height) are niches containing eight seated Buddhas. The first two figures to the left and right of the entrance are the Hindu gods Brahma, with his jar *(Plate 84)*, and Indra, with his thunderbolt *(Plate 85)*.[13] Both are adorned with elongated halos. The second pair appear to be Manjusri, with his tablet, and a Bodhisattva with a bowl *(Plate 87)*. The Eleven-headed Kanseum (Sepilmyon Posal) in the center of the back is one of the most beautiful sculptured figures in all Korean art *(Plate 86)*. It is very tall and slender and elegantly dressed. Scarves and jewelry are arranged in loops, crossed folds, and knots gracefully tied. The lotus pedestal on which the figure stands is simply and naturalistically represented. The garments are done in the Gupta style of the Ajanta caves, which emphasizes the thinness of the fabric and the modeling of the body beneath. The eleven heads connote the all-seeing power of the Bodhisattva to detect and relieve suffering wherever it may be found. This type of symbolism—many heads and many arms—was developed by Tantric Buddhism in Tibet shortly before Sokkuram was built. The style and the symbolism reached Korea with remarkable rapidity.[14] the concept of multiple heads or limbs is artistically difficult to portray, but in this figure the symbolism has been achieved with little esthetic offense. The heads are arranged symmetrically within a caplike curl of hair.

The ten disciples are represented in a simpler fashion than the Bodhisattvas or the Deva Kings *(Plates 88, 89)*. Their heads are turned toward one another as if they were discussing Buddhist doctrine. In contrast to the beautiful but dispassionate and aloof faces of the Bodhisattvas, the faces of the disciples show individual personality as well as racial differences—a reflection of the great fact that the original disciples of Buddha were of many races. The sincerity of these humble religious figures makes them seem to belong more to an earlier style of Chinese sculpture than to the worldly style of the contemporary T'ang schools.

In the center of the cave, a conventional lotus pedestal supports a Sakya Buddha cut from solid granite *(Plate 90)*. It is about eleven feet in height. The left hand is laid palm up on the lap, signifying meditation. The right hand, palm downward, touches the pedestal in the gesture known as the bhumisparsa or "calling the earth to witness" mudra. This mudra signifies Buddha's activity in the universe: his fighting response, as it were, to the challenge of Mara, the Buddhist Satan, who questioned his right to enlighten and save the world. The meditation mudra, on the other hand, symbolizes Buddha's utter tranquillity and peace. Here, as in much Buddhist symbolism, the universal paradox of opposites is acknowledged. The Buddha itself is rendered in almost stark simplicity. Its garment is merely indicated by shallow cuttings; its conventional sacred marks, such as the topknot and the spot between the eyes, are present but inconspicuous. The bhumisparsa mudra is especially pleasing to Korean worshippers, who see in it a pledge that the Buddha will protect them against any invasion from across the eastern sea. The aloof, yet listening, pose of the Sokkuram Buddha has had, and still has, a tremendous appeal to countless Korean worshippers.

The total effect of the temple as a unit makes it a superior example of cave shrines. Sculptured figures cut from living rock are not rare in the Far East; they may be found in many places in China, Japan, and Korea. But the other sculptures, even those at Lungmen and Yunkang in China, are not of such consistently high quality, nor is the overall planning of the other shrines as complete religiously or artistically as it is at Sokkuram. The style of the sculpture is clearly that of T'ang China, but many of the features—the ambulatory arrangement of the chapel, the orderly disposition of the various figures, their proportions, their austerity, the contrast of the strongly individual and particularized earthly figures with the ethereal and generalized divine and semidivine figures—are wholly unique. This shrine is certainly one of the treasures of the ancient Orient.

PAGODAS: Of the dozens of isolated Silla pagodas that remain, a few of the most outstanding have been chosen for comment here.[15] Two from Pulguk-sa have already been mentioned. A dated pagoda at Kuhwang-ni, reputedly belonging to the temple of Hwang-bok-sa,[16] has several features of special interest (Plate 91). In the first place, it was erected upon a rear terrace as a relic repository and not as a pagoda attached to the main hall. In the second place, it contained relics of great intrinsic and artistic value. Finally, the cover of the relic box was inscribed with a dedication giving the date as 706.

The pagoda itself is of the conventional undecorated type with a pedestal and three stories. The bronze relic box (Plate 92), about eight and a half inches square, was found in the second story. The inscription reads as follows:

"King Sinmun died July 2, 692. The succeeding king, his son Hyoso Wang, built a hall of meditation, a Buddhist temple, and a three-storied pagoda. On June 1, 700, the mother of the king died, and King Hyoso himself died two years later on July 27, 702. Thereafter, King Sungdok succeeded to the throne. On May 30, 706, King Sungdok placed four sariras, a pure gold Amitabha figure, and a volume of Buddhist sutras in the second story of the before-mentioned pagoda in commemoration of three deceased royal members: King Sinmun, Queen Mother Sinmok Taehu, and King Hyoso."[17]

The actual contents of the box included two images rather than one. There was also a small sarira box which enclosed a silver-gilt box: a cube of between one and two inches on a side (Plate 93). In addition, there were a number of glass beads, two bracelets, four bronze bowls with stands (Plates 94, 95), some gold strings, and a number of pieces of bamboo.

The Buddhist figurines are the masterpieces of this collection. Both are of gold, one a standing figure and the other a seated one. The seated Buddha (Plates 96, 97) is four and three-fourths inches in height. His legs are concealed by a fall of drapery, and his right hand is raised in the gesture of blessing. The pedestal is made of a downturned lotus, a short column, and an upturned lotus that forms the seat. The outer sections of the halo and the aureole are in low-relief openwork. In the center of the aureole is a medallion decorated with a punched and incised leaf-and-flower design, while the halo has for its center a twelve-petaled lotus flower with seed pods. The standing figure, an Amitabha (Plate 98), is just under six inches in height and stands on an inverted lotus pedestal that is in turn supported

96

by narrow tiers, one circular and the other scalloped. The halo has in its center a lotus design surrounded by bands of light rays that symbolize Amitabha in his role of the Buddha of Boundless Light. The border of the halo shows a flame design executed in low-relief open-work. Figure, halo, and pedestal were cast separately, the figure being left hollow—no doubt to permit the storage of a tiny scroll of sacred text. These little images, shining as brightly as they did twelve hundred years ago, are marvelously appealing from both the religious and the artistic standpoints.

There are numerous other pagodas from the United Silla period. Some are main-hall pagodas, some are stupas, and some are commemorative pagodas. Two of the important ones are at Hwaom-sa. One of these is the main temple pagoda, with a basement and five stories (Plate 272); the other, the Lion Pagoda, which is a stupa (Plate 273). Others include the pagoda at Silluk-sa (Plate 255), which dates from 760, several at Kumsan-sa (Plate 267), one at P'yoch'ung-sa (Plate 280), and one at T'ongdo-sa (Plate 274). Two isolated examples of interest are the pagoda at Sinwol (Plate 99) and the one at the site of Namsan-sa. All of these pagodas conform to the general Silla pattern of base, boxlike stories, and trun-cated cornices.

LANTERNS: Lanterns from this period are scattered about the peninsula in various temple compounds. Two of interest are at Kumsan-sa and Haein-sa (Plate 260). A pagoda and a lantern removed from their original locations to the present Kyongbok Palace grounds (Plate 100) are of typical United Silla shape, proportion, and size, but they are among the better preserved and more skillfully fashioned objects of their type.

TOMBS: In the Kyongju area there are at least thirty-three royal tombs as well as many graves of the nobility. Although these tombs have been well protected by Korean guards, none of them have been excavated. The largest are about sixty feet in height. Eight of them, built after Silla had been subjected to the inflow of T'ang models, were constructed in the Chinese fashion, the tumulus being faced with stone carvings representing the twelve animals of the zodiac.[18] At some tombs, such as those of kings Sungdok and Kyongdok, the figures on the stones are those of warriors with animal heads. At the approaches to the tombs are found the stone figures of lions and of two military and two civilian officials. At the Kaenung tomb (Plate 101) in the east suburb of Kyongju—allegedly the tomb of King Munmu—the guardian figures (Plate 102) have been half-buried in earth during the passing centuries. Although they show the effects of weathering, signs of the once vigorous carving and great skill of execution are still obvious. In the west suburb of Kyongju is the tomb ascribed to the Silla general, Kim Yu-sin, who helped to establish the royal family of Kim on the throne of United Silla. The tomb is of interest because its twelve-animal parapet has been preserved in excellent condition. Five of the mythical figures have been selected for representation here: the ram, the dog, the pig, the horse, and the dragon (Plates 103–7). The figures are both strong and graceful, and the beauty of the execution is such that their fabulous character is forgotten in the realistic and convincing manner of their presentation.

PALACES: Secular architecture once flourished at Kyongju, although at the present time almost all traces of former glory have vanished. A city of at least a million inhabitants at its height, it was laid out in squares on the pattern of Ch'ang-an in China, with wide streets, city walls, twenty great gates, guest houses, and an elite residential section composed of the "great houses" tiled and decorated in keeping with sumptuary laws that granted privileges of this sort to the nobles while forbidding them to commoners.[19] Kyongju contained "cities within cities," monasteries, and palaces. The present city, by contrast, occupies only the western corner of the former area and has a population of about four thousand. According to tradition, Kyongju was founded in the earliest days of the Silla confederation (about 57 B.C.) in a strategic location at the junction of two rivers and three mountain spurs encircling a fertile basin about five by seven miles in area, but it was not built as a city until the third century. The ruined walls of one of the fortresses that guarded the city still remain, and tiles from the many buildings can be found everywhere. Some of these are still intact and show elegant stamped, moulded, and incised designs (Plate 110). The site of one of the palaces is marked by a small artificial lake and the foundation stones of former buildings, but only a Yi dynasty pavilion now stands there. Another palace site, that of the P'osokchong (Abalone-Stone Pavilion), is now marked only by the irregular stone channel through which, at one time, a stream of water was directed during al fresco banquets (Plate 108). Around it, in their heyday, stood gaily painted banquet halls, and the kings of Silla used it for a favorite pastime in which a cup of wine was set afloat and a specified guest challenged to compose or cap a verse before the cup reached a turn in the channel, or to drink the wine as a forfeit if he failed. One of the last kings of Silla is said to have lost his life at this spot, so absorbed that he ignored the warning of messengers reporting the approach of enemies.

Some of the tombs are marked by stone memorial steles. The base and top of one such stele, a splendid piece at the tomb of King Muryol (reigned 654–60), are extant. The dragon, which once occupied the top, signifies the power of heaven or *yang,* while the tortoise base symbolizes the earth or *yin.* The back of the tortoise of the stele of Kim Yang *(Plate 109)* exhibits stylized shell markings and an outer border of cloud designs. The slot which originally held the memorial tablet is bordered by a design of lotus petals. The wrinkled legs and snakelike head of the tortoise are extended in lifelike fashion.

PAINTING: So far, little has been said about Korean painting of the first eight or nine centuries of the Christian era. The reason is that, apart from the tomb murals, examples of this art have perished. Literary evidence gives us the name of the seventh-century painter-priest Solgo, but again we must turn to Japan for a hint of what Korean painting during this period must have been like. A painting of Shotoku Taishi and his sons, attributed to the Korean Prince Asa, is the source of the portrait head of Prince Shotoku that appears on several denominations of Japanese yen notes, but the painting itself is more doubtful than its attribution. The paintings on the Tamamushi miniature shrine at the Horyuji offer a better clue to the skill, style, medium, and subject matter of Korean painting in the Three Kingdoms period.[20] The eighth-century frescoes at the Horyuji, which were almost completely destroyed in a disastrous fire in 1949, are attributed by some to a Korean priest named Doncho (Tamjung in Korean). The controversy over this attribution need not prevent us from regarding the Indian or central Asian techniques displayed in these paintings as clues to the nature of Korean painting, especially since such influences are apparent in the sculpture of Sokkuram and other Buddhist relics of the period in Korea.

Literary evidence from Japanese sources also tells us that Korean excellence in painting continued in Japan after the Asuka "tutelage" period was long over. "The foremost court painter of the first half of the ninth century . . . was the Korean, Kudara Kawanari, by ancestry a man of Paekche. . . . The contemporary history, *Montoku-jitsuroku,* noting that he died in 853 at the age of seventy-two, states that 'because of the excellence of his paintings, he was frequently ordered to exhibit (to the Emperor) his portraits of men of old and his representations of landscapes, grasses, and trees, all of which were like nature itself. . . .' He may have reflected some of the striking achievements of Wu Tao-tzu. He was the first memorable painter in Japan, the first to bring landscape, for example, to the level of a dignified art; and he was a Korean."[21]

CERAMICS: Among the many types of minor arts that flourished at this time, the ceramics industry was by no means the least important. Tiles for roofs, walls, and pavements were moulded, pressed, incised, or carved. A few of these have escaped breakage to testify to the cleanness of line and the delicacy of execution of such humble accessories to the building trade. A group of roof tiles will serve to illustrate the general excellence of this category of the ceramic art *(Plate 110).* Two of the round tiles are decorated with lotus flowers, two with a delicate flower-and-leaf pattern around lotus seed-pod centers, and one with a twenty-four-petaled chrysanthemum. The long tiles exhibit familiar grapevine scrolls and two designs of confronting birds among elegant and painstakingly designed floral scrolls. Still another example of the taste for refinement of detail is found in a tile decorated with a design showing deer among stylized foliage. These intricately ornamented tiles illustrate the high quality of artistic achievement that permeated every medium of art in this creative age. Bowls and other utilitarian objects, many with a yellow-green glaze, display other types of decorative designs.

BRONZES: Among the hundreds of extant examples of bronze casting from this period, two magnificent small Buddhas and an architectural fixture—a door handle—have been selected for comment here. One of the bronze figurines is a slender Avalokitesvara about six inches in height *(Plate 111).* It shows the pinched waist, the free-hanging scarves, and the draped ties across the hips that were typical of the T'ang style. The second figurine is a Yaksa Yorae (Yakushi Nyorai in Japanese) about fifteen inches tall *(Plate 112).* In his left hand he evidently once held the medicine bowl that invariably serves as a distinguishing feature of this representation of the Buddha. The figure shows the tendency of sculptures of this period to look heavy. The bodies are full, the faces are rounder and more fleshy, and the drapery clings to the well-modeled contours in long, sweeping curves. The total effect is one of maturity, dignity, and a full-blown beauty of volume and plasticity. Giant sculptured rock *(Plate 113)* shows similar stylistic qualities, but the most characteristic sculpture of the age was the small bronze figure.

The door handle consists of the mask of a monster with decorative feline eyes and a suggestion of whiskers. The whole head appears in a stylized fleur-de-lis shape balanced by a large ring hanging from the snout of the monster *(Plate 114).*

BELLS: Of the products of the minor arts ministering to the total complex of the Buddhist establishment, the great bells were probably only second in importance to the sacred images themselves. The massive bell of Kyongju, one of the three remaining great bells of Korea, was cast in 771 in honor of the long and peaceful reign of King Sungdok, mentioned above as the patron of the relic pagoda of Kuhwang-ni. The bell, formerly located at the temple of Pongdok-sa, now hangs in an isolated pavilion in the Kyongju Museum grounds *(Plate 115)*. It is some eleven feet high and seven and a half feet in diameter and weighs a hundred and fifty-eight thousand pounds. The bell is struck on the outside by a log hanging loosely on chains. Reputedly its sound on a clear night can travel as far as forty miles. "When struck, it gives out now, as of old, the 'Brahma Sound'—solemn and strong when it called the monks of Pongdok-sa to prayer. If there is another bell in the whole world equal to it, it is probably the bell of Sangwon-sa in Kangwon Province, also cast in Korea under the Great Silla (723)."[22]

The decorations are clear and well cast. Around the crown are located three of the conventional squares, each supplied with nine studs: a design found on Chinese bells as far back as the Chou dynasty. At the top and bottom are bands of stylized honeysuckle and vine designs, and on the waist of the bell are delightful angels playing musical instruments among tossing draperies and flying clouds *(Plate 116)*. There are also conventionalized floral medallions decorating the rounded sides of the bell. The inscription reads:

"True religion lies beyond the realm of visible things; its source is nowhere seen. As a sound is heard through the air without any clue to its whereabouts, so is religion. Thus we hang up this great bell that it may awaken the call of Buddha. So ponderous is it that it can never be moved—a fitting place on which to inscribe the virtues of the king. Great Sungdok was his name, his deeds eternal as the hills and streams, his glory as the sun and moon. He called the true and noble to aid him in his rule. Fitting ceremonies and music accompanied all his ways. He encouraged the farmer to a joy in his work and the merchant to the exercise of honesty. Gold and jewels were accounted as nothing in his sight, while useful knowledge and skill of hand were treasures above compare. His great aim was the right-ordered life. For this reason people came from afar to seek his counsel, and all revered him for his worth."[23]

20: PAGODA, CHONGYIM-SA (page 68). Puyo, South Ch'ungch'ong Province.
Height: 28 1/2'. Paekche, 6th–7th century.

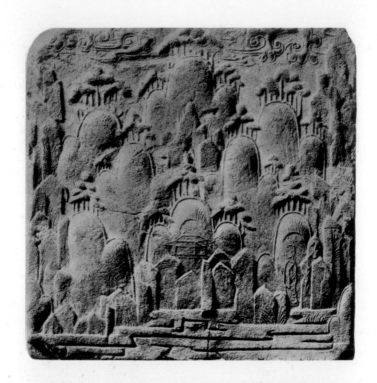

21, 22: TILES WITH LANDSCAPE IN RELIEF (page 68). Gray paste.
Excavated at temple site in Puyo, South Ch'ungch'ong Province.
Height: 11″; width: 11″; thickness: 1 3/4″. Paekche, 7th century.
National Museum of Korea.

23, 24: TILES WITH KWI-HYONG IN RELIEF (page 68). Gray paste. Excavated at temple site, Puyo, South Ch'ungch'ong Province. Height: 11″; width: 11″; thickness: 1 3/4″. Paekche, 7th century. National Museum of Korea.

25, 26: TILES WITH DRAGON AND PHOENIX IN RELIEF (page 68). Gray paste. Excavated at temple site in Puyo, South Ch'ungch'ong Province. Height: 11″; width: 11″; thickness: 1 3/4″. Paekche, 7th century. National Museum of Korea.

27, 28: TILES WITH FLORAL MEDALLIONS IN RELIEF (page 68). Gray paste. Excavated at temple site in Puyo, South Ch'ungch'ong Province. Height: 11″; width: 11″; thickness: 1 3/4″. Paekche, 7th century. National Museum of Korea.

29: BODHISATTVA (page 68). Gilt bronze. Excavated at Kunsu-ri, Puyo, South Ch'ungch'ong Province. Height: 4 1/2″. Paekche, 6th century. National Museum of Korea.

30: PAGODA, KORYANG (page 71). South Kyongsang Province. Height: about 10′. Karak, 6th–7th century.

31: KARAK CERAMICS (page 71). Excavated at Koryang, South Kyongsang Province. Karak, 6th–7th century. Koryang County Seat Headquarters.

32, 33: MONUMENT OF KING KWANGGAE TOJI (page 72). North P'yongan Province. Height: about 21'. Koguryo, 5th century.

34–36: DETAILS FROM GREAT TOMB MURALS (page 75). Near P'yong-yang, North P'yongan Province. Koguryo, 4th–6th century.

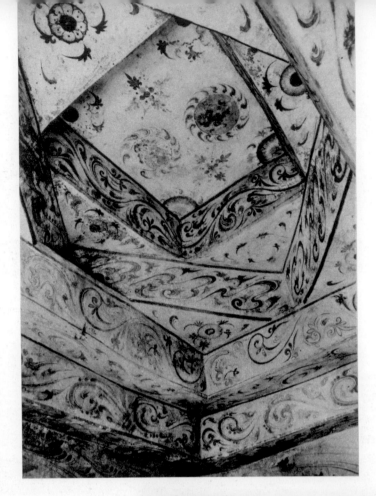

37, 38: CEILING DECORATIONS, SHINBA-RI TOMB NO. I: CORBELED DOME AND DETAIL
OF SUN AND MOON DESIGNS (page 75). Painting on white stucco. South P'yongan
Province, near P'yongyang. Koguryo, 5th–7th century.

39: CORBELED DOME, TOMB OF THE DANCERS (page 75). Painting on plaster.
T'ung-kou, Manchuria. Koguryo, 4th–6th century.

40: MURAL, TOMB OF THE DANCERS: DANCERS AND SINGERS (page 75). Painting on plaster. Height: about 2 1/2'; width: about 3 1/2'. T'ung-kou,
Manchuria. Koguryo, 4th–6th century.

41: DETAIL FROM MURAL, THREE-
CHAMBERED TOMB: CARYATID
(page 75). Painting on plaster.
T'ung-kou, Manchuria. Koguryo, 4th–6th century.

112

42: MURAL, TOMB OF THE FOUR SPIRITS: TORTOISE AND SNAKE (page 76). Painting on stone. Height: 3'; width; 5'. T'ung-kou, Manchuria. Koguryo, 4th–6th century.

43: DETAIL FROM NORTHEAST CORBEL, TOMB OF THE FOUR SPIRITS: SPRITE ON
DRAGON (page 76). Painting on stone. T'ung-kou, Manchuria. Koguryo,
4th–6th century.

44: DETAIL FROM NORTHWEST CORBEL, TOMB OF THE FOUR SPIRITS: SPRITE ON CRANE (page 76). Painting on stone. T'ung-kou, Manchuria. Koguryo, 4th–6th century.

45: DETAIL FROM SIMULATED PILLAR, TOMB OF THE CONCENTRIC CIRCLES (page 76). Painting on plaster. T'ung-kou, Manchuria. Koguryo, 4th–6th century.

46: DETAIL FROM CORBEL, TOMB NO. 17, WUKUAIFEN: SPRITES AND WHEEL
(page 76). Painting on plaster. T'ung-kou, Manchuria. Koguryo, 4th–6th
century.

47: DETAIL, TWIN PILLAR TOMB (page 76). South P'yongan Province.
Koguryo, 5th–6th century.

48–50: DETAILS FROM MURALS, TWIN PILLAR TOMB (page 77). Painting on plaster. South P'yongan Province. Koguryo, 5th–6th century.

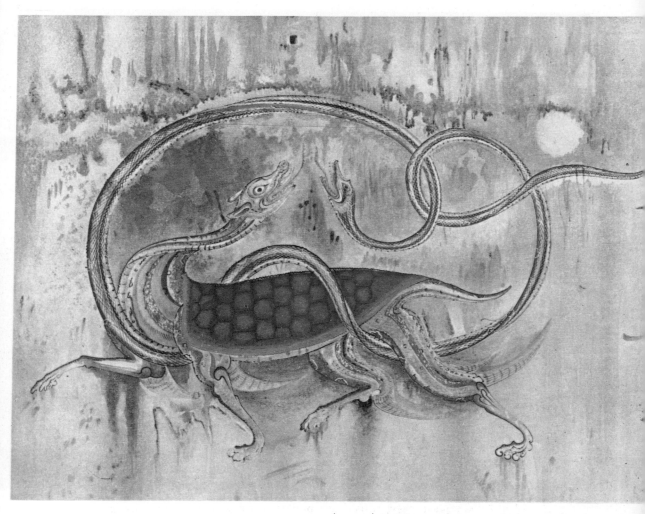

51: MURAL, GREAT TOMB: TORTOISE AND SNAKE (page 77). Painting on plaster.
Height: about 3'; width: about 5'. South P'yongan Province. Koguryo,
6th–7th century.

52: MURAL, GREAT TOMB: AZURE DRAGON OF THE EAST (page 77). Painting on plaster. Height: about 3'; width: about 5'. South P'yongan Province. Koguryo, 6th–7th century.

53: MURAL, GREAT TOMB: WHITE TIGER OF THE WEST (page 77). Painting on plaster. Height: about 3′; width: about 5′. South P'yongan Province. Koguryo, 6th–7th century.

54, 55: WASHING VESSEL AND INSCRIPTION (page 78). Bronze. Excavated from Ho-u (Washing Vessel) Tomb, North Kyongsang Province. Diameter: about 8 1/4″; height: about 6 1/2″. Koguryo, 5th century. National Museum of Korea.

56, 57: SAKYAMUNI (?) AND MOLD (page 78). Terra cotta. Excavated near P'yongyang. Height: image, about 8″; mold, about 6″. Koguryo, 6th century. National Museum of Korea.

63: BELT WITH PENDANTS (page 85). Gold with jade and glass ornaments. Excavated from Gold Crown Tomb, Kyongju. Length of belt: 64″; longest pendant: 27″; shortest pendant: 8 1/16″. Old Silla, 5th–6th century. National Museum of Korea.

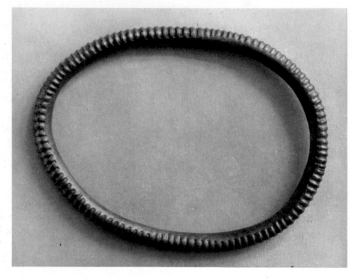

64: BRACELET (page 85). Gold. Excavated from Gold Crown Tomb, Kyongju. Width: about 3/16″; diameter: about 3 1/8″. Old Silla, 5th–6th century. National Museum of Korea.

65: RINGS (page 85). Gold. Excavated from Gold Crown Tomb, Kyong-ju. Width: from 1/4″ to 3/8″; diameter: about 3/4″. Old Silla, 5th–6th century. National Museum of Korea.

66: BOWL (page 86). Gold. Excavated from Gold Crown Tomb, Kyong-ju. Height: about 2 1/8″; diameter: about 4 1/2″. Old Silla, 5th–6th century. National Museum of Korea.

67: VESSEL IN SHAPE OF A HORSEMAN (page 86). Gray stoneware. Excavated from Golden Bell Tomb, Kyongju. Height: 9 3/8″; length: 11 1/2″. Old Silla, 5th–6th century. National Museum of Korea.

68: MAITREYA (page 87). Gilt bronze. Height: 6 9/16″. Old Silla, 6th–7th century. National Museum of Korea.

69: MAITREYA (page 87). Gilt bronze. Height: 8 1/4″. Old Silla (?), 6th–7th century. National Museum of Korea.

71: MAITREYA (page 87). Gilt bronze. Said to be from Andong area. Height: 31 11/16". Old Silla, 6th–7th century. National Museum of Korea.

70: MAITREYA (page 87). Gilt bronze. Height: 35 3/4". Old Silla, early 7th century. Toksu Palace Museum.

72: STONE OBSERVATORY (page 89). Punae-myon, Kyongju-gun, North
Kyongsang Province. Height: about 22′. Old Silla, 7th century.

132

73: PAGODA, PUNHWANG-SA (page 89). Kyongju. Height: 27 1/2'.
Old Silla, 7th century.

74: MAIN ENTRANCE GATE, PULGUK-SA (page 92). North Kyongsang
Province. United Silla, 7th–8th century.

75: PAGODA ("PAGODA THAT CASTS NO SHADOW"), PULGUK-SA (page 93). North Kyongsang Province. Height: about 27'. United Silla, 7th–8th century.

76: PAGODA (TABO-TʻAP), PULGUK-SA (page 93). North Kyongsang Province. Height: about 34'. United Silla, 535; repaired 751.

77: AMITABHA (page 93). Bronze. Pulguk-sa, North Kyongsang Province. Height: 6 1/4'. United Silla, 7th–8th century.

78: DOMED CEILING, SOKKURAM (page 94). North Kyongsang Province. United Silla, 8th century.

79: ENTRANCE, SOKKURAM (page 94). North Kyongsang Province.
United Silla, 8th century.

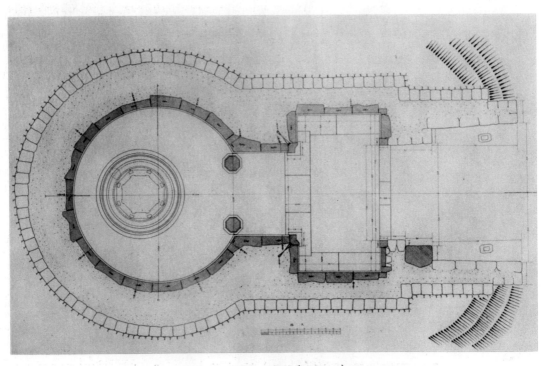

80–82: GROUND PLAN, LEFT AND FRONT (OPPOSITE) ELEVATIONS, SOKKURAM (page 94). North Kyongsang Province. United Silla, 8th century.

83: GUARDIAN FIGURE (page 94). Granite
relief. Sokkuram, North Kyongsang
Province. Height: about 6 1/3'. United
Silla, 8th century.

139

84: BRAHMA (page 95). Granite relief. Sokkuram, North Kyongsang Province. Height: about 7'. United Silla, 8th century.

85: INDRA (page 95). Granite relief. Sokkuram, North Kyongsang Province. Height: about 7'. United Silla, 8th century.

140

86: ELEVEN-HEADED KANSEUM (SEPILMYON POSAL)
(page 95). Granite relief. Sokkuram, North
Kyongsang Province. Height: about 7'. United
Silla, 8th century.

87: BODHISATTVA (page 95). Granite relief. Sokkuram,
North Kyongsang Province. Height: about 7'. United
Silla, 8th century.

88, 89: ARHATS (page 95). Granite relief. Sokkuram, North Kyongsang
Province. Height: about 7′. United Silla, 8th century.

90: SAKYAMUNI (page 95). Granite. Sokkuram, North Kyongsang Province.
Height (overall): about 11′. United Silla, 8th century.

91: PAGODA, SITE OF HWANGBOK-SA (page 96). Kyongju.
Height: about 23′. United Silla, 7th century.

98: AMITABHA (page 96). Gold alloy. Found in pagoda at site of Hwang-bok-sa, Kyongju. Height: 5 3/8″. United Silla, 7th–8th century. National Museum of Korea.

99: PAGODA, SINWOL (page 97). North Kyongsang Province. Height: about 8′. United Silla, 7th–8th century.

100: SILLA PAGODAS AND LANTERNS (page 97). Kyongbok Palace Pagoda Park, Seoul. United Silla, 7th–8th century.

101: ROYAL TOMB (page 97). Kyongju. United Silla, 7th–8th century.

102: GUARDIAN FIGURES AT ROYAL TOMB (page 97). Stone. Kyongju. Height: about 5'. United Silla, 7th–8th century.

149

150

103–7: ANIMAL FIGURES (page 97). Stone relief.
Tomb of Kim Yu-sin, Kyongju. Height: about 3′.
United Silla, 7th–8th century.

151

108: AL FRESCO BANQUET CHANNEL (page 98). Stone. Site of P'osokchong, near Kyongju. Length: 18′ 5″; width: 14′ 5″. United Silla, 8th–9th century.

109: BASE FOR STELE (page 98). Stone. Tomb of Kim Yang, near Kyongju. Height: about 3′. United Silla, 7th–8th century.

152

110: TILES WITH FLORAL DESIGNS IN RELIEF (page 99). Gray earthenware. Excavated at Chongun-ni, Kyongju. About half actual size. United Silla, 7th–8th century. Kyongju Museum.

112: BHAISAJYAGURU (YAKSA YORAE) (page 99). Gilt bronze. Height: about 15″. United Silla, 8th–9th century. National Museum of Korea.

111: AVALOKITESVARA (page 99). Gilt bronze. From Ch'ongdo district, North Kyongsang Province. Height: 6 1/4″. United Silla, 8th century. National Museum of Korea.

154

113: BUDDHA AND BODHISATTVA (page 99). Stone relief. Kulbul-sa, near Kyongju. Height: 12'; width: 12'. United Silla, 8th–9th century.

114: DOOR HANDLE (page 99). Bronze. From a tomb near Kyongju. Length: 6 1/2″; width: 4″. United Silla, 8th–9th century. Kyongju Museum.

115, 116: TEMPLE BELL AND DETAIL (page 100). Bronze. Formerly at Pongdok-sa, Kyongju. Height: 11′; diameter: 7′ 5″. United Silla, 8th century. Kyongju Museum.

PART THREE

# The Koryo Dynasty

WITH PLATES 117–77

FOLLOWING PAGE 183

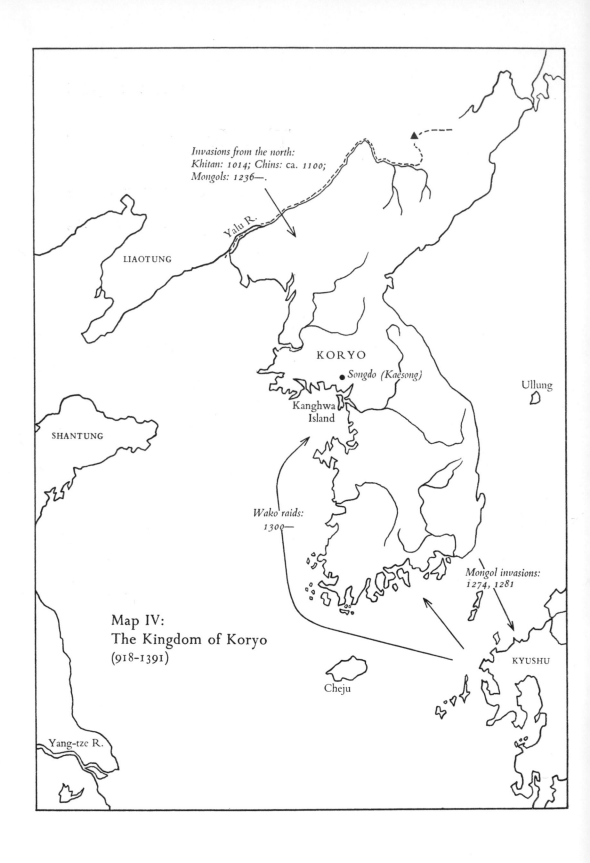

Invasions from the north:
Khitan: 1014; Chins: ca. 1100;
Mongols: 1236—.

Yalu R.

LIAOTUNG

KORYO

Songdo (Kaésong)

Ullung

Kanghwa
Island

SHANTUNG

Wako raids:
1300—

Mongol invasions:
1274, 1281

Map IV:
The Kingdom of Koryo
(918-1391)

KYUSHU

Cheju

Yang-tze R.

# The Kingdom of Koryo:
# History and Architecture

HISTORICAL BACKGROUND  Koryo, beginning in 918 and ending in 1391, retained its vitality for almost five hundred years. It was established in a way unique in the history of Korea. The founder, Wanggon, seized control of the peninsula without assassinating the previous ruler, the last king of Silla, and furthermore accorded him generous treatment, a palace in the capital, and a peaceful old age. The T'ang dynasty in China had collapsed a few years previously (906–7), and a period of confusion in all north China had followed. When T'ang support was withdrawn from Korea, the king of Silla soon found that he had jurisdiction only in the Kyongju area, while robber chiefs controlled the rest of the peninsula. In the southwest a principality called Late Paekche sprang up. In the north, one called Late Koguryo, or Taebong, was organized under the leadership of a strong and rapacious Buddhist chief called Kunye, who regarded himself as semidivine. Wanggon served under this man until an episode that occurred in 918 put Wanggon in Kunye's place, apparently by acclaim of his fellows. Wanggon then established the capital of the dynasty at Songdo and gave the name of Koryo (an abbreviation of Koguryo) to the new kingdom. In China, some forty years later, the founder of the Sung dynasty established his regime with the same unique feudal gesture of amnesty to the displaced royal house.

Perhaps the outstanding feature of the Koryo period was the incidence of foreign invasion. There were five incursions into the peninsula during the Wang dynasty, occurring about a hundred years apart. The dynasty had scarcely become firmly entrenched when, toward the turn of the century, the Khitans rode down into Korea and, in 1014, burned its capital at Songdo. They were eventually repulsed by a General Kim, who negotiated a treaty of peace. Around 1100 the country was invaded by the Chins (Jurchen or Gold Tartars), a Tungusic people living in Manchuria. These people too were dealt with by Korean forces, and an agreement of peace was arranged by a statesman named Yun Kwan. When the Chins became rulers of north China (1113–1234), the Koreans shifted their official allegiance from the Sungs to these new non-Chinese overlords.[1]

In Korea the general reallocation of power in north Asia caused by the Chins in the twelfth century accelerated the process of decentralization. The central government, weakened by less able descendants of Wanggon, was unable to stop the dispersion of political power into the hands of provincial great men who, formerly congregated at the capital, were now located at various monastic and semimilitary feudal estates in the provinces. As a consequence of this dispersion, new cultural centers developed rapidly. Demands for schools, books, and ceramics multiplied, and the result was that the twelfth century saw a blossoming of the native arts, freed from the hothouse influence of superior Sung culture. The Koreans, cut off from Sung markets, were obliged to develop their own products, and this they did, achieving some remarkable original inventions in their time of need.

Among the local achievements was the invention of movable metal type—a device never before developed in Asia, although movable clay types had been developed in China somewhat earlier—and the creation of a new variety of ceramics, the inlaid celadons. The schools that were established in provincial centers to cater to the needs of country people required books, and the demand for a supply of well-printed works, not only of Buddhist scriptures but also of certain Confucian classics, was met by improved printing methods. Block-printed editions were easily financed in China, where quantities of copies of each edition were readily sold, but these were expensive in Korea, where few copies but many different titles were needed. The solution hit upon in Korea was the publication, under royal auspices and in limited editions, of the required number of copies through the use of movable metal types that could be broken down and used again for the next title on the list. Some block printing was also done. For example, Buddhist scriptures were published in costly editions at least four times during the dynasty at moments of severe national crisis as a gesture to beseech divine help.[2] These crises occurred at the time of the Khitan attack in 1014 and the repeated attacks of the Mongols from 1200 to 1250. In 1234, the major book of the Son sect, the *Sangjong Yemun*, was printed in movable type. Later in the Yi dynasty this type of printing was revived, and editions were distributed by the king free of charge.

Local schools that had begun to function as far back as 958 now became, in the twelfth century, stronger and more sophisticated. Classical learning became widespread.[3] For the first time in Korean history, the thirst for Chinese knowledge spread outside the limits of the court. Improved education brought about cultural changes which in turn made the twelfth century a vigorous creative period.

It was during this century that Buddhism also reached its broadest native development. Colorful, artistic, worldly, at the center of all court and community activity in the land, the Buddhist church effectively influenced every aspect of cultural life. Monk-clerks attended to the business details of government; monk-scholars taught in many schools (which were usually affiliated with temples or monasteries and used Buddhist scriptures as the basis of their curricula); and monk-ministers, as the chief learned men of the country, advised the king and carried on much of the diplomacy with the Chins or Khitan Tartars, who themselves relied upon Buddhist-trained officials for these services. Confucian learning and Confucian scholars, as representatives of the refugee Sung court in south China, were in eclipse. Interest in trade and commerce arose in all areas, for even the Sung court, departing from the old Confucian emphasis upon a purely agricultural economy and the cautious, if not hostile, attitude towards a money economy, encouraged trade.

Of the five major Buddhist sects in Korea, the Son, which originated in China as the

Ch'an (called Zen in Japan), was especially congenial to north Asian psychology. Chiefly a meditative sect, disrespectful of ritual, it was soon very popular in China, and after 1097, ✓ when it was introduced into Korea by Prince Cho Taejong, it achieved and maintained overwhelming popularity there also. Son remained the most important of the five Buddhist denominations until the downfall of the dynasty and even later, under the persecution of the Yi government, continued to be the only influential sect in Korea.

Under the Mongols, Lamaism also entered Korea, at least in court circles. This development made Buddhism in Korea more foreign in flavor than ever, and this fact, as much as anything else, brought about the downfall of Buddhism when the Yi dynasty came into power and Korea ceased to be a Buddhist country. Another important factor in the collapse of Buddhism was its internal decay. Early in the Koryo dynasty, peasants began to escape military service by becoming monks, one in four doing so. As times grew more disturbed, the Buddhist establishments weighed more and more heavily upon the diminishing productive class: the farmers. This the Yi monarchs, returning to the policy of encouraging agriculture above all else, corrected by outlawing the religion and all its temporal works.

The period of decentralization, roughly coterminous with the twelfth and the early thirteenth century, was a period of robust military feudalism, internal trade, and a developing money economy—all the features of society considered most unhealthy by the Sung statesman Su T'ung-po. Koryo, however, went its own way, beginning, like Japan in the same century, to develop its own institutions free of Chinese political and cultural interference. But all of this came to an end in the new period of centralization brought on by the Mongol conquest.

Around 1200 came the first wave of Mongol raiders, who were dealt with as the Khitans had been. But as the predatory and rapacious nature of the Mongol domination became better understood, the Korean king and the court withdrew to a haven on Kanghwa Island, where they held out for a full generation without yielding to compromise of any kind. It was not until the Mongols became Sinified under Kublai Khan (1260–94) that the Koreans accepted a tributary relationship with them. Then, around 1300, after the death of Kublai and the relaxation of the Mongol grasp on Korean affairs following the failure of the invasions of Japan in 1274 and 1281, which were launched from Korea, the Koreans became the target for retaliatory piratical raids by the Wako of Japan. From about 1300 on, these raids grew in frequency and daring, and the fourteenth century marked their height. During this century Korea and south China were largely under Mongol control —the latter until 1368, when the Mings came to power, and the former until 1392, when the Yi dynasty was established. At one time in this confused age the Korean statesman Yi Che-hyon was credited with having saved his country from being turned into a province of China.[4]

Although the Mongol domination brought about a new centralization which put an end to the developing feudal life, the new culture and the even more important new class structure were very different from the old. The new culture was colored by the importation of a medley of foreign innovations of many kinds (from the abacus to firearms) which were introduced by the Mongols in their encouragement of a free exchange of goods and persons in the region reaching from Poland to Korea. Society also changed greatly through the democratic hierarchy of Buddhism and through the military hierarchy of the army. Commoners rose to positions of great power. Small armies grew up under local leadership, and the number of common people in leading positions expanded greatly.

The Koryo dynasty thus included in its five-hundred-year span two periods of centralization separated by one of decentralization. During the first two hundred years, Korean culture developed under close and fruitful ties with Sung China. In the twelfth century, however, cut off from Chinese culture and politically associated with non-Chinese rulers no more culturally advanced than themselves, the Koreans progressed greatly in their development of a native culture. Later, under the systematic exploitation of the Mongols, many innovations were introduced into Korean life, but impoverishment soon affected all levels of achievement, and the Koryo dynasty ended in confusion, in the failure of existing institutions to meet the challenge of the times, and in general disillusionment.

ARCHITECTURE    In examining the art and architecture of the Koryo kingdom, it is possible to study still extant monuments of the period, two of which are Buddhist temples of wood construction. We shall therefore begin with an account of Koryo architecture—first, however, placing it in its setting. To do this, it will be necessary to go back to the architecture of ancient China and to relate to this parent tradition the derivative styles of border areas.

Native Korean building has been well adjusted to the needs and tastes of the Korean people. It is suited to the rocky landscape and the temperate-zone climate; it is functional to a high degree; and, though a branch of Chinese architecture in its general features, it has developed particular features of its own. Korean builders used local materials, imported little except certain pigments to be used in the painting of temples and palaces, and took careful account of the contours of a mountainous landscape when designing and erecting their buildings, which ranged in type from farmhouses to royal audience halls. Nevertheless, the major features of the building tradition came from north China.

It is generally accepted that north Asiatic architecture changed slowly in the centuries after the basic features were first developed on the north China plains in the second millennium before Christ, and that these features were essentially the same inside China as in border areas like Korea, Japan, and Indo-China. China was the home of one of the five great building cultures of the ancient world and in its early development progressed, like the other four, into city building and the monumental style. Of the chief building techniques of the ancient world, China shared three: post-and-lintel, arch-and-vault, and corbel or cantilever construction. The Chinese, however, did not develop the fourth principle of construction: the truss. In the opinion of Western architects who have studied Chinese techniques, the neglect of the truss principle was the cause of the Chinese development of the unnecessarily complex roof, a building feature that persisted throughout the whole history of north Asiatic architecture. The elaborate roof evolved in answer to the effort to achieve spacious and monumental building while at the same time depending upon post-and-lintel thinking.

Other major features of the early Chinese tradition were the treatment of pillars and walls —walls as screens and not as supports of the roof—and the treatment of foundation platforms. The transitions between the three elements—roof, walls, and foundation—were handled at the top by means of heavily bracketed eaves and at the bottom by heavy stone socles which, with subbasement support, bore the entire weight of pillars and superstructure. The wooden pillars were aboveground. They were lacquered or varnished and could be kept in good condition, free from unnoticed deterioration due to termites or rot. The walls, not being required to bear weight, could be delicate and light like lattices, while the basements gradually became high platforms composed of great granite blocks, solid and high above the ground to insure dryness within the building and to counterbalance the heavy dominating roof. The complex eaves and upturned corners were, as noted above, results of the transition problems inherent in larger building. In the development of the roof, the supporting brackets became increasingly important. For example, in order "to roof a wide hall, the wooden posts were made to carry great girders straight across it. These girders in turn would each carry two smaller posts of lesser span, and these other smaller posts still closer together, until little by little the triangular shape of the roof was built up. . . . Perhaps it was this trick of construction which helped in the development of the curved roof, for there was no engineering gain in such a construction to be achieved through having the rafters straight."[5] These features are exhibited in the main building at Pusok-sa, which is described below.

The building materials used in carrying out the basic features just reviewed differed greatly in different areas, constituting the first element of local adaptation. The materials available in the Chinese empire were almost unlimited, whereas the Japanese and the Koreans were obliged to use the wood and stone available in their own small kingdoms. In general, all three countries used wood for the superstructure, tile or thatch for the roofs, and stone for the foundations. The Chinese used more brick and marble than the other two countries. The Japanese had little stone suitable for dressing, since much of the rock of Japan was porous and volcanic, so their emphasis was upon wood. Korea, on the other hand, had an abundance of granite of many varieties and colors and was able to build grandly in stone. Korea's wood, however, was generally soft, whereas the Chinese and the Japanese had hardwoods of many varieties. Variety within the general north Asiatic architectural tradition was therefore obtained, even at the outset, by the difference in building materials.

The second difference was in detail. The search for greater perfection of detail was seldom neglected, with the result that one monastery would differ in many interesting particulars from another, even of the same sect, not far away. Major variations within China, for example, may be seen in the difference between the northern and the southern building emphasis on detail, the southern tending (like the Hindu architecture of the tropics) to flamboyance, the northern to suavity and symmetry. The northern type (the tradition preferred by both Japanese and Koreans), which developed in the wide plains of China, was characterized by spacious family homes and large cities laid out in large rectangular patterns, and was built up of aggregations of walls within walls, all organized on a symmetrical basis.

This Chinese arrangement on a chief axis was suited to the plains. In Japan and Korea, adaptation to hilly terrain produced asymmetry, and an esthetic delight in the beautiful landscape scenes caused the grounds around a residence to be treated as an intrinsic part of the whole. The inward-turning house of north China, arranged around one or more courts, was therefore modified greatly in Korea, and the style was used mainly in public buildings (much as the West uses the Greek or the Gothic for such purposes), in Buddhist temples, in the formal units of the great houses, and vestigially in the L- or U-shaped peasant houses.

The use of color in the decoration of buildings also created a major local variation upon the Chinese tradition. Owing perhaps to the monotony of the north China plains, brilliant colors were used there even on the outer walls of public buildings—pinks, yellows, and reds. But in Korea and Japan, color was used sparingly and usually only on the interiors of temples and palaces, except on rafters beneath the roof overhang. In both these countries the taste for uncarved, unpainted wooden surfaces both outside and inside the living areas of all residences was conspicuous. In Korea, emphasis was placed not upon color but upon texture, which meant highly polished wooden beams overhead and highly polished floors beneath in the *maru* rooms, or upon polished oiled paper in the *ondol* rooms.[6]

Other occasions for variation from the central Chinese tradition arose from the philosophy of architecture itself and the goal of keeping the buildings as close as possible to the human needs and customs of the different peoples who occupied north Asia. For example, unlike the north Chinese peasants, south Korean peasants, as far back as the time of Christ, did not live in walled villages but in separate houses near their fields. These houses, built largely of stone and mud, were located then as now on hilly upland areas so as not to encroach upon good farming land. Such farmhouses are still generally found fitted snugly into some fold of the hills, protected from the north and facing south for a maximum of warmth from the sun. The residences of aristocrats were also generally located on hillsides where fine views of mountain peaks were part of the geomancy of the site and where the architects took full and dramatic account of local rocks, trees, or streams that often threw the layout of the inner and outer courts, stables, and the like into an asymmetrical arrangement.

Thus in materials, in emphasis on particulars, in decoration, location, and site, the architecture of border areas differed from the Chinese parent tradition. North Chinese preferences were for symmetry, whereas Korean preferences, except for the most formal of buildings, were for asymmetry, a trend even more conspicuous in Japan. The Chinese preferred solidity even in lower-class dwellings—a solidity that was achieved through a wide use of brick and plaster and an inward-turning arrangement, while the Koreans modified the effect of solidity by a general use of paper-covered lattice doors that were often used as walls between heavy roofs and heavy foundations. The Japanese developed an architectural tradition even further away from the Chinese norms in a native building system in which delicacy and impermanence of construction and lightness of building materials were the rule rather than the exception. Finally, Chinese preferences for impressiveness may be contrasted with the deliberate unpretentiousness of the Koreans and with the Japanese taste for an even greater simplicity.

In spite of the differences between local schools of architecture, we must not lose sight of the fact that the similarities were far more important than the differences. All schools shared certain disadvantages, of which the lack of application of the truss principle was one. Another of the chief problems encountered everywhere, but more in wealthy China than in the poorer countries of Korea and Japan, was the problem of nonfunctionalism, as seen in the complex roof and in the conflict between the material and its use exemplified by the "stone lace" so conspicuous in China. In Korea this sort of flamboyance was noticeable only in the buildings most closely patterned upon Chinese models. In native and informal building, functionalism was the rule.

In closing this brief discussion, it should be noted that all areas shared in the advantages of the Chinese architectural tradition, a building tradition that has solved some of the problems that the West has only begun to think about, particularly in city planning. For example, this tradition developed an "almost final solution of the problem of the relation between house and street"[7] and solved four related problems of architecture: flexibility of plan, decentralization, expansion by aggregation of fixed units, and relative nonpermanence of building materials. The modern West is only beginning to experiment with these features.[8] In all the variations, similarities, disadvantages, and advantages of the Chinese architectural tradition, Korea stood about halfway between Chinese and Japanese practice.

With the establishment of a new dynasty of northerners located in a mountainous capital far away from the flat, spacious plain of Kyongju, new architectural requirements led to new developments. The nonaxial arrangement of the entire city of Songdo (Kaesong) was one of these modifications. The palaces and temples of Songdo clustered along the flanks of Inwang Mountain and were enclosed within a meandering, irregular city wall. Another departure was the unique Korean "radiant heating" system of the ondol floor, which became widely used in this capital of cold winters[9] and soon spread to the whole peninsula, although inexplicably not to Japan. The fact that the kitchen flues often ran under the ondol floors meant that the floors were kept dry and free of damp or mold, which were the two curses of the Chinese house.

In 918, the city of Songdo became the center of Korean political life and remained so for the next five hundred years. The architecture of this period remained to a great degree Buddhist in inspiration and financing. During the first hundred years of the dynasty (the tenth century) much building went on amid tremendous enthusiasm on the part of the newly powerful nobles, both lay and ecclesiastical. The palace of Wanggon, for example, attracted considerable attention in its day for size, elegance, and beauty, and even though it was burned down when the city was destroyed by the Khitans in 1014, a description of it still remains in all the major histories.[10]

The Wanggon palace was laid out according to the Chinese axial plan, but because it was located on the flanks of a mountain it had to be accommodated to the terrain. The series of courts were connected from one level to the next by flights of stone steps which, along with the foundation stones, can still be seen on the now empty mountainside. The palace buildings are said to have covered about 2,600 *kan* in floor space, or approximately 46,400 square feet. Twenty gates provided for egress and ingress. The main building was apparently flanked by two double-storied guest houses constructed in a style that has continued to the present for such structures. The guest houses were painted a gay red and were reputedly situated so as to command a magnificent view of the valley floor and the distant sheen of the Imjin River. Another feature of this famous early palace was its wide stone-paved passageway laid along the central axis for the use of Sung ambassadors. There was also a great banquet hall adorned during festive occasions with silk hangings and official gifts. A small council chamber, watchtowers, an observatory fifty feet high, and conduits constructed to convey cascades of spring water into the palace from above were other features. After the burning by the Khitans, the palace was rebuilt, but apparently not on such a grand scale.

Still extant in Korea are several Koryo buildings. Two wooden halls of Pusok-sa, rebuilt about 1350, are deservedly famous. They are the oldest standing wooden structures in the country. The main hall *(Plates 117–21)* is long and narrow and somewhat low. The roof is curved, but the bracket and beam construction is relatively simple. The interior shows a double row of columns supporting the inner cross beams *(Plates 122, 123)*. These columns show an entasis, a feature of pillars of the whole ancient world. The floor is of brick.[11] Murals in color, though damaged, still decorate the halls and are highly valued as being among the rare relics of Koryo painting. Fortunately, the Buddhist image housed in the main hall of Pusok-sa is also extant: a Sakyamuni in wood with an unusual full-length aureole of carved and gilded wood.

# CHAPTER NINE

# The Kingdom of Koryo: Sculpture and Minor Arts

IT IS safe to say that there were no arts and crafts of any importance—outside of those cater- ing to peasant needs and some producing military equipment for the state—which were not directed or supervised or patronized to a large degree by the Buddhist church. Bud- dhist doctrine, especially as expounded by the Son (Zen) sects, was still strong; Buddhist efforts on behalf of their beliefs were still vigorous; and the art that was produced to serve or to enhance the religion was still profoundly motivated throughout the dynasty. The arts which will be considered in this chapter and the next must be looked upon as largely tinctured throughout by Buddhist ideals, craftsmanship, and designs drawn from three sources: India, China, and the earlier Buddhist tradition in Korea itself. Progress toward secularization, speeded up under Sung influence, was halted during the many troubles of the foreign invasions—a confused period that riveted more firmly than ever the styles and ideals of a rapidly deteriorating religious art upon the workshops of the kingdom.

Among the major products made for the service of religion were, of course, the Buddhist images. The Sakya Buddha now seated in the main hall of Pusok-sa *(Plate 124)* is typical of the category of principal Buddhist figures. Carved out of wood, gilded, and furnished with an elaborate and unusual full-length aureole, this figure is a rare example of religious sculpture in this medium. The Buddha's face is fuller, the head rounder, and the draperies less suavely modeled than corresponding features in late Silla art. The torso is still slender and tapered, however, like those of the late Silla figures.

A good example of the small figures intended for use in household shrines is the rare seated representation of Avalokitesvara (Kanseum in Korean) which was excavated in the Diamond Mountains toward the close of the period of Japanese control of the peninsula *(Plate 125)*. It is about seven inches tall, is made of gilt bronze, and dates from the close of the Koryo dynasty. An elaborate crown adorns the head, and a necklace and bracelets composed of small beads strung together with round, flattish plaques decorate the body. Over the scarf that covers the shoulders and upper arms, the characteristic curls of the Kanseum lie in gentle waves.[1] The feet are placed soles uppermost above the crossed legs. The lotus seat is flat, and the petals are slightly incurved to give the appearance of closely following the lines of the seated figure. The gentle expression of compassion on the face and the restraint and good proportions of this small and elegant figure make it a valuable relic of Koryo sculpture.

An example of the giant images carved in stone, sometimes from previously installed monoliths of the dolmen age, is the Kwonch'ok-sa Maitreya (Miruk) near Nonsan *(Plate 126)*. (The Miruk, Buddha of the Future, departs in iconography from the usual Buddha figure in that it is represented as a Bodhisattva without the adornments of the other Bodhisattvas.) The Kwonch'ok-sa figure is about sixty feet tall and is provided with the double mortar-board hat with little pendent bells characteristic of the Korean Miruk.

The next class of Koryo Buddhist sculpture is represented by the pagodas. Some elegant remnants of Koryo pagoda sculpture are still standing. This preservation of Korean monuments is due to the scarcity of hardwood in Korea and the substitution of stone for wood in the construction of pagodas. An important example of Koryo pagodas is the one standing at Woljong-sa in Kangwon Province *(Plate 127)*. It is a nine-storied, octagonal pagoda set upon a pedestal consisting of a downturned lotus and two tiers of unadorned plaques. The finial is its chief glory. An elaborate crown-and-ball construction topped by a sequence of wrought-iron rings, plates, and a spire, it is an exceedingly graceful and impressive remnant of Koryo art. The pagoda is over forty-eight feet high. Another pagoda still *in situ* is the Kumsan-sa monument, which has six stories and a crown-and-ball finial.

A number of pagodas have been removed from their original temple sites and set up in the Kyongbok Palace grounds in Seoul. These include five Koryo pagodas which are among the best to be found in the entire peninsula.[2] A five-story stone structure erected in 1031, according to the inscription on its base, was brought to the palace grounds from North Kyongsang Province. It is seven and a half feet square at the base and about fifteen feet in height. As an early Koryo pagoda, it shows little modification from the Silla tradition with its high pedestal and boxlike stories crowned by unadorned eaves slightly upturned at the edges. Following a general trend during Koryo times, however, the pagoda is smaller and somewhat more slender than its Silla prototypes.

Twin pagodas dating from 1388 (if we are to accept the inscription found on one of them) formerly stood at the Yongch'on Monastery in Kangwon Province *(Plates 128, 129)*. They are slender three-storied columns placed upon a double pediment very much in the Silla tradition except for a greater slimness and a sharper curve to the eaves. These pagodas were commemorative and contained sacred utensils which are remarkable chiefly because they are dated and thus give us information as to shapes and materials in use in the fourteenth century *(Plate 130)*. The most interesting of the items is a small silver-plated box and lid about two inches in height. It may have been a relic container. Other containers found in the pagodas are of bronze and have fitted lids similar in design to the brass bowls in common use today. A celadon bowl is decorated on the inside with an inlay of concentric circles. Two more bowls show shapes commonly used even now. A stone urn with a lid has a remarkably graceful outline for so small a vessel (about three inches in height). The lid also has a shape with lines that continue those of the body in a pleasing manner.

Another pagoda of exceptional beauty came from North Cholla Province, where it was reputedly built to contain the relics of a court priest, Song Pup *(Plate 131)*. It bears an inscription dating it from the eighth year of King Hyonjong (1017). About eight and a third feet tall and just under five feet across at the base, it is one of the best surviving examples of stupa art. Upon an eight-sided pedestal, a supporting pillar holds a flattened stone ball. This pillar is composed of plinths of upturned and downturned lotus flowers, the upper being the more elegant, and a central band of medallions carved in alternating dragon and cloud patterns. The ball itself is tied with an eye-pleasing double band and circular floral pattern carved in middle relief. The octagonal base is balanced by an octagonal scalloped crown placed on top of the ball. This section is in the shape of a downturned morning-glory whose underside is expertly carved with flying clouds and flower designs. The excellent stone masonry displayed in this piece, its proportions, its lighthearted decorations, and the total impression of balance and harmony make it one of the masterpieces of extant Koryo sculpture.

Without a doubt the most Indian in feeling of the Koryo pagodas is the 1085 Kyonmyo-t'ap containing the ashes of the Buddhist monk Haerin. About twenty-one feet high and twelve feet broad at the base, this elaborate monument of two stories plus pedestal and crown-and-ball finial is unusual in that it combines many of the features generally found in other pagodas and lanterns widely separated in time and space *(Plate 132)*. The boxlike stories and the proportions are of Silla style; the elaborate scalloped crowning piece is typical of Koryo lanterns and ball-urn pagodas; and the lions characteristic of old Silla pagodas, the false door, and the double panels covered with relief are all features of various prototype pagodas. The festoons and tassels of the cornices, the flowers, birds, and Buddhist images—even the small winged angels on the crown—repeat decorative motifs found in other extant pieces of Koryo art, but not in any other single work of stone sculpture. The total effect appears too elaborate and too foreign to reflect Koryo taste of that early date. It is possible that captured Khitan stone masons may have fashioned the pagoda according to Korean designs, or that similar elaborate works in more perishable materials were common but have been destroyed. This one pagoda remains unique in Korea.

Standing in Seoul's Pagoda Park is a tall pagoda of ten stories, some forty feet in height, built of yellowish marble. Constructed in Korea by imported Chinese stone masons, it displays a shape (twenty-sided polygon) that originally came from India and was rarely seen in Korea *(Plate 133)*. Upon a low base of three steps rise three stories arranged in four wings, then seven stories with the boxlike structure of primitive pagodas, the whole crowned by a tiled facsimile of a roof. The tiers are graduated in size. The structure of the cornice of each story represents a roof with rafters and tiles—a new device that appears in miniature pagodas in bronze but rarely in stone. A small veranda runs around each story, and elaborately carved illustrations of Buddhist scripture cover the sides. This pagoda was built in 1466, a copy of one in Songdo. Literary references reveal that the construction was a matter of importance discussed, planned, and executed by ministers of state in honor of the marriage of a royal princess.* The three top stories, which were reportedly taken down during the Japanese invasion in 1592–98, lay on the ground beside the pagoda for some

* See Andreas Eckhardt, *A History of Korean Art* (London, 1929), for easy reference. Accounts in the *Koryo-sa* and the *Taehan Chiri* assign the pagoda to the year 1348, when the king ordered the pagoda built in honor of the wedding of a royal princess, and the ministers in charge brought in Chinese workmen to execute the order.

three hundred and fifty years until American engineers arriving in Korea in 1945 used army equipment to swing them back into position again.

A number of lanterns also date from Koryo. The Hwaom-sa lantern *(Plate 134)* is the largest of its kind in Korea. The Kwonch'ok-sa lantern, which is placed directly before the giant Miruk described above, stands some twenty feet tall *(Plate 126)*. Probably the best example of Koryo lanterns is the Silluk-sa specimen, which dates from 1379 *(Plate 135)*. The pedestal, designed like the conventional Buddha throne, is carefully constructed to appear heavy enough to support the lantern and yet not to be unduly large. The octagonal lantern has eight apertures spanned by arches surrounded by flying devas and figures of animals in high relief. The roof is a scalloped undecorated octagonal piece topped with a simple ball and crown. The proportions, finish, and richness of this Buddhist lantern once again testify to the high level of architectural sculpture in stone during the Koryo period.

Not the least attractive creations of the sculptor's art of this period are the miniature shrines carved of wood or cast in bronze or silver. A silver-plated case and a miniature stupa with a dated inscription are excellent examples of the refinement practiced in this branch of Buddhist art *(Plates 136, 137)*. At some unknown date—probably in 1391—the stupa and case were buried in a stone box on a peak in the Diamond Mountains at a spot "where the moon rises over the village."[3] The objects were unearthed by the Japanese. The stupa, which is actually an urn, is about six inches in height and the case more than eight inches. Similar designs of haloed Buddhist figures performing the *anjali* mudra appear on case and urn. On the urn, these figures are separated by festoons of cloud and lotus designs from which depend patterns of circles, and this decoration is echoed on the case. The urn is topped by a four-storied pagoda and is set on a free-standing lotus-petal base. Both top and base are exquisitely modeled. The lid of the case imitates a tile roof and is crowned by a realistic rendering of a lotus in full bloom. The stupa and its case are historically as well as artistically important, for the inscription indicates that Yi T'aejo, in order to petition for success in his undertaking, placed the stupa in its box one year before he became monarch; that is, in 1391.

A gilt-bronze stupa found in a celadon jar from the stupa of Sujon-sa in Kyonggi Province is another example of miniature sculpture.[4] It is a pagoda of nine stories, about six inches in height *(Plate 138)*. Designed for home use, it is elegantly modeled in every detail. Each story is provided with a veranda and entrances on each of the four sides. In the front of the first story, the chief entrance is indicated by a triple opening, whereas the other three sides, as well as all four sides of the other stories, have only one opening each. The cornices of all stories imitate tile roofs from the corners of which small bells depend. The pagoda is in good condition, the gilt is still fresh, and the whole object appears to have been more the work of a jeweler than of a sculptor. Another set, a case about seven inches high and an urn, was also found in the jar *(Plates 139, 140)*. The case is six-sided and silver-plated. Its panels, formed of the sheet-metal cutouts so popular in Korea in all periods, carry a combination of floral and vine designs. The lid, shaped like a tiled roof, appears to have been ornamented at one time with jewels, while the base is done in a pattern of lotus petals. The hollow case fits over the little urn. Grooves in the stand hold the case in place.

Another gilt-bronze shrine, dating from the thirteenth or fourteenth century, is a somewhat larger example of miniature work *(Plate 141)*. It is constructed in the form of a temple pavilion, rectangular in shape and measuring about eleven inches in height, ten in width, and five in depth. It rests on a simple platform consisting of upturned lotus petals and a plinth. The roof is made to simulate tiles and is painted green. The interior of the shrine is entirely covered by decorations in relief. On the back wall are a Buddha and two Bodhisattvas enthroned on high elaborate lotus seats. Fourteen disciples called Nahan (Arhat in Sanskrit) are depicted attending the deities, each with a plain halo to indicate his sanctity. Cloud designs appear above their heads. The side walls show the Bodhisattva pair, Pohyon and Munsu (Samantabhadra and Manjusri), seated upon an elephant and a lion to right and left respectively. The floor has a pattern of lotus petals; the ceiling, of dragons. The two doors boast robust gate protectors. The outside of the shrine, free of gilding, is decorated only by faintly incised designs, the sides showing the Four Deva Kings (two on a side) and the back depicting eight warders in an upper register with five lotus flowers against an overall leaf background. The front doors, hinged to side pillars, carry peony panels on the lower registers and an overall textile pattern on the upper.

A simple stupa-shaped case in wood, owned by Mr. Chun Hyung-pil, is hinged in the middle and opens to reveal a small Buddhist altar. The wood is highly polished; the carved base is gilded; and the metal hinges and locks are carefully cut, filed, decorated, and affixed.

Other metal objects decorated with sculptured relief or incised design cover a wide range from large, heavy bronze bells to delicate gold and silver utensils. A bronze mirror ornamented with the "Udumbara flower"[5] shows the departure from the rigid compartmentalized designs of early mirrors and displays flowers and leaves fluttering, flying, or falling in all directions over the surface in a free design most refreshing to look at *(Plate 142)*. An inlaid *kundika* or water sprinkler of bronze, now covered by a delightful light-green patina, is another example of the new freedom of design, although traditional decorations still appear within registers marked off as border designs *(Plate 143)*. The kundika was taken from a tomb near Songdo. It has two spouts; the one on top is attached to the lip of the vessel by a band of silver, while the second protrudes from the body and has a cup-shaped mouth with a hinged silver cover of cutout designs. The decoration is in inlaid silver, starting with the veined leaves on the upper spout, continuing in the scattered and turning cloud designs on the neck, and ending in the major scenes of willows, flying birds, blowing grass, swimming ducks, and fishermen arranged in a delightfully free and breezy way on the main body of this Buddhist vessel.[6]

On the whole, except for very formal utensils, ornamentation on small objects was lavish. A taste for overall decorations of vine and floral designs continued to be satisfied by means of openwork, relief, incised, molded, or stamped patterns applied to a variety of materials ranging from metals through stone to clay. A gilt-bronze stirrup decorated in loose scrollwork is an example of this ubiquitous ornamentation, as are a number of floral corner pieces designed as metal fittings and executed in the same medium. These metal fittings were sometimes simulated in incised designs on stone.

Vessels of precious metals were also produced in abundance, both for use in Buddhist temples and as table services in the palaces and the homes of the mighty.[7] A silver ewer and basin in the Boston Museum of Fine Arts are extant examples of great artistic merit

*(Plates 144,145)*. The ewer is about fifteen inches tall, and the basin, into which it fits, about eight inches. The body of the ewer repeats the design of the basin, and its sharply scalloped shoulders exactly match the scalloped top of the vessel. A short neck rises in an upsweep of tapering lobes to a round opening. The cover sweeps grandly upward in a band that continues the lobe design of the neck, bursts into three tiers of elaborately modeled lotus blossoms, and climaxes in a daintily poised phoenix with a graceful array of coiled feathers. The spout and the handle are minutely detailed representations of bundles of bamboo stems. A tiny removable lid is affixed to the spout, and the loop connecting the handle to the cover is in the shape of a bent bamboo. The basin, like the ewer, has lobed sides terminating in a reinforced scalloped edge and rests on a high flaring base with a scalloped foot. Both vessels are ornamented with engraved floral sprays on the lobes and inside the borders along the scalloped rims. Details like the veining of the lotus petals and the skins of the bamboo sprouts appear in delicate incising. The silver of these vessels is enhanced by gilding of the highly modeled parts and the floral sprays.

The formal and detailed elegance of these pieces suggests that they were produced in the more peaceful years of early Koryo. The style suggests the silverwork of the T'ang period—a style inherited by Koryo through Silla—although in general appearance no counterpart of these pieces is found among Chinese examples of the T'ang dynasty. "Nor do existing specimens of the Sung art of China supply any indication that the ewer was inspired by that source. On the other hand, among ceramic wares of the Koryo period, we are confronted with ewers not unlike these silver ones. . . . The Koreans of the Koryo dynasty had ideals and customs of their own. The refinement of feeling and the excellent technique of the ewer—it is one of the most elaborate examples of silverwork of the Koryo period known—are the evidences of a very high attainment in the working of precious metals."[8] A silver cup and stand in the National Museum of Korea, executed in high relief, give us yet another example of the silversmith's art.

Bells continued to constitute an important category of Buddhist workmanship during the Koryo period. One such bell, dated 1223 and standing about twenty inches in height, is large enough to demonstrate the excellence of the bronze casting of this period *(Plate 146)*. Conventional designs featuring flying angels, floral medallions, and nine studs within a bordered rectangle all appear in fine detail. The bands around the rim and the shoulder are decorated with a T'ang border pattern of grapevines and flowers in relief.

The least known of the Koryo fine arts is the painting. A few genuine examples still remain, but these, even when all taken together, can give us only glimpses of the splendors that must have been achieved in murals, temple banners, altarpieces, and the like. Some panels in the Koryo building at Pusok-sa still retain traces of Koryo painting. The figures are those of a protector of Buddhism and a deity *(Plate 147)*. They show distinctly, like the silver ewer and other products of Koryo, T'ang styles adapted to Korean tastes. Here a favorite Korean combination of soft greens and reds is observable.

Illustrated sutras give us examples of outline drawings, one dating from 1007 and another showing Lamaist refinements dating from 1350. The earlier sutra was block-printed on a narrow scroll that was interred with the relics of a famous monk in the *sari-t'ap* (memorial pagoda) of the Chinnyom Kwangje Tae-sa *(Plate 148)*.[9] The other drawing illustrates the

Gandha Vyuha Sutra. It is done in gold ink on dark paper and depicts Buddha at the moment of transfiguration. The border of the scroll is decorated with spirals within circles and with medallions containing stylized thunderbolts. Lamaist features are noticeable in this design— the magic thunderbolt in particular. The picture itself is some seventeen inches long and eight inches wide *(Plate 149)*.

# CHAPTER TEN

# Koryo Pottery

DURING the twelfth century the production of superior ceramic ware reached its highest refinement. Several new varieties appeared simultaneously in the first quarter of the century,[1] one of which, the inlaid ware, must be considered a Korean invention, and another, the celadons, a distinguished Korean rendering of a major Chinese type.[2] The custom of burying special objects with the dead preserved hundreds of superb specimens of this pottery until the present century, when the graves began to be opened. With the appearance of these wares on the market from about 1880 on, came an increased interest in Korean ceramics as distinguished from the Chinese. Japanese collectors on the spot had access to the best of the excavated pieces as they came to light, as well as to deposits of shards surrounding ancient kiln sites, and so were the first to write scholarly articles and to publish illustrations of the rarest pieces. These publications, along with the collections of ceramics themselves that began to appear in Western museums, stimulated interest in a hitherto little known subject. On the whole, both authors and collectors were highly appreciative of the qualities of Korean ware. In the introduction to a small book on the subject published soon after World War II, Mr. Honey of the Victoria and Albert Museum wrote:

"The best Corean wares were not only original, they are the most gracious and unaffected pottery ever made. They have every virtue that pottery can have. . . . It seems to speak at first of a serenely happy people, and only later in a time of extreme poverty does its graciousness give way to a wild austerity which is admirable in a different way. This Corean pottery, in fact, reaches heights hardly attained even by the Chinese."[3]

What, then, was this ware like? Where and when was it produced, under what conditions and, above all, what technical secrets were required to achieve such intriguing results? The answers to some of these questions will be attempted here.

To begin with, the materials available were of the best quality. The Korean peninsula is rich in ceramic clays, every province having pits. Pottery, therefore, was not only an early culture-product but has continued to the present day to be a major one. It has been produced throughout the country for the daily use and enjoyment of every class of society and for all levels of sophistication and income. The ceramics industry can therefore be looked upon as one measuring stick by which to appraise the prosperity or decline of Korean economic conditions throughout the history of the country.

For the last thousand years, pottery manufacturing has been in the hands of families of potters who grouped themselves together in villages and who combined to operate kilns,

174

to market their wares, and to control the industry through their guilds. Each family owned at least one potter's wheel, and each knew how to manufacture anything in the entire range of the potter's craft from tile and household crockery to ceremonial ware of the greatest refinement.[4] These potters' guilds were ranked very low socially—beneath most other artisans because of their alleged "rough manners." Certain master potters located on Kanghwa Island, however, seem to have risen above this social stigma. In the last decade of the sixteenth century whole villages of Korean potters were removed to Japan, where they laid the foundations for the Japanese ceramics industry.

The two areas which produced the most abundantly during the Koryo dynasty were Cholla Province in the extreme southwest and Kanghwa Island on the west coast near the capital.[5] Some thirty to forty kilns were located near Tangjon-ni in Cholla Province and others near Mokpo in the same province.

The first two centuries of the Koryo dynasty are sometimes lumped together for convenience in the study of Koryo ceramics as a period of imitation of the Chinese potters of Shantung, a province which lies only a hundred miles distant from Korea across the Yellow Sea. There the famous kilns of Yüeh-chou produced superior wares of many types. The next three periods in the study of Koryo pottery are roughly coterminous with the centuries: the twelfth (1106–1213), the thirteenth (1214–1308), and the fourteenth (1309–92).[6] The twelfth-century product reached a high-water mark of original and artistic ware; the thirteenth-century pottery began to repeat styles produced in the twelfth century; and the ware of the fourteenth century was frankly retrogressive and crude. One type of ware, the celadons, died out completely during the early Yi dynasty.

Two main classes of pottery were produced during the Koryo dynasty. One was the red, soft-paste, hand-potted ware that formed the bulk of pottery in daily use both before and after Koryo. This type does not interest the connoisseur or the art critic. The other class, however—the gray hard-paste sonant ware that was produced on the potter's wheel and was decorated and glazed—includes the famous colors and patterns that distinguish Koryo ware from all others.[7]

Technical peculiarities which help us to distinguish the Korean product from the Chinese are, first, the treatment of the foot ring, which was usually glazed and baked with spur marks from three to twelve in number,[8] or the presence of sand particles that adhered to the base as a result of resting the piece on props or on a bed of sand within the saggar during baking; second, the presence of dates or marks;[9] and third, the typical Korean shapes, glazes, and decorations. In the West, ceramics are differentiated by the quality of the paste into three general classifications: stoneware, faience, and porcelain. In Asia the distinctions are made according to glazes, shapes, and decorations. It is therefore according to these three categories that Korean wares are discussed below. The first and most important distinction is based upon the quality and color of the glaze. The principal glazes of the twelfth century were six: the blacks and browns; the range of whites, which included the three types of white, cream-colored, and an opaque, "greasy," grayish white; the range of greens included in the celadon glazes; the inlaid types, combining both green and white glazes; the iron underglaze with white overglaze; and the graffito and marbled types.

Some Western collectors and museum curators have felt that, in general, the first two

175

of these six categories of glazes were almost entirely derivative (Chinese techniques and types); that the last two were probably imported; and that the middle two, the celadons and the inlaid ware, were undoubtedly local products.[10] According to Ken Nomori, however, at least four of the six types of glazes appeared as local Korean products within the first decade of the twelfth century.[11] Of these four local types, the chief was the stoneware with the jadelike glaze easily distinguished from Chinese celadon.[12] This "blue of the sky after rain" was the particular glory of the early Korean pottery and has been likened to the lost art of the Chinese Chai Yao. Speculations as to its origins have been a much disputed subject. According to some authorities, the quality of the glaze and the absence of primitive forms of the ware indicate that "the Koreans may have acquired the technique fully developed from the Chinese potters of Yüeh-chou (as suggested by Hsu Ching)."[13] Thus at least a double lineage for Korean celadon is claimed by Ken Nomori, Kyoichi Arimitsu, and Sato Nakino, who ascribe Korean variations upon the conventional methods of the Ju Yao factory in the Yüeh-chou style to the first Koryo period (935–1106) and point to the green glaze of a vase dated 993 as a typical specimen of the Korean proto-celadon, and to specimens like the Paekche vase[14] and the Silla urn[15] as indicative of earlier production of green-glazed ware. No one denies the existence of Chinese prototypes for Korean ware, but such recent studies as those mentioned here have made clear the existence of an internal evolution somewhat slower than that of the Chinese celadons (which were themselves a rather sudden phenomenon of the tenth century) as well as the development stimulated by foreign models. Four ceramic boxes, all discovered in the tombs of Korean high priests and all having the "emerald-color" glaze, are typical examples of the best twelfth-century celadon. A Chinese poem speaks of the impossibility of imitating the color of the Korean ware.[16] Examples of the other glazes may be seen in some of the types described below.

The second consideration in the evolution of the Korean ware is that of shape. Forms which are obviously derived from Chinese models are illustrated in the plates for this chapter. These are, in brief, the universal shallow dish, bowls of a conical or slightly incurved shape, spittoons, headrests, and bottles or vases of mallet, baluster, pear, or foreign shapes like the Tartar water bottle, the Persian ewer, and the Indian sprinkler. Imitations of Chinese ritual bronzes, though they are considered by some Western collectors to be missing from the Korean repertory, nevertheless formed an important category mentioned even by Hsu Ching.[17] Also, possibly because of close Mongol ties, familiar Chinese designs like the paired fish and the *jui* scepter came into fashion in Korea toward the end of the Koryo dynasty. Such fish designs occurred in many ways: against an overall background of waves or other symbols of water, in medallions, and in free arrangements.

Principal Korean shapes seem close to T'ang forms, which were themselves close to primitive and natural forms such as those of the gourd or melon, the bamboo, and flowers. The Korean taste for natural forms may be detected in the treatment of subordinate parts of ceramic pieces. For example, Korean wares emphasize bodies which are lobed, pierced, or modeled; bases which are pleated or flared; and lips which are open, scalloped, or flowerlike. Certain forms with covers, like the domed covered bowl, were in existence in south Korea from neolithic times, while others, like the typical covered boxes and ogee-shaped bowls, were similar to lacquer forms found in Han tombs in north Korea. The boxes were produced in sets or nests faceted and fitted together, and the bowls came with or without handles. The most individual of all Korean forms was the cup and saucer set, the cup of which was fitted to an elevated perch in the center of the saucer, rather than into an indented section.

The third and last criterion by which Korean ware is judged is its decoration. Here one finds hundreds of examples of a simple type of embellishment which consisted of a design cut into the paste before glazing. This was done by means of the incised fine line, relief, stamping, or molding. The first choice for the incised decor was the inexhaustible vine-and-flower pattern or that of small boys among vine leaves—a T'ang motif which itself was borrowed from a Hellenistic cupid design. A second type of decoration, which was hardly less popular than the incised pattern, was that of the inlaid celadon, a technique which was a Korean speciality. By this method an intaglio design, made by hand or mold, was filled flush with the body of the piece by threads of black or white clay, sometimes enhanced by spots of red. The inlay *(sanggam* in Korean) was then inserted, the piece was baked, the overglaze was applied, and the piece was baked again. The invention of this technique is thought by some to have been the work of a single master potter. The dating of the invention is uncertain, but since Hsu Ching did not mention it, some authorities claim that it did not exist in 1124, when he paid his visit to Korea. Nevertheless, the origin of the inlaid ware should probably be assigned to the first decade of the twelfth century.

With the fact in mind that inlaid ware in other materials was familiar to Korean artisans from the time of Lo-lang, and noting the similarity of concurrent inlaid silver and bronze utensils of Koryo like the bronze kundika *(Plate 143)* and the silver ewer *(Plate 144)* to the ceramic pieces, we can assume it quite possible that the transfer of a bronze method to ceramics was a simple development if there were patrons who liked the effect and would order it.

In addition to the methods of decoration mentioned above, there were third and fourth types which were widely employed. The third category was that of pictorial underglaze decoration, an art form fundamentally unsuited to pottery but a type that was nonetheless extremely fashionable in Ming and Ch'ing China. The fourth type included the sculptured pieces, which, in contrast to the pictorial products, were remarkably well suited to the plastic medium of clay and are now regarded as Korean rather than Chinese in development. Both types were brought to perfection during the Koryo period.

The painted ware included all types of painted designs: the delicate, refined, and formal in treatment as well as those of the bold and careless type. Four favorite patterns appeared in the latter half of the twelfth century: the willow-and-waterfowl combination—a design that has been ascribed to Khitan influence (which in itself had a much earlier origin in steppe art); the crane-and-cloud combination; and the wealth of chrysanthemum and peony designs. In all of these pictorial representations, a quiet, gentle concept of the simple beauties of nature was emphasized in a way that was quite different in effect from the contemporary Chinese painted designs of Tz'u-chou derivation. This Korean product, and not that of Tz'u-chou, appears to have been the model for later Japanese *egorai* (picture-Koryo) such as the well-known Satsuma ware. Another original contribution of the Korean potter was his use of underglaze copper oxide, which turned a brilliant red when baked. This was a Korean discovery of great significance for the later pottery of the whole Far East, since the Chinese use of it does not seem to have begun until the Yüan period about a hundred years later.[18]

The modeled pieces and the independently sculptured wares showed a masterly understanding of forms appropriate to clay. Incidental modeling almost absent-mindedly added to conventional objects showed an appreciation of natural animal forms and a delight in their graceful contours that is an altogether charming characteristic of Korean pottery. Covers surmounted by lions, ducks, and pheasants and legs of vessels shaped in the forms of rabbits, mice, and bears add variety and vitality to a ceramic tradition which was a far cry from pure imitation of Chinese models.

A last and very rare form of decoration which should be noted here is regarded by some as the final achievement of Koryo. This is the gold-painted overglaze addition of a spray of blossoms or other simple floral decoration in gold, which was conceived as a finishing touch to enhance or bring out the cool colors of the celadons.[19]

To return to the chief considerations in the study of pottery—shape, decoration, and glaze—for examples and illustrations, one might start with the most common shape in use: the bowl. One bowl in the collection of Mr. Chun Hyung-pil—a shallow vessel carved in relief with two phoenixes amid an overall pattern of *posang* flowers—is a good example of Ting style in shape, decoration, and glaze *(Plate 150)*. An example of local style, on the other hand, is a bowl of inlaid celadon, dating from the twelfth or the thirteenth century, which exhibits the Korean taste for incidental modeling, scalloped rim, and inlay technique *(Plate 151)*. It is about four inches in diameter and just under two inches in height. The glaze is a bluish gray, and the foot is glazed, as is usual with Korean ceramics. There are three spur marks. The shape is that of a lotus flower with eight lobes, and the handle is in the form of a dragon's head, indicating that the bowl was for royal use. A peony design decorates the inside of the bottom, while the lobes are ornamented with asters on the outside. Other examples of drinking bowls may be found in the bowl-and-ewer sets described below.

A great variety of ewers and teapots have come to light in recent years to testify to the popularity of this type of wine (or tea or water) jug. One of these, in a form later copied by European ceramics masters for teapots, is in the Freer Gallery *(Plate 152)*. It has an ovoid body and a stylized lotus-flower cover. The glaze is in two tones of greenish-gray celadon with a light crackle. The bold leaf-and-tendril decoration is done in underglaze reserve on the body (the background having been cut away) and in a white inlay. The spout is in the shape of a curved bamboo stalk; the handle, in that of a vine neatly tied at top and bottom. A second pot with cover and bowl exhibits the persistent Korean liking for openwork *(Plate 153)*. Inside the reticulated outer shell with its interweaving pattern of seven children climbing on "holy image flowers" *(posang-hwa)* is an inner container. The bowl, which fits the body of the pot, is in the shape of a holy image flower whose petals, modeled and incised, are arranged in three tiers of twenty-one each around the outside. The cover bears an incised cloud pattern and a border of Greek fret. On top is a modeled angel. The pot is seven inches high. The celadon glaze seems to date this piece in the twelfth century.

A lobed pot with underglaze decorations featuring lotus sprays and three-flowered chrysanthemum stalks—a design denoting late twelfth-century style—is an example of the inlaid ware *(Plate 154)*. The inlay is black and white; the overglaze, a green celadon. An inlaid ewer-and-bowl set displaying boys amid grapes and vine leaves *(Plate 155)* is highly valued because of its color, its shape, and its perfect condition of preservation. This piece is an unusually good example of an even blue-green glaze so distributed over a complex network of perforated porcelain that it catches light and shadow in dancing patterns deliberately designed by the potter to enhance its beauty. The handle is in the shape of a twisted vine. A delightful pot in still another variation is an inlaid celadon about six inches in height and a little more than six inches in diameter *(Plate 156)*. It is thought to date from a later period (thirteenth or fourteenth century) because the design has already become larger, looser, and more casual, and the glaze has a grayish cast. The piece is crackled in patterns of uneven size and has minute bubbles that reflect the light, giving it an unusually milky appearance. The decoration is a favorite Korean combination of the Greek-fret border and the parallel-line pattern symbolizing rain which, in company with the lotus or other plants, commonly designates fertility. A lotus flower is here depicted circling the knob of the lid.

A third category of popular vessels is the general one of flower vases and bottles. Of these, the baluster-shaped vessels, a variety called *mei-ping* in Chinese and *maebyong* in Korean, appear to have been the most common. One in the Freer Gallery has a design of grasses and willows inlaid in black and white under a crackled celadon glaze *(Plate 157)*. Bands of jui and lotus petals encircle the neck. The mouth has a silver rim. A vase with underglaze inlay in black and white, probably dating from the thirteenth century, is also a good example of the type *(Plate 158)*. The glaze is a bluish green and is evenly crackled; there are no flaws in it. The octagonal shape of the neck is a favorite Korean shape often repeated. The small knob at the top could have served to hold a cord for hanging the jar. The design is of asters, peonies, clouds, and a trefoil pattern. A maebyong vase showing a combination of incised and inlaid decoration under celadon glaze is a twelfth- or thirteenth-century piece *(Plate 159)*. Peony sprays are incised on the bowl, cloud and fungus patterns around the foot. A simulated cloth cover around the mouth and shoulder hangs down the sides, its edging and tassels formed of a beading of white circles with black centers. The "cloth" itself is decorated with chrysanthemums in white inlay. Another style of decoration appears in a maebyong vase with a painted underglaze pattern of six chrysanthemums among fernlike leaves *(Plate 161)*. A ring of chrysanthemum petals is painted around the neck. The design is done in iron over a white slip under a celadon glaze. The vase dates from later in the dynasty—thirteenth or fourteenth century. Another maebyong vase from the same period is a very important piece, since it is an example of the use of both white and celadon glazes on the same vessel *(Plate 160)*. It is shaped like a melon with six lobes, each bearing a panel in its center. The body is covered with a white glaze of bluish cast, and each panel contains a different floral design under a green celadon glaze. This vase, slightly misshapen in firing and valued for that very oddity, is famous for including the several chief Korean techniques and providing the first clear proof that the Koreans produced white ware as well as celadon. Still another maebyong vase dating from the end of the dynasty illustrates the use of decoration in the paired-fish design *(Plate 162)*. It is nearly twelve inches tall and is inlaid under a celadon glaze.

Perhaps the most spectacular Korean maebyong vase in existence is the Thousand Crane Vase in the Chun collection *(Plate 163)*. It is over sixteen inches in height and is covered with a fine light-green celadon glaze. Scattered over the body are medallions containing crane-and-cloud designs. The cranes in the medallions are all depicted flying upward, while outside the medallions are downward-flying cranes scattered among clouds on a clear blue-green background. A band of thirty-eight lotus petals encircles the base, and the neck is clasped by a white collar of eight points. The vase, probably dating from the late twelfth century, is one of the best examples of inlaid ware in the world.

Another common vase shape besides the maebyong is the pear-shaped bottle with slim neck and flaring lip. One in the Freer collection has an inlaid design of four medallions containing different floral pieces and displays borders of jui and circles *(Plate 164)*. A second pear-shaped bottle about twelve inches in height has only an incised underglaze decoration *(Plate 165)*. The color is bluish green, and the decoration, a lotus spray, is elegantly done to suggest a peony blossom and the kingly qualities of the peony. The finial of the spray is a small open flower. Both flowers suggest abundance.

An extremely popular vase shape in Korea was the lobed body with a trumpet lip and a high flaring foot. A beautiful example of this type is a celadon piece dating from the twelfth or the thirteenth century *(Plate 166)*. The body is eight-lobed, and the centers of the lobes display alternating sprays of peony and chrysanthemum. At the base is a circular band of lotus petals and at the neck a band of the jui pattern.

In addition to bowls, wine pots, and vases, a fourth classification in wide use has long been the wide-mouthed food and water storage jar. A celadon water jar about eight inches in height and six in diameter at the base is typical *(Plate 167)*. The handles are modeled in the form of loops ending in the mouths of lion heads, and the body is decorated with two large and splashy peonies, one on each side, incised and filled with black and white slips. The size and number of the decorative motifs already show a new trend toward broad rather than meticulous treatment. Another common shape is that of the round-bodied jar with a somewhat narrower mouth *(Plate 168)*. One such jar, in the collection of the Freer Gallery of Art, is decorated with a phoenix and floral design in black and white inlay.

Rarer, though popular, shapes were the pottery pillows, boxes fitted with trays, incense burners, small modeled water droppers for use in making black ink, and the kundika or water sprinkler—originally a bronze form for use in Buddhist ceremonies. Many examples of the kundika were found preserved in tombs, doubtless because of their rarity and value. Sometimes these vessels are incised and monochrome in color, but more often they are decorated by means of medallions in a floral pattern on a dark ground under a crackled celadon glaze *(Plate 169)* or in popular inlaid designs such as the lotus-and-waterfowl pattern on a Freer Gallery kundika that carries a hinged cover on its spout *(Plate 170)*.

The water droppers were all small and usually deeply modeled, sometimes even sculptured in the round. A four-inch dropper in the shape of a lotus bud is a good example of this type *(Plate 171)*. The petals are incised and are edged with rows of small white dots painted in slip. The spout and the handle are in a twisted vine shape. A clear green glaze covers the vessel.

Headrests of openwork design were popular for summer use—in woven bamboo for the commoner, in glazed and decorated pottery for the aristocrat and churchman. Often pierced-ware headrests were filled with scented flower petals: a refinement in fashion among the classes that enjoyed leisure and had developed esthetic tastes. Pottery headrests were often finished with a celadon glaze over an inlaid decoration. One such pillow *(Plate 172)* is a rectangular shape incurved on all four of the long sides, nine inches in length and about five in height. On the top and bottom are central medallions of the crane-and-cloud pattern in the midst of an overall leaf design done in reverse technique. The somewhat narrower sides are decorated with a peony design placed in a cartouche formed of four ogee arches. Above one of the peonies are two bees. Around the ends of the headrest are two bands formed of lotus petals, also in reverse technique. The two ends repeat the cartouche design; in the center of each is a hole left to facilitate firing and to permit the circulation of air.

Incense burners were also carefully constructed and highly prized by their owners because of their ritual functions. The burners were pierced to allow the smoke to escape and were usually ornamented with sculptured sections. One outstanding incense burner that has survived to the present has an openwork ball cover and is finished with an exceptionally fine lustrous glaze *(Plate 173)*. It is six inches in height and about five inches across at the base. The openwork pattern of the ball is in a design called the Seven Treasures, a widely used, eye-pleasing pattern of petal shapes. The body of the burner is in the lobed form of the holy image flower with four rows of sculptured, incised petals supported by a delightful pedestal on a single flower with five downturned, modeled petals. The base is a triangular lobed platform supported by three feet in the shape of rabbits with eyes done in tiny spots of iron paint. This piece is entirely alone in its class: a truly perfect example of the potter's art.

Another unique form, that of the round cosmetic box with its nest of fitted floral boxes, is important not only for its *chongja* glaze but also as an example of a type of container that continued in popularity from Lo-lang times to the Yi dynasty. A box in the Chun collection is a good specimen of this category of pottery *(Plate 174)*. It is a round receptacle measuring between seven and eight inches in diameter. The lid is decorated in concentric circles which, both in feeling and design, imitate its prototype: the lacquer cosmetic box of the Han period. Even the scroll band on the box itself and the fret band on the lid repeat the Han designs of a thousand years earlier. The center of the lid bears a medallion divided into four lunettes, each containing a flower and a centerpiece in chrysanthemum design, the whole element being very close in feeling to the four-pointed collar of the Han type. Within the receptacle are five boxes designed to resemble a central flower and four leaves. The flower piece has eight lobes, and its cover is ornamented with a spray of peony flowers. The leaf-shaped containers are curved on the inner sides and three-lobed on the outer. Like the central piece, they are decorated with peony sprays.

Another form of toilet case is the rectangular openwork celadon box, the rarest of all Koryo ceramics. There are thought to be only four of these boxes in existence, all found in the tombs of high priests.[20] One of these, which came from a tomb in South Cholla Province, is rendered in an openwork tortoise-shell design on both box and lid *(Plate 175)*. The sides of the cover show a fret and jui-scepter border design outlined in white inlay. A fitted tray has a pierced pattern in peony scrolls similar to the outside of another box now in Japan. The deep, lustrous glaze on the individual interior boxes and the outer container is their chief claim to distinction. The containing box is about nine inches long by five in height. With it were found oil jars and mirrors. It is one of the most superb of all existing examples of Koryo celadon.

The last category of pottery to be discussed here is the unique Korean cup and stand. One example of this type is a lustrous celadon piece dating from the early twelfth century *(Plate 176)*. This set is about four inches in height, and the stand is over seven inches in diameter. The lobed cup, shaped like a flower, is incised with floral sprays both inside and out. On the inside of the bottom is a chrysanthemum. The wide rim of the stand, or saucer, has six indentations and is decorated with lotus designs, both flower and leaf. The raised central perch, with a chrysanthemum in its indented center, carries an incised pattern of leaves. A similar-shaped set, decorated in inlaid design, dates from about a century earlier *(Plate 177)*. Both stand and cup have an eight-lobed base. Each lobe of the cup is ornamented with a chrysanthemum spray: a design repeated in the top of the stand. The perch is encircled with a pattern of twenty lotus petals, while the lobes of the base bear a simple black-and-white floral design.

The thirteenth century saw the Mongol invasion disrupt the cultural and political life of the nation, the court forced into exile on Kanghwa Island, and such major industries as that of ceramics paralyzed into mechanical and repetitious production. The deterioration was marked in the steady and general cultural decline of the fourteenth century. It is easy to understand why a Chinese description of Korean ware published in 1387 describes the unique inlaid ware but states that it was "very little valued"—a statement repeated in later Chinese works.[21] In fact, the whole class of celadon pottery died out altogether and, with it, the secret of the lustrous range of blue-green glazes.

117: MAIN HALL, PUSOK-SA (page 166). Yongju district, North Kyongsang
Province. Koryo (rebuilt about 1350).

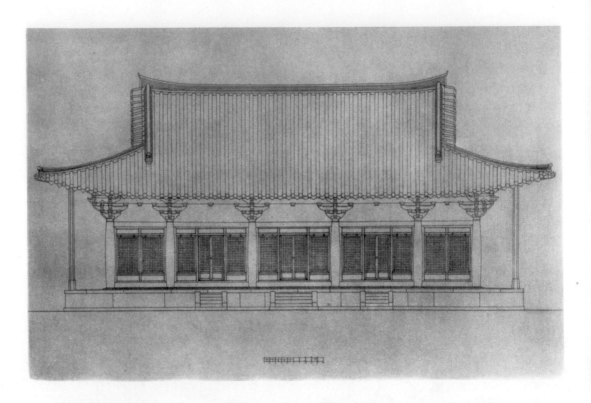

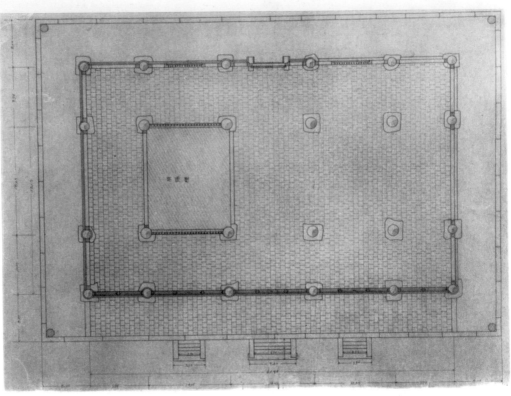

184

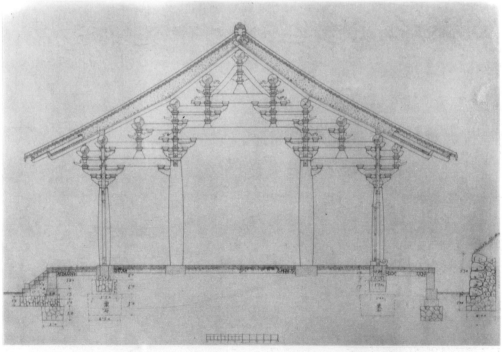

118–21: GROUND PLAN AND ELEVATIONS OF MAIN HALL, PUSOK-SA (page 166).
Yongju district, North Kyongsang Province. Koryo (rebuilt about 1350).

185

122, 123: DETAILS OF INTERIOR STRUC-
TURE, PUSOK-SA (page 166). Yongju
district, North Kyongsang Province.
Koryo, rebuilt about 1350.

124: SAKYAMUNI (page 167). Gilded wood. Pusok-sa, Yongju district, North Kyongsang Province. Height: about 9'. Koryo, 10th century.

125: AVALOKITESVARA (page 167). Gilt bronze. Excavated in the Diamond Mountains, North Korea. Height: about 7″. Koryo, 14th century. National Museum of Korea.

126: MIRUK (MAITREYA) AND LANTERN (page 168). Stone. Kwonch'ok-sa,
near Nonsan, South Ch'ungch'ong Province. Height of Maitreya: about
60'; of lantern; about 20'. Koryo, late 10th century.

127: PAGODA, WOLJONG-SA (page 168). Kangwon Province.
Height: about 48'. Koryo, 11th century.

190

128, 129: TWIN PAGODAS (page 168). Originally at
Yongch'on Monastery, Kangwon Province. Height:
about 13'. Koryo, 14th century. Kyongbok Palace
Pagoda Park, Seoul.

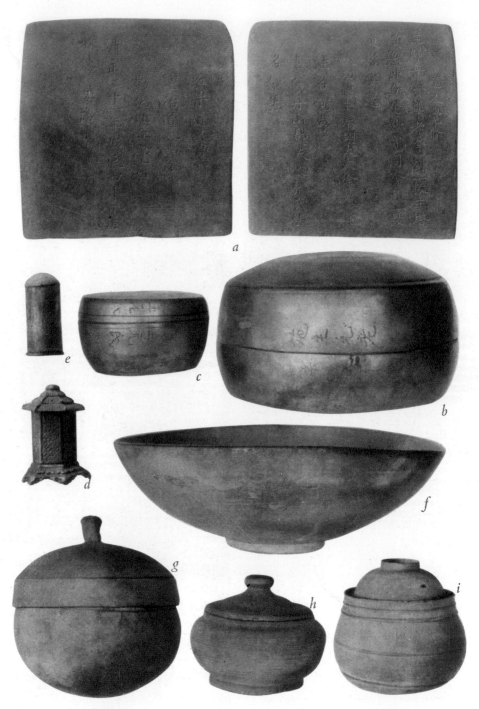

130: SACRED UTENSILS (page 168). From Twin Pagodas at Yongch'on Monastery, Kangwon Province. *a:* Inscribed plaque. Stone. 8″ × 8″ × 1/2″. *b, c, g,* and *h:* Relic containers. Bronze. Height (approx.): *b,* 3″; *c,* 2″; *g,* 3 1/2″. *d:* Lantern-shaped box. Silver. Height: 1 3/4″. *e:* Box. Silver, agalmatolite lid. Height: 1 3/4″. *f:* Bowl. Celadon porcelain. Diameter: about 2 1/2″. *i:* Urn. Agalmatolite. Height: about 3″. Koryo, 14th century. National Museum of Korea.

131: FUNERARY PAGODA (SARI-TʻAP) OF SONG PUP (page 168).  Originally in
North Cholla Province.  Height: about 8 1/3′.  Koryo, 11th century.  Kyongbok Palace Pagoda Park, Seoul.

132: FUNERARY PAGODA (KYONMYO-T'AP) OF HAERIN (page 169). Originally in Kangwon Province, near Wonju. Height: about 21′. Koryo, 11th century. Kyongbok Palace Pagoda Park, Seoul.

133: PAGODA FROM WONGAK-SA (page 169). Originally in Kaesong, Kyong-gi Province. Height: about 40'. Koryo, 14th century. Kyongbok Palace Pagoda Park, Seoul.

134: LANTERN, HWAOM-SA (page 170). Stone. South Cholla Province, near
Kurae. Height: 20'. Koryo, 14th century.

135: LANTERN, SILLUK-SA (page 170). Stone. Kyonggi Province. Height:
about 6'. Koryo, 14th century.

136, 137: STUPA AND CASE (page 170). Silver plate. Height of stupa: 6″; of case, about 8″. Koryo, 14th century. National Museum of Korea.

138: MINIATURE PAGODA (page 170). Gilt bronze. From Sujon-sa, Kyonggi Province. Height: about 6″. Koryo, 11th–12th century. National Museum of Korea.

139, 140: STUPA AND CASE (page 170). Stupa: glass; case: silver plate. From Sujon-sa, Kyonggi Province. (Case) Height: about 7″. (Stupa) Height: about 5″. Koryo, 11th–12th century. National Museum of Korea.

141: MINIATURE SHRINE (page 171). Gilt bronze. Height: 11 1/8"; width: 9 7/8"; depth: 5 3/16". Koryo, 13th–14th century. National Museum of Korea.

142: MIRROR WITH FLORAL DECORATIONS IN RELIEF (page 171). Bronze.
Diameter: about 10 1/3″. Koryo, 12th century. National Museum of Korea.

143: KUNDIKA (page 171). Inlaid bronze with silver fittings. Excavated from
a tomb near Kaesong. Height: 14 3/4″; diameter at base: 3 3/8″. Koryo,
11th–12th century. National Museum of Korea.

144, 145: EWER AND BASIN (page 172). Silver with gold
decorations. Height of ewer: about 13"; of basin: about
7". Koryo, 11th–12th century. Museum of Fine Arts,
Boston.

146: TEMPLE BELL (page 172). Bronze. Originally from Kangwon Province. Height: about 20″. Koryo, 13th century. National Museum of Korea.

147: DETAILS FROM MURAL: BODHISATTVA AND DEVA KING (page 172).
Painting on wood. Pusok-sa, Yongju district, North Kyongsang Province.
Height: about 6'. Koryo, 14th century.

148: ILLUSTRATED SUTRA (page 172). Woodblock printing on paper. Koryo,
11th century. Collection of Judge Kim Wan-sop, Seoul.

149: ILLUSTRATED SUTRA (page 173). Gold ink on dark paper. Length: about
17″; width: 8″. Koryo, 14th century. National Museum of Korea.

PART FOUR

# The Yi Dynasty

WITH PLATES 178–314

FOLLOWING PAGE 297

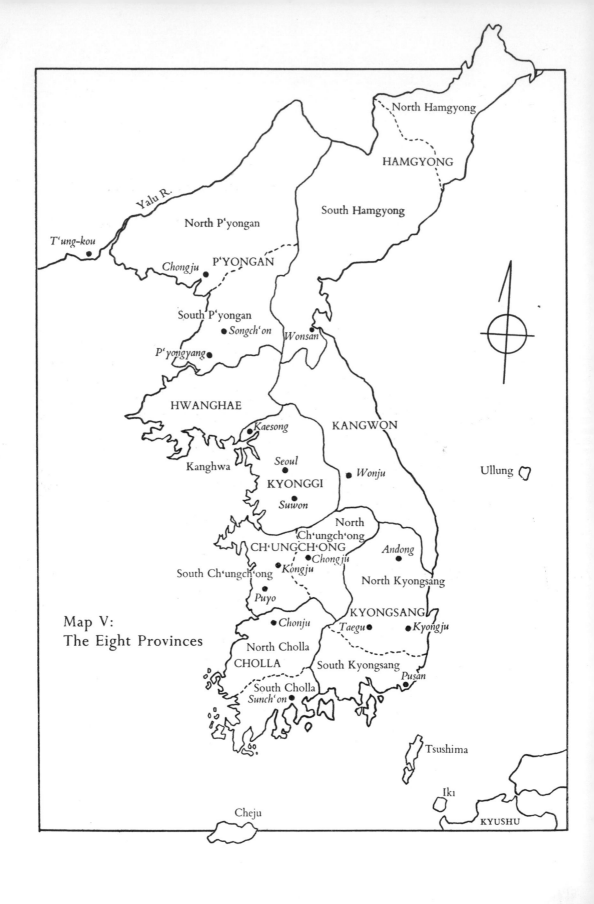

North Hamgyong

HAMGYONG

Yalu R.

South Hamgyong

T'ung-kou

North P'yongan

Chongju ●    P'YONGAN

South P'yongan

Songch'on ●

Wonsan ●

P'yongyang ●

HWANGHAE

Kaesong ●

KANGWON

Kanghwa

Seoul ●

Wonju ●

KYONGGI

Suwon ●

Ullung

North
Ch'ungch'ong

CH'UNGCH'ONG

Andong ●

Chongju ●

South Ch'ungch'ong

Kongju ●

North Kyongsang

Puyo ●

KYONGSANG

Chonju ●

Taegu ●

Kyongju ●

Map V:
The Eight Provinces

North Cholla

South Kyongsang

CHOLLA

Pusan ●

South Cholla

Sunch'on ●

Tsushima

Ikı

Cheju

KYUSHU

CHAPTER ELEVEN

# Fifteenth Century:
# The New Dynasty

HISTORICAL BACKGROUND  The ruling family in Korea for the roughly five hundred years from 1392 to 1910 was the house of Yi. The dynasty was founded, as were all ruling families in northeast Asia, by an ambitious general. In China, such dynastic changes had occurred with cyclical frequency; in Korea, only twice in a span of two thousand years.* By 1368, the Ming dynasty of China had ousted the Mongols from China proper. During the subsequent consolidation process, Ming officials noticed with suspicion the fluctuations in allegiance of the Korean king, who was by birth more Mongol than Korean and who attempted to remain on good terms with both sides. One of the Korean generals of the time, Yi Song-ge (representing the middle generation in a strong grandfather-father-son combination), was popular in Korea because of his success in suppressing Japanese piracy and Manchu raids. He was also successful in keeping as far as possible from the court while his competitors, less astute, became entangled in court intrigue and inevitable political disaster. Because he was supported by his able son, who had made a good impression while acting as diplomatic agent at the Chinese court, General Yi's act of banishing the last Koryo king did not arouse the opposition in the Chinese capital that it might otherwise have done. On the contrary, as soon as Yi Song-ge's pro-Chinese policy was understood by the Ming emperor, investiture of the Yi household as the new royal family of Korea was guaranteed. Later events confirmed the Mings in this stand. The Yi kings organized a Confucian state which not only outdid the Mings themselves in strict adherence to the Confucian code, but outlasted them by several centuries. The Yi royal family and the scholar bureaucracy built upon Ming patterns of government, adopted the Ming legal code, and copied Ming costume.

The first kings attacked their problems with vigor. Inspired by the enthusiasm of the early Ming emperors for reviving the past glories of the Chinese empire and sharing with them a strong reaction against all Mongol practices, the Yi household threw itself with

---

* The first of these was the period of the Five Dynasties, 907–60. After a period of warlord rule in Korea, the country was partially reunited under the rule of Wanggon in 918. He exercised great clemency toward the ruling house of Silla, which did not stop functioning until 935. The second period occurred during the breakdown of Mongol rule in the fourteenth century.

zeal into demolishing the institutions of the immediate past and into the work of establishing a new regimen to take their place.

First, they put an end to the lingering military feudalism that had begun to develop under the Wang kings and organized instead an autocratic, highly centralized monarchy. This they accomplished with such thoroughness that the dynasty was able to weather a number of major shocks both from without and from within before it disintegrated under Japanese attack five hundred years later. Second, they reimposed an agricultural economy upon the nation, killing the budding commercialism and re-establishing self-sufficiency. After the systematic and large-scale drainage of wealth out of Korea during the hundred years of Mongol rule, such austere measures were a necessity, and Spartan conservation became the foundation stone of the new state. The first major act of the new regime, therefore, was a careful redistribution of land for cultivation. Former landownership deeds were canceled, and the king in theory became the sole landowner in Korea.[1] All previous records were destroyed—the fire that consumed them, it is said, burning for three days. The land was then parceled out to government officials who received allotments on a loan basis through a system of cultivator rights.

The significant feature of this system was that the use of the land lasted only so long as the official held his government position, his salary being paid in cultivatorship rights. Moreover, the civil service examinations were made the key to official position. In this way the king tamed his nobles by forcing them to become scholars—or some member of the family to do so—if they wished to remain in the upper class. The legislation that put teeth into the system was the *kwajon-bop* (rank-land law), a direct tax collected by the local magistrates instead of the former indirect tax collected by the nobles. Moreover, a system of both public and secret inspectors enabled the government to detect and punish nobles who evaded the law. In a country that was wholly agrarian, to control so completely the means to wealth by this method was the essence of simplicity. Its immediate effect was to give the state a long period of stable government which, by fourteenth-century standards, was remarkably enlightened, orderly, systematic, and not without benevolence.

This is not to say that in the long run the cost to Korean society for political stability of this sort was negligible. Moreover, owing to population increase, economic stagnation, and eventual political factionalism, the total internal deterioration was very nearly complete by the twentieth century. Korea was too small a country and too easily supervised by a watchful central government to allow any measure of success to that segment of the population which sought to avoid the excesses of despotism by staying as far as possible from the center of it—a success possible in large China. Restrictive regulations of many kinds not found in China were enforced in Korea, and there was little redress or reform as time went on. Two of these restrictions were similar to Hindu caste taboos rather than to practices current in countries neighboring Korea. One was a regulation preventing widows from remarriage; another was one prohibiting the sons of nobles *(yangban)* from attaining official positions of high rank if their mothers were concubines.[2] There were also many sumptuary laws, including periodic prohibitions of the production and sale of liquor. Within the court itself, the besetting evils of Oriental despotism—nepotism and the usurpation of power by women and eunuchs—were at first strictly controlled. King Sejong, for example, banished a concubine who asked for an official position for a relative, and punished eunuchs when they engaged in political activity. The mining of gold was an economic activity that, strangely enough in a gold-rich country, was also prohibited on the theory that products of a luxury type threatened the safety of the state by luring in predatory invaders. When China pressed for tribute in gold, the Yi kings simply replied that "Korea is not a gold-producing country."*

In order to put into operation a restrictive and austere program, a trained bureaucracy was necessary, and as time went on, the body of administrators increased in size and officiousness until it was able to strangle all opposition from any other power group in the country: the military, the Buddhist church, the royal family itself. Finally it began to eliminate members of its own class. If the Yi kings had not destroyed feudalism and had instead allowed it to run its course as it did in Japan—developing a money economy, trading guilds, and cities—Korea's fate upon emergence in the modern world would have been different. As it was, they constricted their country for the best of reasons—economic necessity—into a strait jacket of agrarian practices current in China before the time of Christ; deprived the upper classes of the opportunity to acquire wealth or position except by becoming, through scholarship, lifelong servants of the state; and thus set the stage for the factionalism that the upper classes in their insecurity soon developed. Factionalism, then, appeared as a formidable and unhealthy feature of later Yi dynasty politics.

A brighter side of Yi rule, however, was the handling of foreign affairs. The early Yi kings distinguished themselves by astute adjustments with China. The relationship was called *sadae* (honoring the great), and it was carried out by annual trade and tribute missions to Peking.[3] Relations with Japan were called *kyorin* (friendly relations) and were implemented in terms of trading centers in the port of Pusan, where specified numbers of Japanese called each year to trade.[4] Border markets were established to regulate trade with Manchuria, and the piracy menace was abated though not entirely halted by these prudent measures. A small but meaningful exchange of goods and ideas between Korea and her neighbors continued to provide her with the latest novelties.

Confucianism took the place of Buddhism as the official cult, and its reach into the life of the people was carefully fostered by the government through making ancestor worship in each household the most significant act of the individual's life.† The enthusiasm with which the early Yi kings set about the reconversion of the people is seen at its best in the personality and life of King Sejong (1419–50).

This king realized that in order to implement his program a trained officialdom was needed for the sake of efficient administration if for nothing else. He established a Confucian college in Seoul and subsidiary colleges in the provinces and looked into the matter of publication, "because our scholar class has but few books." He and his father, King T'aejong,

* This was partially in line with the ancient Chinese theory that "gold drives out grain." See also Fred H. Harrington, *God, Mammon, and the Japanese* (Madison, Wisconsin, 1944), p. 128. "Religious and political restrictions and ignorance of Western methods had restricted exploitation by the natives."

† According to family law regarding inheritance, the first matter to be considered was the inheritance of the religious function of ancestor worship. Next was the inheritance of the estate and, third, the headship of the family. See Judge Keun Kun-chang, "Korean Family Law" (unpublished paper delivered before the Korean-American Bar Association, 1946).

perfected and financed the casting of movable metal types, the first ever used in such a project in the world.[5] Many fine editions were published by these two kings and their successors and were distributed free of charge to officials and institutions on the royal list.* The acquisition of new reading material was highly stimulating to the upper classes.

In order, however, that the lower classes might be provided with books in a language they could read (the editions mentioned above were all written in Chinese), the king appointed a board of scholars to develop a Korean alphabet. The task occupied the board for nearly fifteen years and necessitated thirteen trips to Liaotung to consult Chinese scholars. The result was the simple but nearly perfect alphabet called *chongun* (correct sound) or *onmun*, which was made a "gift to the people" in 1443.

Not that the gift was appreciated by all. Many scholars were offended that "literature should be lowered to the dust" by becoming available to the masses, and they were more than reluctant to lose their chief prerogative, the ability to read and write. They were also reluctant to see the king seek an ally in the common people. Therefore, during periods of weak kings and dominant officials, onmun was proscribed, and at all other times its use in government offices or in Confucian schools was severely limited.

Nevertheless, the new writing took hold. The common people received it with joy, learned it quickly, and used it to record folk tales, wise sayings, market ditties, love songs, diaries, and household accounts.[6] Chinese literature became available in translation and began to penetrate for the first time to any depth in Korean culture, stimulating the people to experiment with the problems of creating a broader native literature.

ART    In the fifteenth century the Ming empire of China was at its height. New solutions for old problems were being sought in economic, political, and artistic fields. New foreign contacts enriched the nation and were welcomed by Emperor Yung Lo and his immediate successors. The expansive spirit of the Chinese court was also felt in Korea, where the art-hungry leisure classes, deprived by the new dynasty of the contributions that Buddhism had formerly rendered, turned with enthusiasm toward developing a taste for, and an ability to produce, highly imaginative, sensitive, and technically satisfying paintings of their own, without relying upon professional artists to do it for them. The most popular form was landscape painting rendered in ink or in the new medium, water colors.

Art patronage had become a badge of success in the middle classes in China and Japan. In Korea, however, there was no wealthy middle class, and those who were wealthy—the aristocrats—did not patronize art; they produced it. Therefore the usual way for a talented unknown artist to succeed in the painting profession was to put himself under the protection of the king. If the king was knowledgeable, he allowed the young painter a great deal

* Kim Won-yong, *Early Movable Type in Korea* (Seoul, 1954), p. 8. "King T'aejong said, 'In order to have a good government, we must read widely. Since Korea is far to the east of China, books are seldom to be obtained. To reprint books, block printing is too laborious; even after being engraved the blocks are easily broken and it is very hard to print all the books we need. I therefore intend to cast movable types with bronze so that whenever we come to get new books we can reprint them. If we succeed, it would do a great service to the nation. However, I do not want to impose the burden of expenditure involved in making the types upon the people. You courtiers and I will finance the expense.'"

of freedom and protected him from the jealousy of competitors both amateur and professional. The professional artist, in return, was obliged to produce official portraits, to paint
murals (usually in the officially recognized neoclassic styles of T'ang and Sung), and to
do fan and album paintings at parties. Otherwise, he was free to practice any style that
appealed to him.

The early Yi kings, like the Ming emperors, took an active interest in the arts by founding
an academy. In Korea, the Tohwa-so was established at the outset of the dynasty for the
recruitment and encouragement of the best artistic talent in the country. From the start,
the Academy was a success, most of the best artists in the country belonging to it, regardless
of whether they were amateurs or professionals, or whether they held other official positions, or were rich or poor. Honorary titles, similar to that of poet laureate (for example,
*kuksu* or "best in the country"), were awarded to those who excelled,[7] and as further
reward, high rank was bestowed upon successful painters. The rank of *hyongnam* (magistrate of a county), however, was the highest available to professional painters. A few artists
had higher ranks, but they were either members of the royal family or of families whose
fathers had held high rank, thereby making the sons eligible for another classification.

Though long-lived, the Academy was never free from internal antagonisms, the most
serious of which was the rivalry between the amateur painter who was often a gentleman
and the talented professional who had to be very good at his art or "lose his rice bowl."
This rivalry was camouflaged in later times by the arbitrary assignment of all artists to one
of the three main Chinese schools of painting—Northern, Southern, and Gentlemen Painters—to which all artists were at first assigned regardless of individual styles. The underlying
objective of this move seems to have been to separate amateurs from professionals. In
Korea, the painter of the Northern school came to be identified with Chinese traditional
painting as opposed to Southern or "Korean" painting (which was also supposedly the
style of the true artist who painted for the love of it, not for hire). The professional was
thus fairly easily labeled Northern, since he was obliged by his patrons to paint in traditional or Chinese styles, and the amateur came to be labeled Southern.

Art in China, as it interested the aristocrats more and more, came to be intellectualized,
and the term Gentleman Painter was defined as applying to the artist who, "caring less for
the external appearance of things than for the inner meaning,"[8] achieved the expression
of inner meaning by means of rapidly executed ink paintings which could be completed
in a few moments of creative impulse. It is obvious that this noble ideal could hardly be
lived up to at all times by any one class of artist, much less by the gentlemen artists, and
that this method could hardly be reserved for their exclusive use alone.* In Korea the

* This method was closest to calligraphy. It was also ideally suited to the needs of Son (Zen in Japanese,
Ch'an in Chinese) Buddhism, which stressed the importance of sudden illumination after meditation and a
systematic approach to intuitive knowledge by means of controlled meditation. The Ch'anists also despised
learning by means of words, spoken or written, and therefore welcomed the use of pictorial symbol. It is
useful for the art student to note that two fundamentally different groups of people (Confucian scholars and
Ch'an Buddhist priests) found their best artistic outlet in the same method: black ink speedily employed by
means of calligraphic techniques. One of the best presentations in English of the roles and styles of the Gentleman Painter and of the Southern and Northern styles is to be found in Yoshio Yonezawa, *Painting in the
Ming Dynasty* (Tokyo, 1956), pp. 5–32.

pretense was, for a long time, that the school of the Gentleman Painter and the school of Southern landscape painting were one. By virtue, therefore, of its aristocratic element, of its nationalistic element as well, of the art practices of Son (Zen) Buddhism, and of the natural Korean taste for emotional expression provided by the Southern style, there was soon only one important school in Korea, the Southern.

The professed contempt for outward appearances in favor of emphasis upon inner meaning sponsored by the Southern school had greater importance in Korea than was first apparent. Korean court artists, less sophisticated than their Chinese counterparts, actually did bring wholehearted, natural creative effort to bear upon their work, even if this effort was sometimes naive. With a complete art language at their disposal, they did not feel the necessity for original, novel forms with which to clothe the "appearance of things." They felt free, rather, to concentrate on new combinations, new interpretations of old themes, new experiments in brushwork, and finally, in the late eighteenth century, to blend Western art methods with their own.

To conclude, the Tohwa-so landscape painters included the best artists in the country. They expressed in the simple media of ink and silk, by means of oft-repeated symbols, fresh and deeply felt versions of the unrolling panorama of the world about them. What they accomplished, at their best and within their own rather austere frame of reference, was, like the ceramics of the same period, a superlative contribution to Asiatic art.

There were three chief styles which continued throughout the dynasty. The first was the traditional or neoclassic (the exact forms and bright colors of T'ang painting), a style learned by all artists as a part of their training but employed in practice mainly by painters of sacred pictures for temples, of ancestral portraits, and of historical scenes and official ceremonies. The second was an advanced style which emphasized breakdown of form and relied for effect chiefly upon the employment of pulsating monochrome washes or upon multitudes of small dots which, giving up tonality and the smooth, continuous line altogether, substituted for them shapes built up of particles. Artists in this style, freeing themselves from line and exact form, often turned away from representing the likeness of things, or even from trying to express "inner meaning," and ended by becoming manneristic, picturesque, and slick. The third style was created by the Gentleman Painter, who formed a picture the way he would paint a line of ideograms: by carefully planning out the linear composition and the relationship of forms within it. Frequently elements from all three styles would be combined in one painting, particularly during the eclectic eighteenth century.

The early Yi painters experimented freely. The closeness of the Korean capital to the Ming court meant that Ming fashions in art were popular. At first there was much study of Chinese masters and much painting of copies and paraphrases of T'ang and Sung landscapes, but the greatest artists soon freed themselves of dependence upon the masters, as noted above, and began to create compositions of their own inspiration.

Chief of the fifteenth-century artists were the three masters, An Kyon, Ch'oe Kyong, and Kang Hui-an, and the younger artists, Yi Pur-hae, Sin Se-rim, and Sok Kyong. There were others whose works remain but whose names are unknown. Kang Hui-an belonged

234

to a leading family and in his youth was given a good education. He passed all the examinations and traveled to China, where he was able to see and study Ming paintings. The
influence of Son (Zen) Buddhist ideas is seen in his painting of a sage in meditation on a
rock *(Plate 178)*. The hanging foliage overhead and the water beneath give the viewer the
illusion that the world is not real and that only the thoughts of the sage, suspended as it
were in space, are real—a central concept of Buddhist doctrine. The seal on the upper left
side of the painting reads "Injae," one of Kang's pen names. A skilled calligrapher as well
as an artist, he was called upon by King Sejong to paint the ideograms for a new set of
metal types. He loved flowers and gardening, and wrote what was in his day a unique
contribution to Korean literature: a book on horticulture called the *Yanghwa-rok.*

The most gifted of these artists was An Kyon (Hyondongja), said by some to be the
foremost landscapist of the dynasty. He was honored even in his lifetime as the outstanding
artist to paint in the grand manner. Little has been recorded of his life. His birth date was
probably around 1400, and he died between 1464 and 1470. He was a "professional"
attached to the courts of Kings Sejong, Sejo, and Songjong, where one of his duties seems
to have been to uphold the honor of the country in painting contests with visiting Chinese
artists and to supply the king with commemorative pieces, official portraits, palace murals,
and the like. Not much is known about his training other than that he had the opportunity
to see many excellent Chinese landscapes and that he studied them and copied some of
them until he thoroughly understood the principles of their construction. He must have
begun his career at an early date as a member of the Academy, for he was given an assignment by King Sejong in 1446 when he already had the rank of *hogun* (commandant, fifth
rank). At court he practiced the neoclassical style of painting, which was officially recognized and was therefore "safe." Other information about his life is scanty; his work was
valued as a "golden treasure," and when he died his family was left destitute, his house
being seized, presumably for debt, so that "not even a duster remained."[9]

Although An's extant work demonstrates his talent, there was also a political reason for
the esteem in which he was held. The following story illustrates this phase of his career
very well. A Ming envoy to the Korean court in 1464 was a specialist in the painting of
bamboo. He asked the king to show him specimens of Korean paintings of bamboo, and
the king complied by searching the country for the best examples. The envoy was not
satisfied with any of these. He maintained that they were all paintings of rushes or reeds,
not bamboo. An Kyon was hurriedly sent for, although by this time he must have been
a very old man, and was asked to do a painting on the spot to please the visitor. The
Chinese official was impressed and congratulated the artist on his skill, but said that the
painting depicted rushes, not bamboo. At this point the king, "who understood the art
of painting,"* suggested that the leaves be stripped from the stalk and that it alone be
painted. An Kyon, very much on his mettle, accepted the challenge and painted the bare
stem with all his skill, taking care to depict only the essential characteristics of the bamboo

---

* This is doubtless a reference to the concept that the essence of a subject is best presented without distracting
detail. For a review of this concept see Osvald Sirén, *The Chinese on the Art of Painting* (Peiping, 1936), pp. 221,
227.

stalk. The result pleased the envoy, and he admitted at last that the painting represented bamboo exactly and that even in China there were few painters who could equal An Kyon.[10]

Although little information about An Kyon's life is available, there is more than enough in the record by way of panegyric. Fortunately, some of his large paintings have survived, and these serve to give the modern critic a clue as to what was meant by the extravagant praise heaped upon him. First, he could handle a complex and imaginary subject with a deftness that had wide appeal in the Orient. One such painting, called "Spring Dream" *(Plate 179),* is much admired in Japan, where it was taken by its Japanese owner.[11] It is a magnificent scroll, four and a half feet by one and a half feet, depicting in color the artist's concept of the "never-never land" of magic mountains, valleys, blossoming groves, and inviting empty cottages.* It is an outstanding painting still. The gorgeous colors and embellishments in gold have been remarkably well preserved.

Another painting, a fragment called "The Fisherman" *(Plate 180),* illustrates in a simple way other characteristics of An Kyon's art: his skill at interpreting the essence of a subject, his mastery of brushwork, and his exuberance of spirit. In "The Fisherman" the artist has caught and conveyed a mood of universal appeal. It is a painting of a man in contented, though solitary, communication with nature, where the mood of the day is as important as the mood of the man.[12] Here the coldness of the day is emphasized, and this idea is expressed in every line of the picture: the huddled pose, the mantle-wrapped hand protecting the jaw, the tilt of the hat, the fur mantle. Thick strokes describe rough fabric; hairlines depict the fur. The man does not seem to mind the cold. He is not depicted in struggle with nature—a feature often stressed in such themes in the West; on the contrary, he is enjoying himself.

Criticism of An Kyon's work by contemporaries is valuable, all the more because he lived during a period that was one of the most productive of the Yi dynasty. Mention is made of favorable comments on his painting by Chong In-ji, the head of the Confucian College, who was also one of the inventors of the Korean alphabet. A form of artistic achievement popular at the time was the combination of the "three excellences"—a painting, a poem, and calligraphy. An Kyon's paintings were frequently in demand for this type of trilogy. One such was ordered by the heir apparent in honor of the king's visit to a scenic province. The literary description of the painting has been preserved, but the painting itself has been lost. An Kyon's work was described in conventional terms: it was "inspired by heaven," the artist must have been an "immortal," his "hand was genuinely in accord with his subject," he produced "effortlessly," and his paintings had a "life of their own" in that they were reputed to have power to convey their inner meaning to later generations. The effect of this magic on later generations may be seen in the prose-poem written by the poet-statesman T'oege a hundred years after An Kyon's death. The following paraphrase is from the description found in the *T'oege Chip* (The Collected Works of T'oege):

"The cottage and trees in front of the mountain are as calm as if they were sleeping, and the brushwood gate is open. An aged man who went to the market to sell his wares is on the way back, and a boy is spreading his net upon the sands. The mountains slope gently:

* The cottage symbolizes the superior man and his practice of the noble virtues.

they seem to sheathe a mighty sword. The vast expanse of sea and sky join in the distance . . . in a bamboo thicket . . . there is an empty cottage. Who is to retire from the world to live here? Smoke is rising from a quiet pavilion at a late hour. The rice wine is mellow and the returning one is eager to drink . . . guests call to one another from a distance and stop. Driving a donkey up the steep trail, they visit the village in the forest. A boat on the sea is sailing towards the misty landing. A grotesque tree leans against a rock and the water embraces the mountain. How can a man manage to remain in a fairyland like this? If the hut has no occupant, I will become its master. . . . I look up at the hills and streams and everything is as cold as ice in the moonlight. Houses in the distance are dim. Someone riding on a donkey is reciting elegant poetry and I wonder who he is. . . . Seriously, and putting an end to this, I find him to be myself."[13]

# CHAPTER TWELVE

# Sixteenth Century: Century of the Scholar

HISTORICAL BACKGROUND    A conspicuous feature of the political and social reforms of the early Yi kings was, as we have just seen, their promotion of Confucian learning. As a result of these measures, however, Confucian cliques arose which in the sixteenth century became strong enough to challenge the authority of the king himself. Pacifist and economy-minded, the Confucian civil officials began their deadly drainage of funds from rival establishments, such as the army, so that by the century's end the military arm was demoralized and unprepared to defend the country. On the other hand they were responsible for vigorous and inventive contributions to the country's culture in many fields, especially in public works, public morals, art, and literature.

The original purpose of the royal emphasis upon learning was to create an enlightened and educated official class, but the success of this program brought on a countermovement. The reign of a nonconformist king, Prince Yunsan (1495–1506), saw a purge of many important scholar-officials. Yunsan's first act, upon coronation, had been to behead his tutor and to sponsor, by way of reaction, what amounted to a cult of ignorance. Officials (and with them the people at large) were forbidden to use the new writing; dancing girls were housed in the Confucian shrines in Seoul; and many of the most cherished practices of the early Yi kings were thrown into discard by the tenth king of the line. The result of his twelve-year rule could have been foretold. When it was over, there was an equally violent swing back to conformity. The scholars rallied their forces and, headed by the prime minister, deposed the king and established another more docile member of the royal family in his place. Quick to perceive the advantages of being in control of the state through control of the king, the officials then began to frown upon royal "interference" in administrative details, and encouraged the royal family to spend its time in cultural instead of political pursuits. By the beginning of the sixteenth century the Yi kings had lost their supremacy, not to regain it until some two centuries later.

The encouragement of the arts began once more to have the blessing of the powerful. During the reigns of King Chungjong (1506–45) and King Myongjong (1545–68) occurred what Confucian chroniclers have called the Golden Age. Modern historians, however, characterize the period as one of division and rivalry within the Confucian scholar class itself.* Politically and socially supreme, the scholars also controlled the country's economy. They held the rights of cultivatorship of most of the rice land and monopolized the lucrative positions at the court and in the government. At the *kun* (district) level, moreover, the civil service system gave them control of local affairs through the magistracies. They were also able to put themselves out of reach of the common law, to make of themselves an untouchable group,† and to curtail the rise of merchant, military, or professional classes when the interests of such groups seemed to threaten official monopolies. The possibilities for profitable and important careers were few in Korea; official positions were limited; and the number of educated men who wanted rank and income from the state was far greater by the sixteenth century than the small Korean bureaucracy could absorb. Increasingly savage ruptures appeared in the ranks of the scholars. Remedies were devised and applied, but the splintering process, once begun, did not stop. There was little outlet for the energies of the nobles except competition for official position.

The most serious rupture, as far as the state was concerned, was the conflict that developed between the civil administrators of the bureaucracy and the censorate.‡ In 1518–19 a third purge of scholars took place, avowedly because of the interference by an ambitious young civil official named Cho in the conduct of a military campaign in the north, but actually because of the efforts of the top echelon of blooded aristocrats to weaken the talented and Confucian-trained young members of the censorate and other official "organs of remonstrance" led by Cho. The outcome of this clash was that the censorate was purged of the Cho group through a betrayal from within the censorate, and though it survived the attack of 1519, it was eventually frustrated in its attempt to break through the upper crust of the specially privileged aristocracy. The organs of remonstrance were accused of preaching good government but not having to practice it. This split in the civilian government exacerbated the split between military and civilian officials, and the division was surreptitiously encouraged by China—a shortsighted policy, considering the military skills of the rising Manchus and the powerful centralized military state that was evolving in Japan under Nobunaga.

By mid-century another rift in the solidarity of the scholar class appeared, this time on

---

* Dr. L. George Paik, in his lectures on Korean history at the University of California (1951), designated the period 1495–1567 as a "reign of terror."

† A change in criminal procedure occurred during King Songjong's reign (1470–95). The literati were given the privilege of being tried by the Confucian College, and not by the state, for their crimes. This was an important turning point in the rise of sharp class distinctions that characterized the Yi dynasty period. See *Songjong Sillok* (Historical Records of King Songjong) and Homer B. Hulbert, *The History of Korea* (Seoul, 1905), Vol. I, p. 319.

‡ *Chungjong Sillok* (Historical Records of King Chungjong). James S. Gale, "A History of the Korean People," *The Korean Mission Field* (Seoul, July, 1924—September, 1927), chap. xxvi, makes the statement that from "this slight irritation . . . a deadly feud began." Owing partly to the Yi kings' policy of preventing the rise of a military feudalism in Korea such as had developed in Japan, the military versus civilian competition was exploited and encouraged. There is some speculation among modern historians as to whether Korea would have been subjected to the two hideous and long-drawn-out wars with the Japanese and the Manchus, had a better balance between civilian and military interests been preserved. See Edward Wagner, "The Purge of Korean Literati" (Ph.D. thesis, Harvard University, 1959).

an intellectual basis; that is, the separation of the formalists, or legalists, from the humanists. The legalists were scholars who trained primarily for careers in the government. As a group they were in theory committed to the Confucian agnostic concept of a mechanistic universe which operated with but little concern for the welfare of man, and in practice to a life of somewhat dull routine. This body attracted more of its kind into official position. Once in the majority, they began to feel that they had a monopoly of office. The humanists, or scholars who did not study for public office, found themselves in positions of less influence, since they were removed from intimate daily contact with the king. They filled educational and religious positions and lived in the country, whence they were often hastily recruited for service whenever the visit of a learned Chinese envoy required the presence of a man of broad learning. It was primarily the humanist who created the institution of the widespread *sowon* or literary schools, the first of which was built in Kyongsang Province in 1541,* and the number of which soon reached the thousands. It was also this class of Confucianist which provided Korea with its cultural leadership during the four hundred years that remained of the dynasty.

A third phase in the breakdown of the Confucian scholar class began with the formation, about 1575, of political factions.† The rivalries of these factions so absorbed the attention of officialdom that matters of national concern began to take second place. Before the Japanese invasion of 1592, the Korean king—warned by spies of Japanese preparations— sent a mission to Japan headed by the chief men of the two leading factions. They could not agree in their reports about the question of a possible attack, and the government, paralyzed by indecision, neglected to prepare for such an eventuality. The formative period of the factions or political pressure groups (called the Tongin, So-in, etc.) lasted for a space of about eighty years (1568–1649), included the disturbances of two wars, and finally merged into a new period of contest for power among the fully matured factions late in the seventeenth century.

Although by fits and starts Korean society was culturally progressive under the guidance of the scholars, politically the country retrogressed. Three of the safeguards against official corruption and incompetence insisted upon by the early kings were abandoned; the army shriveled, eunuchs were active in palace politics, and nepotism was freely practiced. Worst

---

* The sowon became important centers for the dispersal of culture to provincial centers. They rapidly increased in number. The government gave subsidies to these schools and thus made it possible for the humanists to train their sons for office, to compete with the formalists for office, and thus to retain their hold upon their property. The sowon were also endowed by the literati who patronized them. In course of time they became centers for political intrigue. They rose to their highest point of influence in the eighteenth century. Most of them were closed in the 1860's by the regent, who then regarded them as hotbeds of anti-government activity. The sowon are important to the art historian because they became centers for the production of much of the painting and calligraphy of Korea in the three-hundred-year period between 1550 and 1850.

† The episode to which Korean historians refer as marking the beginning of factional struggle in Korea occurred during the regency of the Queen Mother Sim, when a personal feud developed between two men who lived in the eastern and western parts of the city. The factions that arose around these two men were called the Tongin (Easterners) and the So-in (Westerners). The formative period of these factions lasted for a space of eighty years and then emerged into a new period of contest for power among the fully matured factions: the Noron (Old Men's Party), the Soron (Young Men's Party), the Namin (Southerners), and the Pukin (Northerners).

of all was the emergence of factionalism. The most prosperous and productive period of the Yi dynasty, therefore, came to an end with the close of the sixteenth century.

CULTURE    King Chungjong, as did his successors, Kings Myongjong and Sukchong, actively discouraged Buddhism and Buddhist learning and encouraged the spread of Confucian literature. He accomplished this by means of new publications supplied with onmun explanations and by sponsoring the preparation of a Sino-Korean dictionary, a great event in the cultural life of the kingdom. With this dictionary the Koreans had the means for translating Chinese into their native tongue, a step second only in importance to the creation of the alphabet. Progress in all the arts was marked.

In this period flourished two of Korea's most highly esteemed philosophers, Yi Hwang (T'oege) and Yi I (Yulgok). These men served the country both in public capacity as diplomats, college chancellors, and counselors, and in private capacity as political thinkers and religious leaders. By the opening of the sixteenth century many Korean philosophers were even more oppressed than the Chinese by the imprisoning effect of the Chu Hsi philosophy upon the intellectual life of their class. The concept of the universe and man's role in it that had been "so efficiently cemented together by Chu Hsi that the final edifice shows no sign of crack or fissure,"[1] was too bleak for the already emotionally deprived Koreans. Therefore, in order to meet the needs of their countrymen for more substantial satisfaction than they were getting from Chinese Confucianism, T'oege and Yulgok undertook to "perfect the system" by developing its spiritual aspects.

Encouraged by the example of Wang Yang-ming (1472–1528), who had focused attention upon the intuitive side of man's nature, they developed the idea of a personal God which Chu Hsi had ruled out of the Chinese system. Many Koreans besides T'oege and Yulgok were dissatisfied with the avoidance by the Chinese of the problems of the soul, immortality, and the nature of God. The Chinese philosophical system, as it existed in practice in Korea, they thought did nothing "but nourish pride and cater to the ego" of one class.* It taught no higher ideal than that of the superior man, ignored the problems of the inferior man—his poverty and the general degradation of women—and callously destroyed the faculty of faith.

Both T'oege and Yulgok rallied to the cause of broadening the application of Confucianism to everyday problems by recommending, above all, the intuitive approach (which is often the creative approach)[2] to the solution of many Korean injustices and inequities. A significant comment upon Yulgok and his teaching was made by the scholar Yi Hang-bok: "He never laboured to find out anything but seemed to know it by intuition —because of his loving heart he never feared to disagree with others. He made straightforwardness his rule in life and, as his duties presented themselves, did each and every thing to the profit of all."[3] There was more than a hint of a new and stimulating social philosophy

* This statement is frequently made by modern Korean historians. Nevertheless, it should be remembered that Confucian morality was of a very high order and was of great value in setting up standards of behavior. To cite one example, Korean women who have been well brought up in Confucian behavior will not indulge in gossip. When a woman does so indulge, it is generally recognized that she is not entitled, by Confucian standards, to the honorary epithet.

in Yulgok's teaching. Another aspect of the practical application of his theories was a remedy which acted like a blood transfusion to the dying economy. This was his experiment with rural cooperatives called the *hyangyak*.*

During his youth Yulgok's mother died. In compliance with the custom of mourning for parents, he withdrew from active life and lived in a hut at her grave for three years. The act was of great importance in forming his character, for he then put into practice the habits of observation of nature and of basing his thinking upon the results of direct observation, habits that he had learned from his artist mother. These habits of thought colored all his writings and influenced later generations of Korean scholars in the beginnings of scientific questioning and original thinking based on personal experience and experiment. It was Yulgok who first broke air holes through the thick crust of the imported Chu Hsi doctrine, the dead weight of which had been stifling the development of intellectual initiative in Korea for more than a century.

In spite of political retrogression and subservience to China, Koreans at all levels enjoyed a lively culture which they were maturing on their own initiative at their own rate. Misunderstanding in the outside world about the nature of this culture can be laid to the Japanese invasion which occurred at the end of the century. Japanese chroniclers, as well as the Spanish Jesuits who were then active in Japan, recorded their contempt for the Korean lack of warlike skills and laid it all to what they supposed was total Korean degeneracy.

ART    The sixteenth century saw in China the beginning of an emphasis upon decorative styles, a change designated by William Cohn as the shift from the "infinite to the intimate,"[4] largely to cater to the tastes of the middle classes. In Korea the new styles were immediately imitated in occasional pieces,[5] but they did not take the place of the old, well-established traditions, which remained dominant.

Many first-class painters were at work during this century. Yi Sang-jwa was a slave whose talent brought him to the attention of the king. He was admitted to the Academy as a professional painter and was thereafter classified as a *chungin* or member of the minute middle class. His work covered a wide range from landscapes to illustrations for books, the most interesting of which was the set of illustrations for the *Yolyo Chon* (Book of Virtuous Widows). He also painted the portrait of King Chungjong. An extant painting of his, that of a wind-blown pine jutting from a crag beneath a moon just perceptible at the top of the painting is one of the main treasures of the Toksu Palace Museum *(Plate 181)*. The darkness and stillness of night and the smallness of the sage and his attendant portrayed in the opposite corner from the moon are tellingly caught in this old scroll. There is no signature or seal on the painting. It has been frequently reproduced in Japanese publications.

Most other artists of the century were paired: O Mong-nyong (Solgok), the painter of plum blossoms, with Yi Chong (T'anun), the painter of bamboo; Kimji, the figure painter, with Yi Sung-hyo (a prince of the royal house, father of Hoju), who was a versatile figure-

---

* See "Haeju Hyangyak" (The Cooperatives of Haeju) in the *Yulgok Chip* (The Collected Works of Yulgok). They were first proposed by the famous Cho Kwang-jo as mutual assistance societies on a village level. Cf. Paek Nam-un, *Chosen Hoken Shakai Keizai Shi* (Social and Economic History of Feudalistic Korea) (Tokyo, 1933).

and-landscape painter. Then there were Yi Ching (Hoju), the artist prince, and Munch'ong, the Buddhist painter. Last of all, there was the talented Madame Sin. Four of these painters have been selected for comment below. Madame Sin was from an impoverished but accomplished family of scholars; T'anun and Hoju were from the royal family itself; and Munch'ong represented the class of priest-artist. All four painted for enjoyment and devotion to art or religion, but never for money. Because of Munch'ong's commitment to a religious congregation, nothing is known about his life except that he lived in the sixteenth century. His painting, "Temple in the Mountains" *(Plate 182),* is a good example of the vigor of the Buddhist painting of the period. A landscape done in black ink, it depicts a monastery located high in splendid mountainous country in accordance with the Buddhist emphasis on detachment from the turmoil of daily life. The effect of remoteness is further emphasized by the absence of the foreground usually found in such landscape scrolls.

There is a dearth of information about the lives of most Korean artists, but about the life and work of Madame Sin, who was probably the most distinguished woman of the Yi dynasty, much is known. Madame Sin (Sa Im-dang) was entitled to fame in the opinion of her countrymen because of her influence upon her son Yulgok. The praise that is bestowed upon her is meted out in the cautious terms reserved by Confucianists for deserving women. Comments upon her paintings and other accomplishments are mixed with comments on her good character and her model behavior as daughter, wife, and mother. Fortunately, some of her paintings remain to speak for themselves, and these, although faded by the passage of time, are masterly. Madame Sin had other talents besides her skill at painting. She was known for her needlework, her elegant calligraphy, and her scholarship. Also important was her practice of the Confucian virtues in her family life, her care of her sons, and the instruction that she gave them.

Information about her is drawn from two sources, literary and artistic. The written information comes from a biography, prepared by Yulgok himself, and from biographies of the other members of the family: her father, grandfather, husband, and son, all of whom distinguished themselves in one way or another as scholars and statesmen. Her mother also was known for her piety, a memorial shrine having been raised in her honor by the king. Other written sources are the inscriptions on Madame Sin's paintings; the colophons written long after her death by such statesmen as Song Si-yol and Kwon Sang-ha; and information gleaned from the inscription on the memorial stone near Munsan, which was composed by the scholar Yi Hang-bok in honor of her son. These names are all well known in Korea's hall of fame, and passing praise from them is worthy of notice.

The facts of Madame Sin's life are prosaic. She was born in 1512 in a remote and beautiful part of Korea's central east coast, and was given the name Tongyang. She was the second of five daughters born to a Confucian scholar who, though one of the most celebrated of his day, was poor. His assets, however, were his learning and his library of heirloom books, and of these he contributed generously to his family. His brilliant second daughter learned to write flawlessly and to compose. She became acquainted with the ancient history of China and of Korea and with the Chinese classics, which were the sacred books of her class and times. All this was unusual education for a girl, and one biographer notes, by way of apology, that she did "not indulge in poetry or essay writing," which were male prerogatives.* She also learned the household arts which were necessary requirements for marriage, and at the proper time, in her late teens, was married to a young official named Yi Wŏn-su, who had the rank of *kamch'al* (inspector of the censorate).

Fortune seems to have favored her in everything, including the sex and number of her children—four sons, named Son, Pon, I, and U. The third son, I (or Yulgok), born when she was twenty-four years old, had an extraordinary career as statesman, official (he was chief of the Confucian College), religionist, and original thinker. According to the story on the memorial stone raised in his honor, Madame Sin dreamed of a dragon before his birth, and the room he was born in was then named Dragon Dream Room and later kept intact as a memorial to the great statesman.† Madame Sin died in 1559 at the age of forty-eight. Mourning for parents was so strict that few people undertook full observance, as Yulgok, however, did at this time.

These are the main facts about Madame Sin's life, her work, and her influence upon others. Nothing is said about her personal characteristics to show what sort of person she was in private life. Nevertheless, even a superficial analysis of her life gives some clue as to her personal qualities, such as frugality, good taste, simplicity, reticence, distaste for the sentimental, sensitivity, habits of keen observation, and a taste for wide reading. These qualities were to a great extent transmitted to her sons. An anecdote concerning the clothes that Yulgok once wore to receive a Chinese dignitary illustrates the family's Quaker-like preference for simplicity. He appeared in peasant dress. The envoy's reaction to this was to ask: "Has Korea no scholars, that she must call a farmer from the plow?" "Far from it," replied the interpreter. "This gentleman is the first scholar in the land. His appearance is his own choice."

Simplicity and clarity of statement were Madame Sin's chief qualities in her art. Her simplicity, however, was achieved by a knowledge of her subject and an unerring sense of selection and appreciation for design. Although her early training consisted of imitating the paintings of great artists, especially those of An Kyŏn, she was eventually able to discontinue the copying of the style of others. She began to paint when she was seven and from then on trained herself until she could paint any subject that might be given her. In her constant efforts to perfect her painting, she created a style that was difficult to imitate,

---

* Madame Sin did nevertheless write some poetry. From the *Choya Chibyo* (Official and Unofficial History) comes the following lyric:

> Far from the lush mountains of my native place,
> A thousand *li* away I dream of home
> Where breezes blow across the Kyong Podae
> And snowy herons come to earth and fly away again
> The livelong day,
> Where fishing boats lie east and west
> Upon the sea. . . .
> When may I go back along the Imyong road
> And once again take up my needle
> Beneath my parents' roof,
> Clothed once more in gay and vivid
> Silks? . . . [the bright clothes of childhood]

† The dragon symbolizes the birth of a superior man.

244

although many, including her son Oksan, tried. She did every kind of painting in demand—pieces for albums, folding screens, fans, scrolls. None of her greater works have survived; we have only the lesser ones devoted to depicting the world of animal and plant life.

The best of the extant pieces is undoubtedly the painting of ducks and millet in the Yi household collection.[6] Another, a painting of a purple carp, is done in hairlines and washes with a nonchalant and expert carelessness that is perfection itself, and incidently seems highly modern. Her painting of grapes *(Plate 183)* is not a still life in the Western sense, but, in line with the Oriental feeling that the world of nature has its own life and that this could best be portrayed in a living state, the grapes are painted on the vine. The possibilities of the design effect of black and white are explored here in a selective but felicitous way. In a set of water colors of plant, flower, and insect life, Madame Sin demonstrates, even more clearly than in her black and white studies, her sensitivity to the harmonies of line and color. The cucumber is rendered in soft purple, enhanced by the white of the starlike asters; the orange-red of the chinaberries is contrasted with the soft greens of the dandelion; and the national flower, done in white, is dramatized by being surrounded by other objects in white—the buds, moths, and butterflies. She varied her brush stroke with her subject: delicate lines to depict the fragility of the hibiscus petals, spiked lines for the dandelion, and so on, done with an economy and ease that came from much practice and keen observation. It is evident from her work that she painted from life, not from other paintings.

The result of her efforts was that, in the judgment of contemporary critics, she rivaled the great An Kyon in importance. "She is next to An Kyon. How dare we ignore her work merely because she is a woman? How can we belittle her because we think painting is inappropriate for a woman?"[7] Comments by critics a hundred years after her death, and down to the present day, give her credit, albeit a bit grudgingly at times. Long after her death an album of her calligraphy was considered to be so valuable that a magistrate of Kangnung, a certain Yun, ordered it to be transferred to wood blocks for preservation and study in the local literary school. A modern Korean art critic, Pak Kyu-su, lauded the etching-like quality of some of her paintings but added that they seemed unfinished because of the lack of her usual color.

The conservative nature of Madame Sin's academic training was apparent in her devotion to tradition. When she was young, she chose her pen name from the name of a famous Chinese empress whom she admired and modeled her behavior in accordance with the noble character of that lady. Along with her reverence for tradition, however, was a pronounced drive to break with tradition, to establish her own style and repertoire out of the facts of her everyday Korean experience, and it is this which endeared her to her countrymen as much as anything else. In conclusion, therefore, it is worthy of note that Madame Sin's prestige rested first upon her success in her family life—the plain living and high thinking which was, and still is, the Korean ideal though it is only too often neglected by the official class—and second, upon her very substantial success as a gifted and sensitive artist.

Yi Chong was the best known and possibly the best loved of the artists of the sixteenth century. His art career, however, marked the end of the epoch. The great Ming upsurge in artistic endeavor that had produced the revival of interest in the great painting of the past and initiated new media and styles, was still alive and developing its own fashions in China. In Korea the old styles lingered on in spite of wars and political confusion, but the grand manner was lost. Yi Chong (T'anun) was a member of the royal family and one of the most genuinely admired painters of the entire Gentleman Painter class. His prestige was due partly to his talent, partly to his urbane and dauntless personality. It is a well-known fact that Asiatic art tradition puts an unduly high emphasis upon the total personality of the artist, but in the case of T'anun the esteem was warranted. Both talent and personality were considerable, and the conventional expressions of praise in his case carry an overtone of genuine appreciation.

According to one record, T'anun was born in 1541. His early life was unmarred by the shadows of war. He lived in contentment, with plenty of leisure to devote to his hobbies. Not the least of his attractions in the eyes of his fellows were his high birth, his superior education, and his princely rank. Like the other gentlemen of his class, he practiced the arts of painting, calligraphy, and poetry, but he had more to say than the others.

Overnight, however, his fortunes changed. The sudden invasion of the country by alien armies, who lived on the land, caused the destruction of his property and, what was worse, the loss of his right arm. T'anun was over fifty when this happened. Nevertheless, he started to practice painting with his left hand and was eventually able to do better with that hand than he had formerly done with his right.

The following excerpt from the preface to an album was written by a friend of T'anun who had also suffered the distractions and discomforts of the refugee life of those days:

"But during the war we were scattered in all directions in order to save our lives, like fleeing birds and animals. Chungsop (T'anun) was unable to escape the enemy's sword, losing his arm. One day we met each other at temporary headquarters, but we were so absorbed in congratulating each other on escaping death, and in mourning for those who had not escaped, that I had no time to ask whether he had saved any of his paintings. Later some of us met in Seoul but . . . to our sorrow it was soon apparent that none of us had saved any of the paintings of our friends. But Chungsop himself at that moment pulled out from his bottomless bag an album of bamboos, which looked like orchids, and plum blossoms that he had painted before he lost the use of his right arm. We opened the album and found that not only were the bamboos as good as formerly but better. . . . Chungsop asked me to write a preface to his album criticizing his work. I said that I would. Seeing the painting of the thinly spaced bamboo, I felt that I liked it best; but the one of the thickly grouped bamboo I did not dislike either. I felt that I could hear it rustling even though it was silent. Although the color was not lifelike,* yet the painting looked real, and I seemed to feel the fresh breeze blowing. . . . Chungsop, you can be content with your painting. It has come out of your inner heart. Now I can say that I understand the meaning of your bamboo. How can I pretend to pass judgment on your paintings, saying this is good, that is better, spilling out much ink in order to differentiate one work from another? Those who are not able to create like to criticize the work of the truly gifted man, and those who do not know how to judge art, take their cue from the man who does. Are you not forcing

* This is a reference to the use of black and white. It was thought that the inner meaning of a painting could be better presented in black and white than in color, which tends to distract.

me to play the part of such a one? Chungsop just smiled when I said this. . . .[8] His paintings are much more spirited now than they were before. . . . Once I told him, in a joke, that the way to rise above vulgarity and to achieve real spirituality was to break an arm."[9]

T'anun's painting was conventional in every respect: in his choice of subject, his manner of presentation, his brushwork. His only deviation was the use of gold ink upon a black silk canvas—a royal prerogative of which he took full advantage. His range was narrow and his drawing simple, but it was always elegant, always selective, and wonderfully light and easy. In one of his albums he presented the bamboo in eight different aspects: the tall, the sturdy, the young, the dew-pearled, the windblown, the dead, the bamboo in the rain, and the bamboo in the snow. The inscriptions accompanying the paintings were varied. A moral, for instance, on the dead bamboo went as follows: "It is easy to feel dispirited when one sees the bamboo foliage dry out day by day, to become at last only dead stems . . . but one should recall the story of Ei Mu-gong (Wei Wu-kong), who devoted himself to keeping his spirit encouraged by regulating his conduct even after he was ninety years old." On the dew-drenched bamboo, the thought is lighter: "Although I am looking for it, I cannot see the dew on the leaves, but they must be wet because the leaves are drooping with weight." The painting of bamboo included here *(Plate 184)* is a good example of his style. It is simple and expressive. Depth is achieved by depicting the foreground stalk with its fanlike clumps of leaves in dark ink, while the stalks behind are only faintly indicated. In this painting, the signature "T'anun" is in the upper right corner; below it are two seals giving Yi Chong's pen names, T'anun and Subun Ungyok. (Another of his pen names was Chungsop.) This silk scroll shows clearly the delicacy and rhythm of the master at his best. Presumbly all of his extant paintings were done with the left hand, since the earlier paintings were lost.

The appreciation accorded to T'anun's work was as great as if the paintings had been nobler creations. Even the king, it is said, valued T'anun's paintings so highly that he always responded with generous gifts whenever he received one of them. One admirer is credited with the tribute: "Now I wonder whether the bamboo has turned into black ink or the black ink into bamboo!" From another came the encomium: "His handling of the paintbrush must have mysterious and heavenly qualities to make the results so reviving. . . . Whenever we appreciate his painting, it refreshes and clears our minds. I think that there is nothing more appropriate than his painting to comfort my old age." The environment in which these paintings were produced could hardly have been tranquil or even comfortable, but there is no hint of sadness or turmoil in the gay works that have survived.

T'anun himself was grateful when his paintings succeeded, and he said so. He was particularly pleased at kind remarks about paintings that he had done with his left hand. He liked to paint bamboo because he admired its qualities: it always grew straight and was never crooked; it was inflexible, stiff, and unyielding, but at the same time it was graceful and was thus associated with the supreme Confucian virtues of loyalty, integrity, and sweet reasonableness.

T'anun was undoubtedly the Korean aristocrat at his best. He participated actively in the duties of his class. He contributed substantially to the artistic and intellectual life of his time, and he was not found wanting during the dark days of the invasion. Not a great artist or even a great man, the prince nevertheless came closer to embodying the virtues of his class than any other artist. The following poem, included in the *Osan Chip* (The Collected Works of Osan), was written about him soon after his death. It is entitled "A Word of Longing for T'anun."

" He was a wanderer with his sword and his poet's brush for ten years.
Though the grass is green again, we have longed for him for a year in vain.
The darkening day is gloomy with rain.
I wonder if his soul is wandering yonder in the clouds
Where the wild geese fly. . . ."

Yi Ching (Hoju) was another member of the royal family who lived and worked during this troubled period. Born in 1578, he was only eleven when the Japanese landing took place. His family fled to the northern border when the invaders swept through the peninsula in the summer of 1592. They finally returned to Seoul to rebuild their burned-out palaces when the Japanese armies left Korea in 1598. Hoju's education was therefore interrupted. One of the gentlemanly pursuits he particularly liked was the study of painting. Other things he neglected, but not painting. It was his meat and drink and his escape from the troubled world in which he lived. Once, during his childhood, he disappeared from home for a day or two, and search parties had to be sent out for him. When he was found, he received a beating from his father for the trouble he had caused. He explained that he had been out watching birds and had become so interested that he had forgotten the time. Then, to prove his point, he painted a picture of the bird he had been studying, while "tears fell from his eyes upon his paper."

According to his biographers, Hoju continued to concentrate upon his art throughout his life, forgetful of everything else—even forgetful of his own "honor or dishonor." He died young, at the age of twenty-nine. He served as a *chubu* (official in the central government), presumably using his leisure time to paint.

He is known by the Koreans as a painter in the Chinese style. His paintings are deliberate and detailed, and all have the same mood of dreamy tranquillity. His work is like that of the Chinese painter Shen Chou (1427–1509). Because he painted in the Chinese manner, Hoju is not highly thought of in Korea; or it may be that his status as the son of a concubine influenced the critics. The comments of two admirers and critics, both of whom lived about hundred years after Hoju's death, are given below, since they reveal the dimensions of the artist's talent. Nam T'ae-ung said that Hoju followed in the footsteps of his artistic forebears; that he had mastered all of their styles, developing at the same time his own; and that he could honestly be called a master. The critic felt, nevertheless, that Hoju was too trapped by tradition and rules and that his paintings, though large, were not magnificent and, though carefully and painstakingly executed, lacked true sensitivity.[10] On the other hand, King Sukchong (1675–1721), who was one of the Yi dynasty's few scholar-kings, wrote in the *Yolsong Oje* (Selected Prose and Poetry):

"Korean painting has succeeded wonderfully in following the basic art principles. Confronted with a piece of plain silk, Hoju has created a magic landscape. A few houses are visible in the blue haze. Fishing boats are floating on the tranquil water, green leaves show signs of changing color, and autumnal tints are everywhere. The red ball of the sun is sinking towards the horizon, and the glow of evening fills the sky. One can enjoy this beauty which is proffered to the eyes in a moment endlessly extended by the artist without having the trouble of lifting one's heels. . . . There is a cloud upon the mountain. There are no waves upon the sea. I can imagine the boatman's song as I stroll beneath the pine trees watching the flocks of water birds collect upon the long line of the seashore."[11]

The landscape in the Chun collection *(Plate 185)* is an excellent example of Hoju at his best. It is a landscape poem: a lovely decorative thing done in gold upon black silk (the royal medium) which depicts with careful minuteness an enchanting scene of mountains, trees, pagodas, and temples. The Chun collection also contains an album of eighteen paintings in water color depicting the same pallid dream world. They were obviously done by the same hand, and they have a charm and dignity that satisfied in a special way the longing of the overconfined city man for the soothing spectacles of nature before which his troubles could dwindle. It is true that Hoju did not present nature in its productive aspects—fertile fields and the like—but in the romantic moods most likely to appeal to the gentleman, who could enjoy them without having to "lift his heels."

His work, though detached from the Korean scene in inspiration and in manner, and rendered even more exotic by the gold ink he so often used, has remained as a delightful memento of some of the best of the scholar tradition in painting. There was no peace or security to be found in Korea in Hoju's time. The major crises that the dynasty faced in its long five hundred years were compressed into the period spanned by his lifetime. Hoju's dream-world painting shows no trace of the disturbance of the world about him. Aloofness was a part of the scholar's code.

# CHAPTER THIRTEEN

# Seventeenth Century:
# Century of Change and
# Growing Seclusion

HISTORICAL BACKGROUND     In 1592 occurred the Japanese invasion. This was a war in which everyone lost, the Koreans most of all. It was a war marked by stalemate, confusion of aim, and a high amount of treachery on all sides. The Japanese armies were supposedly fighting in Korea to gain a foothold for their conquest of China. The Chinese came to Korea in haste to prevent the Japanese from invading their country, and both sides intrigued with the Koreans to gain their ends. When the Japanese gave up first, on the occasion of the death of Hideyoshi, they withdrew from the peninsula, taking with them anything movable upon which they could lay hands, including whole colonies of artisans.[1] Then the Chinese, in a discreet way, did the same thing. Therefore it was not surprising that art collections disappeared—destroyed, looted, or just scattered in the mêlée.

Korea's recovery from the destruction caused by this war was slow. Many slaves took advantage of the confusion to escape from their masters and remained free afterwards, thus forcing the aristocrats to make efforts to hire laborers and at the same time get more land to cultivate in order to make ends meet. Tenantry became more feasible under the new system than the operation of farms by a diminished slave-labor supply. New men, who had taken over the business of national defense while many of the former officials were in hiding, joined the ranks of the upper classes. Social changes of this sort meant that the ruling class was enlarged without enough expansion of the economy to accommodate the change. The lower classes were still further reduced in numbers with more of an upper class to support. The scholars had lost their monopoly of government business and their positions of dominance in the economic and social structure, and were obliged to compete even more ferociously with one another for the privileges of collecting rents and taxes. They could, however, sabotage any innovations which might further threaten their interests (or what they regarded as their interests in a purely agrarian economy) by the simple means of withholding support from an incipient commerce which had started up in the long years of the presence of Chinese and Japanese soldiers upon Korean soil. Thus it was not long before the weight of yangban conservatism was felt and Korea again fell back into the patterns of life which favored the scholar gentry.

The Mings, impoverished by the costly campaigns in Korea, were beginning to watch with alarm the rise of the Manchus. In Korea, the king (Prince Kwanghae, 1609–23) was also watching the rise of the Manchus, and it was not long before he conceived the idea that it might be advisable for Korea to join them against the Mings. The proposition, however, was unacceptable to the Confucian ministers, who had convinced themselves that their only security lay in firm alliance with the Confucian ministers of the Ming regime, who had "come to their aid" during the Japanese invasion. What really frightened the Korean officials was the possibility that a change in the power balance in northeast Asia would change their own status. Consequently they contrived to depose their king and go to the aid of the declining Mings, a move which was disastrous for Korea. It is possible that an early alliance with the Manchus would have spared the Koreans the second invasion that the affront now brought down upon them.

A rebellion led by General Yi Kwal (1623) very nearly put an end to the Yi dynasty, an event which, coupled with the country's defeat at the hands of the Manchus (1636), brought the kingdom to a new low point in general demoralization. For once, the king and the officials saw eye to eye in the formulation of the decision to isolate themselves, to close their borders, and to control with great care all intercourse with Ch'ing China and Tokugawa Japan. The desire for isolation was carried to the extent of stripping the trees and shrubbery from the hillsides facing the sea so as to present a bleak, uninviting picture to passing ships. The ensuing period of withdrawal, of seclusion, was unlike the seclusion of either China or Japan in that it was primarily directed against Korea's neighbors, not against the West. It lasted for two hundred years, roughly from 1650 to 1850.

It was a very different Korea in 1650 from what it had been seventy-five years earlier. The political factions, by mid-century, were ready to engage in organized struggles for power. The dynasty was at its lowest ebb, its prestige almost nil from the disgrace of the king's public prostration before the Manchu emperor, its power over the nobles negligible, and its treasury empty. From this nadir point, the Korean kings, by playing off one party against another, began to regain their power. Tensions across the borders eased as the Manchus established themselves in Peking in 1644, and from then on, conditions in all of northeast Asia began to stabilize. It was at this time also that the early shipwrecks of Western trading vessels began to occur on Korean coasts, and Korea got its first glimpse of Westerners.[2]

CULTURE     Far from being shattered culturally, the Koreans emerged from their wars with a revival of energies. During the campaigns, military and naval officers had devised some ingenious and highly successful war machines, and after the war there was a burgeoning of literature on and about the war, some in the form of memoirs, some as treatises on military strategy and tactics.

The most conspicuous figure, dominating the whole century in his eighty-five years of life, was the influential scholar, man of letters, and chief of the Noron Party, Song Si-yol.

He was highly esteemed by the Korean scholar class, partly because of his anti-Manchu stand and the tremendous knowledge of the Chinese classics that he brought into play in support of it. His career illustrates the policy pursued by Korean statesmen in arming themselves with knowledge of the history and ethics of China to use against the Manchus. It was owing to Song that a greater assiduity than ever was directed to a study of Chinese rather than Manchu literature.

Unfortunately, the emphasis upon the far past slowed down the rate of development of Korean literature and put an end to the creative spirit which had started so well but which from Song's time died down to a mediocre restatement of the same tired but politically safe ideas. No novelty was admitted, no deviation encouraged. Literature was almost wholly Confucian-bound.

The portrait of Song Si-yol by an unknown artist—no doubt a member of the Tohwa-so—is an excellent example of the formal yet sensitive art of portraiture as practiced by Yi dynasty painters (Plate 186). Song's enormous prestige is subtly suggested by the larger-than-life depiction of the white robe of office. The two inscriptions, both in the same calligraphic style, were added long after the portrait was painted. The inscription to the right, dated 1651, is a whimsical poetical admonition written by Song Si-yol to himself. The second inscription, dated 1778, is signed with King Chongjo's posthumous name. According to the inscription, this portrait was installed in the Confucian shrine in Seoul.

ART    In art, as contrasted with the literature of the period, there was more room for the expression of personality. Rapidly executed ink paintings were still fashionable. They were produced in the inspiration of the moment, and in the employment of this method the door was left open for the play of genuine inspiration even in themes that were already dull from overuse. Painting and calligraphy continued to be practiced as a basic part of the intellectual and religious life of the sowon as well as of the remote Buddhist temples where many educated people found refuge during the wars. The culture of the capital began to be disseminated in yet another wave to provincial centers, and much painting was done by the country artists. New sources of inspiration also became available to Korean artists at this time in Western art and the Japanese color print. A rare painting in the collection of Mr. Philip Han was done in Japan by Pak Che-ga, who employed Western perspective and modeling, as well as the general composition of the Japanese print, including Mt. Fuji in the background. The painting depicts a girl sitting in her garden against the backdrop of a Western-style portico.

Another of the scholar-painters of the times was Cho Sok, who was born during the war, in 1595, and died at an unknown date. He was a scholar who specialized in the painting of birds. One of his works, now owned by the Toksu Palace Museum, is called "Birds in a Tree" (Plate 187). Two magpies sit boldly on the branch of a tree near the center of the scroll while just below them are perched two smaller birds from among the few who are not afraid of the magpie. The scroll is painted in ink and faint color on silk. It is without signature or seal.

Among court artists were Kim Myong-guk (Yondam), Han Si-gak (Solt'an), and Yi Myong-uk. Yondam was noted for his versatility; his range was from meticulous landscapes that would please an early Sung master to simple one-stroke figures that were the ultimate in suggestiveness, a product of the school of thought that developed the art of devising the simplest part to suggest the most complex whole. Solt'an was a master of the perishable painting of the ink-and-rice-paper variety, while Yi Myong-uk preferred the neoclassic style on silk or grass cloth. Toward the end of the century, within a space of about ten years, a galaxy of the dynasty's most distinguished painters were born. These artists came to maturity during the reign of King Sukchong (1675-1721) and are thus more properly included under the subject of eighteenth-century painting.

An understanding of the trends in seventeenth-century art may best be obtained from a review of the life and work of Yondam, who was undoubtedly the most colorful artistic figure of his generation. He was active during the reign of King Injo (1623-50), whom he served as a court painter and as a member of the Royal Academy. He spent much time on specifically political assignments. At a time when there was no photographic coverage of important occasions, the artist was important as an intelligence officer. He had to record the details of what he saw and to put them down in pictorial form. Yondam appears to have been very popular in Japan, where he went on at least two missions, in 1636 and 1643. He was greatly in demand at the Tokugawa court, no doubt as much for his convivial spirit as for the dashing and amusing "thrown-ink" paintings he did on the fans and album leaves of the samurai. As for the Japanese opinion of Yondam's paintings, it is recorded that "those who got them thought of them as jewels."[3]

Nothing is told us about Yondam's early life, his family, or his birth and death dates; in fact, there is little information besides anecdotes about his drinking habits. From this evidence of official snobbery toward recording biographical data about Yondam, we gather that he did not belong to the gentleman class. He was, nonetheless, a very talented artist, as his extant paintings—although they are not his masterpieces—sufficiently demonstrate. His specialties were landscape and figure paintings which he executed with a vigor and a willfulness that suited the temper of the times. Yondam was an eccentric person who would not, perhaps could not, take the world too seriously, possibly because he had seen too much violence and despair and national humiliation in his day.

It was believed that he could not paint except under the stimulus of wine, which he drank, it is said, by the tok (the approximate equivalent of a barrel). Those noblemen who wanted pictures painted by him understood that they stood a better chance if they brought him wine first. They never knew how their requests would be treated, because Yondam had a directness that overwhelmed the timid. His paintings were superior, "implying defects in other paintings so that Yondam was anathema to the old-fashioned artists."[4]

One of Yondam's most noticeable characteristics was his sense of humor. Few of his paintings are entirely solemn, and most have some twist to them which displays his appreciation of the droll. The Susong No-in or god of longevity (Plate 188) is presented as a laughing monk with long eyebrows, windswept whiskers, and a bald head. His lower anatomy is made to seem stumpy by way of compensation for the tall head, and the god's symbol of long life, the turtle, is here represented by a few strokes which make it seem like a small pet.

Yondam's unpredictable manners often intimidated his associates, as the following anec-

253

dote will show. A Buddhist priest called upon him to commission him to paint an important mural, a "hell" scroll, for the walls of a temple and left several hundred feet of fine cloth with him for the purpose. When the priest had departed, Yondam called to his wife: "Exchange this cloth for wine and let me stay drunk for several months."

At the time appointed for the completion of the painting, the priest returned to call for it, but it was not ready. "I have not yet had the inspiration," said Yondam, and the priest departed in disappointment. This scene was re-enacted four times. Finally, when Yondam had "taken more wine than usual," he sat gazing at the spread of blank cloth for some time. Then he suddenly seized his brushes and completed the entire painting in one sitting. It was a gloomy scene: the palaces of the dead were painted amid dense clumps of trees, and the dead themselves were depicted in the drab shapes and colors appropriate to their condition. The victims were exhibited with their torturers, who were cutting and burning them, pounding them in mortars, and grinding them between millstones. The torturers were depicted as monks and nuns.

When the priest returned to take delivery, he became angry. "Why do you shame us like this?" he exclaimed. "It is preposterous!" But Yondam only laughed. "You rascal priest," he said, "you do nothing your whole life but deceive the people and take advantage of their misery. You are the one to go to hell!" The priest became threatening: "You have betrayed us. Obliterate the painting and give me back my cloth!" Again Yondam only laughed. "If you want the mural finished to suit you," he said, "you must buy me more wine. I will alter it for you."

The priest reluctantly did as he was bidden, and Yondam cheerfully took up his brushes again, added hair to the bald heads and whiskers to the chins, and painted the robes in bright colors. The painting had taken on brightness and a decorative charm. Nothing more could be asked of it. Grudgingly the priest expressed admiration and carried it off to his monastery, where it remained for a long time one of the principal treasures of the sect.[5]

Humorous, unpredictable, and contrary, Yondam could also be imaginative and tender. He liked to paint scenes which depicted Taoist Immortals enjoying for eternity the freedoms of a life of simple joy lived in an idealized place somewhere among the mountain peaks. The ink painting of the "Search for the Immortals," although small and faded, shows in a sympathetic way the very human urge to shake off the ills and humiliations of old age for the sake of living, forever robust and happy, as one of the Immortals. In this scene, mountain mists are swirling about the tiny cottage of a hermit. An old man has climbed the mountains to find the Immortals, and the implication from the inscription is that he is trying to find out how to be transformed into one of them. A boy points into the mists. "They are there," he tells the old man.

Criticisms concerning Yondam's carelessness could be appropriately applied to most of the slapdash paintings of the so-called Southern-style painters. They certainly do not apply to his more sensitive and meticulously organized landscapes.[6] From Nam T'ae-ung's *Ch'ongjuk Hwasa* (History of the Bamboo Painters), the following comments should be noted: "The smaller Yondam's paintings were, the more wonderful they were. The larger they became, the more exotic and mysterious. . . . But all, large or small, lacked detail and clarity because of this emphasis upon mystery. Furthermore, he could not paint unless he was drunk, and when he was drunk he could not handle his brush carefully, so that his paintings were a mixture of 'the dragon and the snake.'* Some say that he was a traitor to his profession."

Yondam's genuine talent was nevertheless recognized. A poem inspired by one of his landscapes, and paraphrased below, puts into words the feelings of the poet:

> "In the pine tree's shade creep
> A thousand feet of vine.
> On the mountain peaks the pine-tree roots
> Impregnate the black rock.
> The hair of two old men is white as frost,
> Their mantles flutter in the gentle
> Pine-scented breeze.
> A song comes faintly from the distant river,
> A cascade falls into a pool of rippling waves . . .
> And flowing streams run swiftly
> As horses run,
> Their clear waters slipping easily
> Over white sands.
> White-crested ripples beat softly
> Beneath the pavilion porch.
> All travelers, rested in the wayside hut,
> Go on into the forest.
> Alone, one returns with a book."[7]

The second painter of the above-named trio of court artists was Solt'an. His outline painting of the monk Podae *(Plate 189)* was done in the conventional mode for figure drawing: the outline in ink, hallowed by Liang K'ai, Shih K'o, and others. Here the caricature of the monk exhibits the artist's interpretation of the Son (Zen) philosopher and his failure to accept things as they are, as well as his failure to sweep away the hypocrisies and pretenses of life for the sake of wholeheartedness. His legs are pictured as wobbly, and the smirk on his face is intended to show the monk's ambivalence. A complex philosophy is thus indicated in a simple painting, easy for most Orientals to understand but difficult for the Westerner to appreciate until he comprehends the meaning.

The "Dialogue between the Fisherman and the Woodcutter" *(Plate 190)* by the third court painter, Yi Myong-uk, depicts another widely understood concept, that of the unity of mankind in spite of the diversity of man's experience. The fisherman is sunburned, his clothes are tied up, and his hair, in a topknot, is exposed to the sun, while his face is shaded by a broad-brimmed straw hat without a crown. In contrast, the woodcutter is pale from working in the shade, his body is covered to protect him from thorns and the stings of insects, and his topknot is hidden. The fisherman carries his catch, the woodcutter his axe. The one thing they have in common, the symbol of their status as workers, is the pole each

* *Yongdu samm'i,* literally "a dragon's head and a snake's tail": a good beginning and a poor ending.

man is carrying. Man's essential loneliness is the theme: a loneliness that is nevertheless assuaged by the joys of companionship and the moment of relaxation at the end of the day. The painting is done on a large canvas, the composition covering the whole area—its forms clearly articulated in the style of Lin Liang, a Chinese artist who lived a hundred and fifty years earlier than Yi Myong-uk.

CHAPTER FOURTEEN

# Eighteenth Century:
# Century of Peace and Stability

HISTORICAL BACKGROUND    The eighteenth century saw Korea freed from the fear
and the fact of invasion. In imperial China, the reigns
of K'ang-hsi (1662–1722) and Ch'ien-lung (1736–96) brought the country to the largest
size in its history and to a peak of general prosperity. In Japan, the Tokugawa shoguns were
firmly enforcing a policy of isolation and self-sufficiency—a policy also followed by the
Koreans. The Far East was finally at peace.

In Korea the two kings Sukchong (1675–1721) and Yongjo (1725–76) between them
reigned a hundred years. Externally, their relations with the Manchus had stabilized, and
the two states had adjusted to a peaceful, if not a mutually respectful, relationship. Contact
with Japan continued to be restricted to a limited trade through the Daimyo of Tsushima
and to the dispatch, over a period of years, of four large missions to Edo. Internally, factional conflict persisted, reaching its peak during the reign of Sukchong.* The situation became
so intolerable that the next ruler, King Yongjo, attempted to put an end to party politics
by the simple expedient of distributing the offices equally among the main factions by
means of the *tang pyong chaek* (policy of equal opportunity). Nevertheless, one faction, the
Noron, soon monopolized all the positions of importance. Another of Yongjo's reforms was
the establishment of a standard tax which, at one stroke, decreased the possibilities of
official corruption and increased state income.

CULTURE    During the reigns of Yongjo and Chongjo, the second cultural revival of the
dynasty took place. Stirrings of dissatisfaction with the Confucianism of
Chu Hsi—a discontent that had started in the fifteenth century with Yulgok—now developed into marked breaks with the past under the stimulus of Western concepts which
came into Korea through the Jesuits. Korean scholars who were attached to the annual
tribute missions to Peking brought back Jesuit books and maps and earnestly studied their
contents. The new learning, *silhak pa,* based its approach to education on the scientific, or
inductive, method called *silsa kusi:* a motto of four characters meaning "in real things find
truth." Books describing Western inventions were written in Korean, and Pak Che-won's

* There were two major shifts in factional control: from Soron to Noron and back again. Both were
occasions for the execution of about two thousand yangban.

*Yenam Chip* (The Collected Works of Yenam) introduced Western achievements in such sciences as physics and mathematics, Western religion, and devices like the clock and the organ. Other books were written about new concepts of political theory, one even beginning by courageously discrediting the Korean founding myths such as that of Tangun. The leaders of this new scholarship were Pak Che-ga, Yu Hyang-won, and Yi Ik.

Cultural contacts with Japan were less rewarding. Several shoguns spent enormous sums on the entertainment of large Korean missions, since they were eager to learn Confucian political strategy from the Koreans, or at least those refinements that led to a more secure hold upon the people.* This international contact catered to the egotism of Korean officialdom without contributing anything fresh and creative to stimulate it in return.

Another outside influence which breached the intellectual isolation of the Hermit Kingdom was the introduction of the forbidden religion, Christianity, which, with its concepts of social equality, uplift of women, personal salvation from sin, and belief in a loving God, was irresistible to many. A phenomenon occurred, new in the history of world Christianity: a sizable Korean church arose without missionary stimulus. Koreans became self-Christianized by means of Chinese translations of the Bible furnished to visiting Koreans by the Jesuits in Peking. Within one generation, from 1775 to 1800, several thousand Koreans were converted. As an immediate result, persecution by the government began, the Korean Confucian bureaucracy having become alarmed because Korean Christians were being instructed from Peking that ancestor worship was incompatible with the practice of Christianity. As a Confucian state, the Yi dynasty was adamant in its sponsorship of ancestor worship. Many Koreans clung to their new religion, however, and numerous arrests and executions took place. All of this occurred before a foreign missionary had yet entered the country.[1]

Korean literature, in general under the dominance of shopworn Confucian concepts, sank to the level of pedantic essays and pious treatises on morals. In poetry the older Chinese forms of the ode and epigram still prevailed and were used repeatedly whenever funerals, banquets, births, or other events requiring the services of the man of letters took place. In those studies, however, that were removed from the main interest of the strict Confucian scholar class and that treated specialized subjects such as medicine, law, and language,

---

* The Hideyoshi invasion and its aftermath brought about a change in Korean-Japanese relations. At first, all contact was forbidden by the Koreans for a period of about ten years. Then the Korean king agreed to deal with the Tokugawa shoguns (newly established as rulers in Japan) on a basis of equality. During the seventeenth and eighteenth centuries, twelve Korean missions traveled to Japan, each consisting of from three hundred to five hundred persons. The shoguns were interested in studying the devices by which the Korean royal house played off the factions against each other and those used by the yangban in extorting money from the people. The mission of 1711 was the largest. At that time the shogunate prohibited the Japanese crowds from watching the Korean procession in mixed groups of men and women for fear that the Korean envoys would get the impression that the Japanese lacked Confucian manners. Korean animosity never quite yielded to the blandishments of hospitality. In the early seventeenth century in Korea, even civil officials were required to wear swords to remind them of their animosity. For a review of this subject, see Sohn Pow-key, "The Opening of Korea: A Conflict of Tradition," *Transactions of the Korea Branch of the Royal Asiatic Society*, Vol. XXXVI (Seoul, 1960). See also Kiyoshi Tabohashi, *Kindai Nissen Kankei no Kenkyu* (Study of Japanese-Korean Relations in Modern Times), 2 vols. (Seoul, 1940), for an authoritative account of Korean-Japanese rivalry. The Sohn study is primarily concerned with the mission of 1786 but also treats background materials.

where a precise style and orderly arrangement were necessary, a new spirit was apparent. In such studies as these, authors felt safe from political interference or the need to conform, and free to employ original solutions to the problems they experienced.

The eighteenth century was a period of development of family life and of amusements that could be shared by all. Festivals and games—mild ones for the elderly, risky ones involving excitement for the young—were enjoyed by all classes of society. It was the period when the custom of long visits to one's friends developed, and the *sarang pang* (guest rooms) became centers for the interchange of ideas all over the country.*

The handicrafts were practiced chiefly under royal patrons who used the products as "gifts" with which to reward the yangban. The manufacture of certain types of pottery was reserved for royal use and all guilds were regulated as to colors and glazes permitted for household use in the lower classes.[2] The same regulations prevailed in the other arts: lacquer making, silver working, enameling, wood carving. Painting, as was noted above, was commonly regarded as a yangban prerogative. Therefore, new art forms least associated with the Confucian aristocracy were the only safe ones for the people at large to enjoy. But new forms could not easily develop under the puritan watch of the Confucian officials, and so old forms, innocently repeated but with new connotations, had to do. The fear of innovation therefore penetrated, for different reasons, all of Korean society.

But the desire for creation, for innovation, was in the air. Koreans were becoming conscious of themselves and their own culture and were ready to express their ideas in Korean forms instead of the outworn, though respectable, Chinese patterns. As a result, there was a marked rise in the demand for skills which had a temporary value—those which could be exhibited before audiences and enjoyed by all. There was safety in community activity that was absent in individual creation. Therefore the arts which lent themselves to these conditions thrived: music, dancing, and painting, which could be practiced in the presence of one's friends; drama, which permitted ad-libbing; and poetry, which could be produced at social gatherings. Flower raising, as long as it did not aspire to the peony or the regal chrysanthemum, was also permitted to all. It was a rare household, therefore, that did not raise flowers of some sort.

It is not surprising that the creative urge of the people, repressed so sternly, found vent in oft-repeated themes in every art, in the songs of the dancing girls, in the harvest dances of the farmers, even in the black-ink paintings of the literati. These themes were repeated with a variation, a timely twist, a local touch that delighted the audience and kept the subjects from becoming dulled by repetition.

The device of the repetition of old themes with attached hidden meanings, apparent only to the initiated, was adopted by all classes. It was used even by the officials who conducted missions abroad or who entertained visiting officials. Three chief forms of diplomatic entertainment were the production, on the spot, of gift scrolls of calligraphy, of painting, and of poetry. The skill of the poet at this sort of thing was developed by versemaking (or, as the case required, picturemaking) at banquets where the game consisted of filling timeworn poetic forms with ready-made expressions. No one was very much worried

---

* The sarang pang were an important means for the spreading of Christianity.

over the banalities. What mattered was the hidden meaning and the deftness of the artist in implying something which only a few could catch.*

An anecdote about the entertainment of a noted Chinese official illustrates the way diversions of this type developed in the eighteenth century. The Korean chancellor of the Confucian College was sent north to the city of P'yongyang to meet a Chinese envoy who had never been in Korea before and who was interested in its scenic and other attractions. He was also, doubtless, not above putting his Korean hosts on the defensive as soon as he entered their country. As he stepped out of his sedan chair upon arrival, he asked the chancellor to supply him before morning with a poem of a hundred stanzas describing the beauties of the city. The Korean hosts were much taken aback at such short notice, but they withdrew and consulted. One of their number who had proved to be deft at rapid versemaking was selected to fulfill the request. He called for a brazier of charcoal, a fan, and a bottle of wine. A skilled calligrapher was settled near him, ready with a scroll of beautiful paper, an inkstone, and brushes. The main act of the little drama then unfolded as follows:

"Cha took a long drink from the bowl and then began a deep mumbling hum to collect his thoughts, tuning up as it were. He beat time with measured fan on the rim of his brazier and then, springing to his feet, shouted, 'Ready!' Like a rippling stream from a fairy fountain the soft couplets came tripping forth in song. . . . Off went coat and outer garb to clear the decks for action. . . . It was done, rolled beautifully, sealed as a picture is sealed, and carried to the Chinese envoy, who had just entered upon his first delightful sleep. 'Who is it?' inquired he. 'And why am I awakened at this hour?' 'The poem,' they said, 'the poem is here.' 'Already? So soon?' said Chu. 'Impossible.' But there it was. He unrolled it with his attendants around him and, taking up his fan, beat notes to its rhythm on the rim of his brazier. . . . Chu gathered inspiration as he went sailing along and sang out so clearly that all could hear. . . . We are told that he beat his fan into flinders before he reached the climax at the end. 'A wonderful poem!' said Chu. 'Korea is indeed the land of the Superior Man.'"[3]

The art forms used by the educated, as has just been noted, had to perform the primary function of serving the state in order to satisfy the Korean craving to be recognized as "superior men" by the Chinese. Other functions were subsidiary.[4] One of these other functions was to meet the need of the people for emotional expression. Cut off from the satisfying outlets provided by Buddhism, the upper classes were forced to patronize secretly the deteriorating Buddhist monasteries or, even more surreptitiously, the witch doctors and sorcerers, or to coax their arts into giving them emotional satisfactions that Confucianism failed to give.

To summarize, the chief characteristics of the fine arts of the eighteenth century were their political and religious functions, as indicated above, the presence of hidden meanings and double talk, an insistence upon old Asiatic art forms often supplied with new Korean

* The popular song "Arirang," for example, has a rich array of associated meanings, from the lighthearted theme of love in spring, through the somber themes of execution and death, to the tragic themes of political and national destruction. Hwajae's "Fowls" *(Plate 200)* may be interpreted in three ways: light satire and take-off on human vanity, political irony, and barnyard humor directed at the sexual impotence of the yangban.

content, and the employment of perishable media. Music was not written down; speeches were not preserved; and dramatic events and ceremonies of great artistic merit were not recorded. It is safe to say that many vigorous new developments were the ones most carefully camouflaged and the first to perish.

ART     The practice of painting was limited in all the ways mentioned above. It was best appreciated when it was done in public without previous warning to the artist. Tanwon, for instance, who was the most celebrated artist of his day, although something of a rebel throughout his life, was challenged one day while at court to paint a large mural. The king had had a wall whitewashed for the purpose, and a theme was set: the Sennin or Immortals at the seashore. Tanwon, it is said, did not hesitate. He at once doffed his court clothes and "took off his hat" (a daring act of disrespect in the royal presence), and rolling up his sleeves, prepared to paint. The servants made his ink and held it up where he could dip into it while he painted "like a storm." In a few hours the picture was completed, and the king was pleased. It is recorded that in the painting "the sea waves were crashing as if to overwhelm the palace itself." This tour de force was almost certainly an expression of Tanwon's ability to make covert fun of the futile, parasitical courtiers who were jealous of his powers.

Resentful of Manchu overlordship and mindful of old ties with Ming China, the Korean Gentleman Painters found excuses for ignoring current art fashions of the Manchu court and for continuing to follow the aristocratic traditions of the Mings. They lacked means, for one thing, to imitate many of the tasteless extravagances of the Manchu court or even those indulged in by the wealthy middle class and, for another, were inclined to proceed upon a course of their own. Whereas in China artists catered more and more to middle-class taste, as they did also in Japan, where there was a new moneyed class to patronize the production of the color prints and other innovations, in Korea there was no middle class, and art remained a prerogative of the cultured elite.

But it did not remain static. At almost all previous periods, the country had been inundated by the finished products of a discouragingly superior civilization. During the eighteenth century, in isolation, Korean art was freed to some extent to concentrate on the development of local ideals. Significant innovations using perspective and chiaroscuro were only occasionally seen, as in Pak Che-ga's "Lady in the Garden" and in "The Fighting Dog," long attributed to Tanwon. Old forms remained in use, since they contained all the symbols that were needed by the Koreans for the expression of their most complex, profound, and even contradictory feelings.

Some of the best painting was produced by the professional artists who belonged to the fringe gentry (the chungin class, recruited largely from the children of concubines) and whose passionate but repressed resentment of social injustice provided fuel for the creation of their greatest paintings. During this period of awakening and self-consciousness, Korean painting, which hitherto had lagged behind the Chinese schools, began to catch up with them in the work of four masters: Kongjae, Kyomjae, Hyonjae, and Tanwon. Korean painting, as a graft upon the main stem of Chinese art, now began to produce a distinctively Korean flowering.[5]

The first Korean artist to set Korea on an independent course was Kyomjae (Chong Son), the art-hungry old man who painted "daily for eighty years." Kyomjae was a trail blazer. He removed his art from the exotic heights of Chinese-inspired models (depicting only Chinese concepts and employing Chinese methods) and by means of the simple expedient of basing landscapes upon actual Korean scenes and Korean subjects, did a great deal toward changing painting in Korea from a transplantation to a home-grown product. Painting took on a new life. It became lively and comprehensible and was nourished by the springs of Korean culture itself. It is true that in China there was, at this time, a strong trend toward popularization in art, but in Korea a similar trend was not so much a popularization as a nationalization. Kyomjae was honored by his contemporaries because he was able to present lofty concepts in simple Korean terms.

The attempt in Sung landscape painting to conceive of nature's infinite resources—lavishly expended through centuries of time or leagues of space—in terms of tangible forms that could be grasped by the artist in moments of beauty, was as important an ideal to Koreans as it was to Chinese. Nevertheless, infinity as seen in a moment of summer tranquillity meant more to a Korean when the artist presented it in terms of a familiar scene on a summer-warmed Korean river, or when he represented eternity in the ceaseless plunging of a well-known Korean waterfall.

Kyomjae also recommended painting from nature, based on a direct and close study of it. This was a departure from the scholar's painting done in the privacy of his studio. A third significant reform of Kyomjae's was his emphasis upon content rather than form, a challenge to the trivial art based on copies of Chinese paintings. He himself could depict an intricate scene like the "ten thousand peaks" of the Diamond Mountains, which were famous in Korea for their crystalline formation, with simple means and great truth (Plate 192). It is a commentary on the vitality not only of the artists but also of the art patrons that Kyomjae's innovations were not merely tolerated in his lifetime but were adopted by his admirers. All that his detractors could find to say in their biographies of him was that he died poor.

Kyomjae was born of old and impoverished parents. His birth date is said to have been 1676 and that of his death, 1759, making him eighty-four (in Korean count) when he died. His early promise of ability, his energy, and his resourcefulness impressed an aristocratic neighbor enough to help him obtain a position at court. There he had the opportunity to serve as official artist with the rank of hyongam (magistrate of a county) for over fifty years and to associate with the most brilliant and prominent personages of his time. He painted up to the day of his death, some of his best work reportedly having been done when he was past eighty. "He had to use two convex glasses; still his paintings were as real as the mountains themselves," wrote Pak Yon-am in the Yorha Ilgi (Jehol Diary).[6] "The older he became, the more wonderful grew his painting" was repeated in all accounts of his life.

Other laudatory remarks about Kyomjae are worth noting. The Songho Chip (The Collected Works of Songho) has a passage referring to an album of Kyomjae's paintings treasured by one Pak Yu-do, "not because he understood painting but because he appreciated the master's spirit revealed in his treatment of figures, trees, stones, flowers, and grasses." The passage goes on to say: "In poetry, one learns the kind of nature a man has; in calligraphy, the mind is revealed; in painting, the whole personality."[7] A later admirer reports: "We have not had such a great painter in a hundred years. Recognition of his genius will live as long as the mountains and remain as alive as the ever-running streams." It is evident that Kyomjae's influence over his admirers owed something to his strength of suggestibility. For example, the following: "The strokes depicting the water are so correct that they force us to take a few steps backward from the picture so as not to have the water sprayed upon us."[8]

Present-day critics do not share the same enthusiasm for Kyomjae's work that his friends and followers felt. His work is eccentric, and his restless compositions often impart a sensation of disintegration and incoherence. His contrasts are often too startling, his transitions too abrupt, and his message blunt. But there is no doubt about the influence that Kyomjae had upon his colleagues and upon all Korean painters who came after him. The wonder world that he created seemed to the people of his day to come from a magic brush. The magic is gone today, but enough remains to show that it was once there.

The "Mountain Retreat at Losan" is a large hanging scroll painted in colors on silk *(Plate 191)*. The colors, in greens and rusts, are fresh and delightfully harmonized, as exemplified in the range of greens used to depict a stand of pines in the lower foreground. The painting has none of the mist-filled spaces and dreamy quality of studio landscapes. It is straightforward and explicit. A path beginning in the lower foreground leads the eye across a small bridge, past a lotus pond (usually present in the forecourts of Buddhist temples), and to a simple thatched mountain hut that serves as a retreat for the gentleman who is there enjoying the view. There is an asymmetry in the composition, a tilt to the left, which is typical of many of Kyomjae's mountain pictures.

Another landscape, a small one done on a fan, is called "Diamond Mountain Scene" *(Plate 192)*. It is characteristic of Kyomjae to startle his audience by opposing strong contrasts in black and white, in horizontal and vertical, in broad and fine lines, and so on. The tree-covered lower mountains in this scene are depicted in cone-shaped masses rendered by many little horizontal lines. There is a deliberate cultivation of formlessness by means of washes and dots, a sacrifice of careful drawing for the sake of an impressionistic evocation of a mood—a style credited to the eleventh-century Chinese painter Mi Fei and perhaps closer to its sister art of calligraphy than any technique in art ever devised. The "ten thousand peaks" are presented with a multiplicity of vertical lines. The cones set off the strange formations of the pointed peaks with a remarkable fidelity to the psychological effect that these mountains have upon the viewer. Kyomjae's stark little landscape—entirely without benefit of human presence—shows what a long way landscape painting had come from its origin in the maplike arrangements of eighth-century T'ang painting.

The "Winter Landscape" is different in mood and technique from the other Kyomjae paintings *(Plate 193)*. It is banal in subject but is saved from sentimentality by its symbolism. The theme here is the sadness of parting, symbolized by the traveler crossing the bridge. This has an associated meaning of death. The painting recalls the simplicity of the early Sung landscapists, who experimented in using snow as a unifying element in their landscapes when they were trying to achieve the unity of coherence by depicting an element common to the whole painting.

One of Kyomjae's most forceful and memory-evoking paintings is his black-ink depiction of the granite cliffs of Inwang Mountain, which stands just behind the city of Seoul, curving in an arm from north to west *(Plate 194)*. Kyomjae depicts the mountain wet with rain, and he captures so successfully the essential timelessness of this great barricade of rock that anyone who has ever seen it will instantly recognize its grim slopes and its formidable outline. The painting is signed, and it bears the date of May 1751.

Besides the above-noted use of snow as a unifying element, Kyomjae was familiar with many other devices for attaining unity of composition. A line of poetry inscribed on one of his paintings refers to the "mountain of clouds" in the painting. He could just as easily have painted a "cloud of mountains." The use of similar strokes, in varying relationships, to represent clouds, mountains, and waves was a device for achieving unity of consonance. To cite another example, Kyomjae's painting of a sage floating on the waves shows this device of similar pen strokes in depicting diversified objects: the spray at the sage's feet is rendered in the same way as the cloud above his head.

In summary, Kyomjae's chief contributions to Korean painting were his emphasis on Korean themes, his insistence upon painting from life, and his experiments with new forms which, though not always successful, were the result of a reconsideration of the whole approach to painting and a refocusing of attention upon the essentials in representation. Kyomjae's name has been linked with the names of two contemporaries in the following jingle: "Korea has three painters: Kyomjae, Hyonjae, and Kongjae, but the greatest of these is Kyomjae."

Hyonjae (Sim Sa-jong) was a student of Kyomjae. He was born in 1707 and died in poverty at the age of sixty-three, the most conspicuous "painting fool" of his times. From the inscription on his tombstone come the following statements about his personal life. He was born in 1707 in Ch'ongsong, South Kyongsang Province, in south Korea, of a family that had distinguished itself in scholarship for several generations. He added to the family reputation. He could paint before he was five—he knew how to outline "the square or round" of things—and when he was still young he was taught landscape painting by Kyomjae. At his prime, all his paintings were masterpieces which were highly valued, even in China. When he died, relatives and friends collected money for his funeral and buried him at P'aju. Shortly after his death, the family's fortunes came to an end in political disaster, and in 1776 several of its members were executed. As for Hyonjae himself, from his youth to his old age, he "never laid his brush down, and although he sometimes went in rags, he continued to try to excel himself, heedless of poverty or dishonor."

Hyonjae's painting showed no evidence of the political troubles of his day, or of any other trouble. It was always tranquil in mood and deliberate in execution—the antithesis of Kyomjae's style. Hyonjae was not original; he could not attain Kyomjae's vivid expressionism; and his portraits were always poor. In short, he could not handle exaggeration or caricature at all. But he could harmonize better than Kyomjae, and he could present in a subtler and more complex way the "inner realities" that Kyomjae too often simplified. Hyonjae's work was therefore more even in quality than Kyomjae's. Above all, he had a fastidious taste in the use of color and line harmonies, and his work was, as a result, reticent rather than flamboyant, and subtle rather than explicit.

An interesting statement about Hyonjae's training is that under his tutor Sokchon he began his art lessons by using the illustrated *Migadaehon Chombop* (Treatise on the Use of the "Mixed Dot" Method of the Mi School). This mention appears to be the first indication of a primer of art in Korea, a fashion that had become quite popular in China.

An album painting called "Viewing the Spring Blossoms" *(Plate 195)* is an example of the happy pieces that Hyonjae could do in his less serious moments. Three gentlemen are seated on the bank of a river under three pine trees. Each one has an attendant who is standing about waiting to be of assistance. In the foreground, absorbed in the task of procuring fresh fish for the gentlemen's al fresco dinner, three fishermen are manipulating a net. Upstream another fisherman stores the catch in a basket trap. Interest is centered on the seated figures. The eye is carried up and out of the picture plane by the mountains in the background. The painting is done in colors on paper, and the blossoms are in a strong pink. The theme is simple: it depicts men in communion with nature. The implication is that the communion is being accomplished in company with others, and in great comfort— a contrast to the solitary vigil pictured in An Kyon's "Fisherman."

Also done in colors on paper is Hyonjae's "Falcon and Pheasant" *(Plate 196)*, a large hanging scroll. The bird of prey is perched on a rock watching the pheasant, which is unaware of its danger. Small birds on the branch at the top of the picture—where the eye is supposed to start—appear to be trying to warn the pheasant. The warm colors of the pheasant's plumage are skillfully rendered and make of this area of the picture a highly decorative center of attention. The falcon, on the other hand, though placed in the center of the painting, is depicted somberly and sketchily—in fact, clumsily—so that it looks like a hen rather than a falcon. Heavy black lines are used to outline the branches, not as shadows but as accents—a device for the balancing of pictorial tensions. This painting is said to have symbolized Korea's political position externally, the falcon being Ch'ing China; the pheasand, Korea; and the little birds, Korea's well-wishers. On the other hand, the hidden meaning could refer to an internal situation, the falcon being the mighty yangban; the pheasant, the farmers trying to eat their own grain while the predatory yangban wait to pounce; and the little birds, the chungin or middle group.

In the landscape, "Moonlight through a Brushwood Gate" *(Plate 197)*, Hyonjae's dependence upon Chinese models—no doubt instilled in him by those painting primers—is revealed. Here he painted in the manner of Ni Tsan, the idol of the Gentleman Painter school whose compositions tended to be frail and scattered. In this painting a number of empty spaces occur, giving it a falling-apart look. The empty spaces do not, as in Sung painting, suggest depth, with the washes gradually fading into space. Here the transitions are abrupt, and there is no attempt to keep dark areas to the foreground and dim areas to the background. The most remote peaks at the top of the painting carry dark areas of equal value with the closest objects in the foreground at the bottom. The light and dark areas, distributed over the whole surface, nevertheless produce a pleasing decorative effect. The washes are soft and satiny, and the mood of dreamy tranquillity is soothing. The painting represents a familiar scene in Korea: mountains tower over terraced rice paddies; streams and clusters of thatched huts fold into the mountainsides; and the inevitable boy with a bullock is playing his flute—a scene marking the time of day as nightfall, with its moment of restful ease. It is a familiar theme presented in a delicate way. The picturesque quality of this painting again shows the influence of Chinese ideals, for an emphasis upon design was characteristic of similar trends which were producing the gay wallpapers and decorated porcelains that were fascinating Western purchasers of Chinese products at this time.

In his "Winter Landscape" *(Plate 198)* Hyonjae consciously executes the painting in the style of a Chinese artist of the Ming dynasty, according to what we are told in the inscription. It is a vertical scroll done on silk in ink and embellished with slight color. It shows a still and silent winter landscape with mountain peaks receding into the background and a stream falling from the heights into a foreground pool. A small man sits alone in a tiny hut on the banks of the stream.

Earlier in time, but belonging also to the Sukchong age, was the third in the trio headed by Kyomjae. This was Kongjae (Yun Tu-so), who was born in 1668. Unlike the other two, Kongjae was far from being mild-mannered and simplehearted. Born into one of the most celebrated scholarly families in Korea (his great-grandfather was Kosan, one of the two most outstanding poets of the dynasty), Kongjae early received a thorough education. He excelled in every branch of learning, including calligraphy and painting. As a calligrapher, he was one of Korea's most notable exponents, ranking with Wandang and Paek Ir-ha. He was involved with his family in party politics (it was impossible for prominent families to avoid such involvement), and this meant that if one member of the family fell out of favor, the entire family suffered.

Kongjae was selective in his social relations and intolerant of requests for his paintings made by anyone outside his narrow circle of friends. An unfortunate occurrence closed his art career, and he died soon after at about the age of fifty. The episode occurred while he was observing strict mourning for his father. King Sukchong had decided to have his portrait painted and had assembled for the purpose the best artists in the kingdom. Kongjae's name was on the list, but the prime minister petitioned the king to have it taken off on the grounds that Kongjae was in mourning and that it would be highly improper to call him out of it—an act "not in keeping with our peaceful and flourishing times." The king may not have taken this advice in good part because the next thing we are told is that Kongjae, "in shame, broke up his brushes, retired to his birthplace, and never painted again." In view of the fierce party struggles that characterized Sukchong's reign and the king's known reluctance to be thwarted, Kongjae's act of renunciation may have been only discretion on his part. It is possible, also, that his act was simply a matter of hurt pride because the king's invitation was sent and then withdrawn. Whatever the cause, the act was an abrupt end to a productive career.

Kongjae's aloofness earned him the resentment of those who wanted to exploit his talent and could not. Nam T'ae-ung wrote in the *Ch'ongjuk Hwasa:* "Tu-so was so proud that he complied with only a few requests for paintings. He favored Yi Ha-gon and Min Yong-gyon, and whenever they asked, readily supplied them so that each had albums and a number of screens. Ha-gon had the 'Manma-do' (Picture of Ten Thousand Horses). All three belonged to the So-in party." From the *Yonnyo Sil Pyol Chip* (Supplementary of the Works of the Yonnyo Collection) came another dry comment: "He was too proud to show any of his paintings unless they were first class, and all his life he painted no more than picture albums and very few screens and scrolls, so very little of his work has been handed down. . . . His style lacked simple taste, and his compositions were sometimes unexpectedly jarring and disagreeable."

Kongjae practiced his art as a hobby, "indifferent to worldly gain." His son, Yun Tok-hi, learned his father's style of painting and became equally deft, especially in painting animals and people. His grandson, Yun Yong (see Plate 204), was an excellent landscapist.

Kongjae, like Kyomjae, cultivated the habit of close study of the object he intended to paint. Special mention is made of his method of observing his subject for long hours before he painted it. Once started, he would not stop until he had completed his picture. His forte was portrait and animal painting, both being handled with a keen appreciation of essential characteristics. The horses that appear in Kongjae's paintings are depicted in movement, usually at a fast trot and with silky tails and flowing manes. A hanging scroll entitled "Storm on the Mountain Pass" (Plate 199) is an example of Kongjae's interest in movement. Everything about this piece is elegant. It is done in black ink on ivory-colored silk and is in an excellent state of preservation. The horse and his rider are heading into the wind, apparently with equal enjoyment. The willow branches, the grasses, and the other mountain plants seem to be partaking of the same motion and the same aliveness. The interest is focused on the rider, and the vitality of the whole centers in the crossing axes of the bodies of the horse and the horseman in a swastika-like movement that keeps the eye in motion within the picture plane. Starting at the top of the painting with the point at which the willow tree moves out of the frame, the eye travels down the trunk, across the two figures, is caught and turned by the stump in the lower right foreground to the horse's head, and continues in two directions again, following the major movement along the animal's stretched-out body and via the hanging willows back to the starting point, while the minor movement, after a jump, returns via the mountain bushes to the starting point. The decorative details of saddle blanket, boots, stirrups, and rider's clothes are subordinated to the larger theme of the oneness of nature, where man, beast, and trees share in common and enjoy in common the same stimulating experience—that of an oncoming storm.

Another painting by Yun Tu-so which displays a similar theme—the idea of the oneness of nature by means of the unity of mood of horse, rider, and tree—is in the collection of the Yi household.[9] Here the ruggedness and endurance of the pine is reaffirmed in the stout body of the rider, who is portrayed as a man in his prime, and is restated again in the sturdiness of his mount. In still another presentation of this theme, a painting also in the Yi household collection,[10] exultation in a moment of conquest seems to be suggested. The heads of rider and horse are held up with pride, their attitudes expressing confidence and victory. The outthrust branch of the paulownia tree above their heads is so far-flung as to suggest unusual inner strength. The branch also introduces the idea that even extreme strength fails: the paulownia is the first tree to lose its leaves in the fall.

To conclude, Kongjae's painting tended to be intellectual rather than eye-catching, requiring in the observer an educated rather than an emotional response. It consisted of a precision of statement rather than the diffuseness of a general mood. There was no room for approximation in Kongjae's painting; his meaning was not all on the surface, but it was unmistakable. He achieved animation and vitality by means of careful composition that seemed simplicity itself, but which was actually imbued with profound and complex associations. Kongjae's style illustrates a significant feature of Oriental painting in that it "relies too much on suggestion, presuming in the spectator a sensibility and a fineness of organization which are found in choice societies; on the other hand it avoids that laborious accumulation of unessential phenomena which in European art has proved the death of so many pictures by accomplished hands."[11]

Also active during King Sukchong's reign were the artists Hwajae (Pyon Sang-byok), noted for his painting of fowl; Kwanajae (Cho Yong-u), eccentric painter of baroque landscapes; and Ch'oe Puk (Hosaenggwan), painter of idyllic scenes.

Hwajae was born in a family originating in Miryang in the far south. Nothing is known about his birth or death dates or his early life. He was active at court as a professional painter of portraits, of which he painted over a hundred. He was rewarded with the rank of hyongam and was additionally honored by being given the title of kuksu or "best in the country." Several of his portraits are still extant. One of these pictured the minister Yun Kup.[12] It was apparently admired because of its idealization of the official in his personification of remote, detached, and supermundane wisdom, which indicated his superiority and fitness to govern. But the artist was also required to achieve a likeness. Portrait painting demanded a rigidly limited style that had as its goal the service of Confucianism, with its emphasis upon social duty and reverence. For this reason, Hwajae turned to the painting of kittens and puppies and barnyard fowl as a relief. These he rendered with such gaiety that he is now known chiefly for this by-product of his artistic career. In his painting of small animals he allowed himself humor and playfulness and gentle ridicule—all qualities that were most conspicuously absent from the ancestor portraits. It is of interest to note that one of Hwajae's nicknames was Koyang, which has the double meaning of "monstrous fellow" and "cat" and is an allusion to his dexterity in the painting of cats.

The painting of a magnificent cock depicted with his two hens and a brood of chicks (Plate 200) is Hwajae at his best. The kingliness of the cock is expressed in the superb plumage, the crownlike spread of the tail feathers, and the glossy blacks and reds of the wings and wattle, which are all the more spectacular because of their contrast with the frightened-looking white hen in the background. The brown hen at the left is, on the other hand, full of complacency. She is the hen who has the chicks, and this proud awareness makes her fluff out her feathers and compete with the cock for the limelight. At least two interpretations of this scene have been derived from the inscription. One of these is that a love philter of great potency can be concocted out of chicken eggs and meat—a philter even more effective than the aristocrat's potion of ginseng. The other is that the common people, representented by the dark chicken, have more sexual potency than the aristocrats (the white chicken), even though the latter are bolstered by their favorite ginseng tonic.

Ch'oe Puk, like Hwajae, had a nickname: Ch'il-ch'il (Seven-seven).* He was a one-eyed scholar who loved outings, loved wine, loved people, and was loved in return. His paintings were immensely popular but difficult to obtain, for he was likely to erupt in anger if anyone offered him money for his work, thereby implying that he was not a gentleman. Seven-

* This may refer to the two "sevens" of which the character puk (meaning "north") in his pen name is composed, or it may refer to the festival held on the seventh day of the seventh moon.

268

seven was not his only nickname. He was also known as Ch'oe the Artist, Ch'oe the Drunkard, and Crazy Ch'oe.

His painting, "An Outing on the River," is a good expression of his own happy nature. The scene depicts a bend in a river from whose right bank a cliff rises abruptly and extends beyond the plane of the picture at the top, thus creating a sensation of space. Four figures are seated under a canopy in a boat that is floating in the shallows at the foot of the cliff. Rocks dot the shoreline, and three trees on the bank at the lower right add interest. A boatman, pole in hand, stands behind the canopy, but there is no movement. The time seems to be a hot August day. The painting is done in the dot technique in ink on grass cloth.

Ch'oe Puk's "Pavilion and Landscape" (Plate 201) is a handsome scroll done in ink with added touches of color. It indicates rather than depicts a mountainous landscape, emphasizing the verdure and giving prominence to a small pavilion set on high stilts beside what appears to be a body of water. Inside the pavilion sit two figures, while at the left another figure is shown approaching along a narrow path. The painting is signed with the name Hosaenggwan (one of Ch'oe Puk's pen names), and the seal bears the same name. The inscription reads: "Both got up and approached the shadow of the pine and wu-t'ung trees. The midnight moonlight is clear, and the waves are not yet calm."

Cho Yong-u (Kwanajae), a contemporary and friend of Ch'oe Puk, was primarily a painter of portraits. Born in 1687, he was active during the reigns of both Sukchong and Yongjo and received a title from the former. His death occurred in 1761. His "Landscape" (Plate 202) is out of the ordinary. It is a hanging scroll, ink on paper, exceptionally long and narrow. There are two distinct centers of interest: one at the edge of the cliff in the upper part, the other in the great tree that overhangs and dominates the small hurrying figure of the man in the lower part of the painting. The device of emphasizing the foreground in order to propel the eye into space is here employed to force the eye upward, to make the observer feel the tremendous weight and height of the rock. The disproportionate sizes of the trees and the human figure and the narrowness of the picture plane do the same thing. The rocks are depicted in a hard, almost brutal fashion, as is the large tree. Exaggeration of this type is a characteristic mannerism of the Sukchong period.

One of the most admired calligrapher-artists of the dynasty, Wongyo (Yi Kwang-sa), also lived in this century. He was born in 1705 and died in exile on an island in southwest Korea in 1777. According to the information on his tombstone, Wongyo, like Kongjae and Hyonjae, was trapped in the factional politics of the times. He was a specialist in calligraphy and mastered the four chief styles of writing, including the difficult "grass writing." In collaboration with his son, he wrote a long dissertation on calligraphy, a book which could be useful only to the advanced or skillful student. One of his criticisms of Korean calligraphy might be noted: he said that Koreans always tended to slant their brushes. This defect was always clearly evident in the result, said Wongyo, since the brush must be held vertically if the proper flow of the ink was not to be impeded. Wongyo kept his inkslab and brushes with him in exile, carrying them in an "old and worn" box.

Wongyo's "Old Man Viewing a Painting" (Plate 203) was an illustration for the above-mentioned book. In addition to displaying his calligraphic style, it is similar to many paintings depicting the life of the leisure classes which were popular in China; for example, the Freer Gallery painting of the fifteenth or sixteenth century entitled "Poet at Ease." In Wongyo's picture, an old gentleman is shown seated before a screen with a woven mat at his back and a stool at his feet. Two young men are in attendance. A servant holds up a scroll which the old man criticizes for the benefit of his young companions, explaining the linear style, the dot style, the washes, and so forth. A fantastic rock in the background is typical of the taste of the times for strange shapes to add interest to the gardens of the rich. The rattan stool and the screen are Chinese, not Korean. The scene is one of quiet charm and the theme one of universal appeal. It is not difficult to understand the joy an old man feels in passing on his wisdom to the young. Wongyo was one of the artists who interpreted the Confucian tradition to his countrymen—a tradition which, at its best, was characterized by easy suavity and worldliness.

Kang Se-hwang or P'yo-am (1713–91), who flourished during the reign of Yongjo, was noted for his landscapes. His "River Scene" is a landscape in miniature done in black ink on paper. The cliff in the foreground, with the ravine and the half-hidden village behind it, is the center of interest. The river and the low hills of the middle ground carry the eye deep into the picture in a perspective treatment of space that is Western. There is no background of mountain crags to shift the point of view as there is in most Oriental landscapes.

A landscape that displays another type of new treatment is Yun Yong's "Spring River" *(Plate 204)*. The vitality of the Korean countryside during the early growing season is fully presented. The center of interest is the double-roofed pavilion framed by a luxuriant stand of spring willows. A wine bottle is placed hospitably upon a table. Spring mists hide the far islands, and the whole scene illustrates the poetic concept of spring, which, like the river, widens as it approaches the sea and then spills headlong into it, just as spring spills over the land.

A student of Kyomjae, Sin Yun-bok (Hewon) carried on and developed Kyomjae's interest in local subjects and went much further by specializing in genre paintings, a subject that his master never touched. Born into a Koryong family in 1758, he died at about the age of sixty. Both Hewon and his father were military officials with the rank of *chomsa* (commandant, fourth rank). Hewon also served as a member of the Academy. He painted lighthearted and frivolous scenes from Korean life which gave offense to the sensibilities of the scholar-painters. The inclusion of women of doubtful virtue in his paintings was a further outrage. Similar subjects had long before entered the artists' ateliers in China, but in conservative Korea such fashions had a hard time taking hold. In his "Women's Visiting Hour" *(Plate 205)*, Hewon sketches with lively brush a scene at the gate of a Korean cottage. Two women stand in the street at the hour when women's work is done. The younger is covered by a green cloak; the older carries a lantern. They have cinched up their skirts in order to walk without soiling the hems of their long dresses. Their long and baggy pants are seen—a daring touch—as well as their turned-up shoes, the style of which exhibits an ancient connection with the Turki tribes of the Asiatic steppes, whatever the origin. The watchdog is on the alert, his stance eager and expectant. The picture is an album piece painted in water colors on paper.

In another album piece, "Ladies' School" *(Plate 206)*, Hewon paints the typical sarang pang (guest room) raised on pillars overlooking the garden and used only in summertime. A young scholar with a fashionable long goatee is leaning out of the sarang pang. With him are three girls, slightly detached. Also detached is the young visitor seated below in solitude. The play of tensions among the five figures is apparent. The picture is a satire on women's education. The garden is the usual formal Korean garden made up of lotus pond, granite-faced terraces hung with ivy and blossoms, and the inevitable evergreens.* The scene is another instance of the type of outdoor living that was so important a feature of Korean life.

In his "Girl Stringing a Lute" *(Plate 207)*, Hewon again paints a subject dear to his heart: the activities of women. The girl's hair is braided in the style reserved for court ladies and courtesans. One end of the lute rests on the girl's lap, and at the other end are seated two other young girls. The painting is done in ink and color on a silk album leaf. It is signed with the name Hewon and has two seals which read "Ippu."

A set of Hewon's paintings illustrating Korean customs, in Mr. Chun's possession, is undoubtedly the freshest, most unself-conscious, and most purely Korean series in the whole collection. It is an album of thirty double pages of genre scenes showing the life and manners of the late eighteenth century. A vigorous and exciting use of color and subject matter distinguishes these paintings from the traditional art of the day. The tenth picture, "Boating Scene" *(Plate 208)*, bears an inscription that reads: "The evening breeze cannot be heard. White gulls fly in the spray of the boat." Another leaf from the same album *(Plate 209)* shows a *kisaeng* (geisha) party with two dancing girls performing the vigorous sword dance to the music of a seven-piece orchestra, while three noblemen in their wide black hats and one with the white hat of mourning look on.

Also active during King Yongjo's reign were the brothers Kungjae (Kim Tuk-sin) and Chowon (Kim Sok-sin). Kungjae lived from 1754 to 1822; his brother was four years younger. Country life is depicted by Kungjae in his "Threshing Scene" *(Plate 210)*, a rural vignette rendered with the utmost simplicity. In painting the figures, Kungjae resorted to the outline method, the method that is as old as the history of painting. For the tree, he used the splashy monochrome ink style of the so-called Southern school. The subject matter is also simple: the landlord on the left watches to see that no one robs him of his due, while on the right three chickens steal grain without being noticed. Kungjae's landscape, "Evening Rain on Lake Hsiao-Hsiang" *(Plate 211)*—probably the only extant painting from his series called "The Famous Eight Views of Lake Hsiao-Hsiang"—depicts a simple rainy-day scene. A boat is moored to the shore close to a summer hut. The river mist conceals the trees in the middle ground. The heavy leaves of the trees are contrasted with the spiky appearance of the bamboos. The mood is one of nostalgia and longing.

Chowon's "Han River Scene" *(Plate 212)*, on the other hand, is full of liveliness and activity. It is in colors combined with a black-ink crisscross of horizontal and vertical lines.

---

* Such terraces were important parts of Korean gardens. They were often built with southern exposures, sheltering the peony bushes, which were thus more dramatically displayed during the blossoming season and protected from frost during the winter. At other times, potted flowers—for example, hanging chrysanthemums—were arranged along the rims of the terraces.

Pleasure pavilions, painted here with their names above the roof peaks, dominate the scene in obvious invitation to visiting noblemen. Fishing boats are clustered at the foot of the cliff, and on the rocks women are beating their wash with paddles. A fleet of boats on the opposite bank is indicated only by masts, their vertical lines merging into the curving sweep of the willows, which are painted in a faint chartreuse to signify spring. The other colors in the painting are light blues and greens.

Yi In-mun (Yuch'un) was another landscapist of note who was active during King Yongjo's reign. He was born in 1745 in Haeju, northwest of Seoul, and died at the age of seventy-one. He was a member of the Academy. His "River in Spring" *(Plate 213)* is fresh and stimulating. The colors—a light green wash for the willows and light blue for water and sky—indicate a new trend: the use of water color, long employed in painting flowers, now rather cautiously applied in landscapes. Like the early Sung landscapes, this scene is clear-cut. The composition is coherent and unified, unlike that of the dispersed and dream-like landscapes of Hyonjae. There is an attempt at Western perspective: the mountain in the background recedes to a smaller size instead of towering at the top of the painting. In a summer house in the lower foreground a gentleman is seated alone, enjoying the view. It is a pretty scene, saved from sentimentality by the suppleness of the design, the strength and confidence of the brush stroke.

Yi In-mun's landscape, "Mountains and Rivers without End" *(Plate 214),* is a horizontal scroll a little over thirty inches in length and seventeen and a half inches in width. It is done in ink and colors on silk. Although this panorama is rendered in the conventional Chinese manner, it shows the Korean departure from idealized Chinese painting that characterized the times in which Yi In-mun painted. The close-up view of the harbor with its many ships and many masts is one of the details that add to the originality and freshness of this picture. The mountain crags and towering cliffs, though stylized, might well have been painted from nature in a land so rich in granite outcrops of all varieties and shapes as Korea.

Kim Hong-do (Tanwon) was born to the Kimhae Kim family sometime between 1750 and 1760. His biographers make a point of the fact that he was a good-looking man, large and handsome and affable.[13] They also note that, owing to the rank and reputation of his father and grandfather, he was given the rank of hyongam and some income from rents in Yonpung, as well as the honor of belonging to the Academy. But they go on to say that he was so poor that his family often lacked food and that the reason for this was his failure ever to plan in advance. It is somewhat maliciously indicated in the following anecdote that Tanwon took money for his painting.

One day in early spring Tanwon noticed a very lovely plum tree for sale, but he had no money to buy it. So he did a quick painting for an admirer who gave him three thousand *yang* for it. He immediately went out and bought the plum tree for two thousand yang, and with eight hundred more he bought wine and gathered his friends to enjoy the magnificent blossoms with him. The remaining two hundred yang he spent on rice and firewood for his family. Tanwon's son did not seem to be adversely influenced by his father's irresponsibility, for he also became an artist, painting under the nom d'artiste of Kungwon and using all the styles affected by his father.

Tanwon painted landscapes, flowers, and portraits in traditional styles, although in his

272

genre paintings he used only the ancient linear style. He was especially noted for his painting of the Sennin (Immortals), whom he presented in a new way that was full-figured and robust. The drapery of their clothing he also treated in novel way, departing conspicuously from the conventional jagged lines usually used to depict textiles.

Moved by "righteous indignation," he once painted an official portrait of the great General Im, who had been beaten to death during the Japanese invasion by order of a jealous minister. This painting, which was done by way of protest against some current official injustice that Tanwon did not dare to criticize openly, was likened by a sympathetic biographer to the literature of Szuma Ch'ien, the great Han historian, because it was "brave and heroic."[14]

Tanwon was apparently the first artist after An Kyon to develop a heroic style. It appears that he used it only when he was deeply moved. Some of his paintings of the Immortals portray the healthy looks, generous nature, and carefree manner of supernatural men as an implied criticism of the meanness, physical frailty, and cruelty of the literati of his class and times.

His painting of a lotus *(Plate 215)*, on the other hand, shows him in a gentle mood. Most Koreans have an almost reverential regard for flowers, and therefore the representation of the life of a flower becomes a far more significant motif for them than for Western-ers. This painting of a gaudy pink lotus is an elegant thing. The composition seems simple, but the blossom, the lily pads, and the seed pod depict the full life cycle of the lotus and are presented in all their curving, curling, flattening, and bulging propensities in front, back, and side views. The contrasting colors and the texture of the lacquer-smooth upper surface of the leaf and its fuzzy lower side are emphasized in a way that is lighthearted and delight-ful and that, moreover, makes good design. The associated meaning of fertility, always connected with the pink lotus, is underlined by the detail of the dragonflies in embrace.

"Spring Journey" *(Plate 216)* makes use of a theme that means spring to every Korean. The interest in this painting is centered upon the attentive pose and facial expression of the young nobleman who stops to look at the swallow. The budding willow and the swallow are associated in the minds of Koreans with the delights of returning warm weather and the feeling of release that an essentially outdoor people experience when they can escape from their imprisoning little houses. The composition of this picture is simple. There is no diverting background detail. The theme is presented by means of fine lines and washes, and the pictorial quality is heightened by spotting.

"Falcon Hunt" *(Plate 217)* is another scene that captures the moment of greatest interest from an episode in the life of the yangban. Again Tanwon has chosen a fresh theme. The gentleman is leaning forward as he watches with intense interest the outcome of the strike. The retainers and the dogs share this interest, as their poses show. Characteristically, as in all Korean crowds, there is one person who is not attentive to what is going on. In the back-ground, in order to call attention to the fact that a nobleman is never very far separated from his lunch, is depicted a woman carrying food in bowls upon her head.

An example of Tanwon's eclecticism is his "Sea Gulls and Waves" *(Plate 218)*, which is a simple, unstudied, gay, and altogether charming piece. The theme could not be less uncomplicated: it is a picture of some rocks amid ocean waves and some birds. That is all. It is done in black and blue water color. An effect of coldness is imparted by the blue washes depicting the heaving water, as well as by the wet-looking black ink used for the rocks. Imperturbability to the cold is indicated by the little gulls seated close together in a row and by the flight of the cormorants away from the rocks. They are undaunted by the coldness or the wildness; they are in their element. Unity of consonance is achieved in this composition by the repetition of similar forms for dissimilar substances. The curlicues indicating foam could be called Tanwon's signature, since he used them to depict clouds, water, bark on trees, and rocks—without confusing his meaning.

"The Picnic" *(Plate 219)* illustrates one of Tanwon's favorite themes. Here a day on the dunes is being enjoyed by several gentlemen, each in his own way. One stands watching the fishermen, one is seated off in his corner sipping a bowl of wine, one is gazing out over the landscape. The wine bottle and the beach fire with its kettle of rice are indications that the gentlemen are not to be deprived of meat and drink in their communings with nature.

Tanwon was much struck by the story of a Chinese Confucian scholar of the Sung dynasty named Hu An-kuo, who lived from 1074 to 1138, and he painted an episode from his life as a tribute. Hu's pseudonym was Wu-i, and the picture is entitled "Wu-i Sailing Home" *(Plate 220)*. A boat bearing the scholar is seen sailing along through the rapids formed by a narrow gorge. Two men carry poles to keep the boat off the rocks. Jutting crags topped by trees and a single house dwarf the boat but at the same time in a curious way enhance its importance.

Many inscriptions have been added at later dates to Tanwon's paintings. An example of these is an unpretentious poem from Hong Yang-hi's *Ige Chip* (The Collected Works of Ige) which is paraphrased as follows:

"As the summer ripens,
Movement in the heat
Makes one feel as if
Roasted on a hearth.
Tu Fu once said:
'Girdling myself up discomforts
Me. I want to cry out in rage.'
Perhaps it is just that this season
Maddens one.
Unexpectedly a fan comes to my hands.
I see bamboo upon it,
Graceful and slender, rustling in the breeze.
The cool breeze also strikes my chest
The fans my sleeve:
A heavenly gift of nature.
How to express this beauty—
Tanwon could do it."[15]

274

CHAPTER FIFTEEN

# Nineteenth Century:
# Century of Decline

HISTORICAL BACKGROUND    After the death of King Chongjo in 1801, every ruler to the end of the dynasty was a boy king whose reign began with a long regency. Internally, this was a period of *sedo* politics, or the dominance of the government by powerful clans like the Kims and the Mins who came into control through the regents. The political parties were in existence, but they were old lions whose teeth were gone. Their chief strength lay in social tabus: no Soron was supposed to marry a Noron, and so on. Externally, the most shocking occurrence was the disturbance of the customary ceremonial relationships with China and Japan. China's defeats in the small wars of 1840–42, 1858–60, 1894–95 were shattering to the morale of Korean officialdom, which could not accustom itself to the idea that its protection from the outside world was gone. Only less shocking was the obligation to abandon the customary isolation in favor of Western-style treaties of amity and commerce, first with Japan in 1876 and then with the United States in 1882. Attempts by Western nations to establish trade relations earlier in the century had been repulsed, in some cases by means of small-scale warfare.* A new relationship also began with China whereby the Chinese, by means of a resident located in Seoul, interfered directly in Korean internal politics for the first time.†

Economically, the country went into an even sharper decline. The continued increase in the size of nonproductive groups dependent upon an impoverished and undernourished peasant class, as well as a series of natural disasters caused by soil erosion, deforestation, floods, and famines, reduced the country to a general state of poverty. No one lived a life of luxury, not even the king. Economic penetration by the Japanese from 1876 on was the opening wedge of the eventual overlay of modernization upon the country by and through Japan. After two wars over Korea, in 1894–95 and 1904–05, Japan incorporated the peninsula into her empire on August 26, 1910.

* Battles on Kanghwa Island with the French (1866), the Americans (1871), and the Japanese (1875).

† L. Carrington Goodrich, "Sino-Korean Relations at the End of the Fourteenth Century," *Transactions of the Korea Branch of the Royal Asiatic Society,* Vol. XXX (Seoul, 1940), presents another view: that the first Ming emperor indirectly interfered with Korean internal affairs just as surely as if he had done so directly.

CULTURE    The cultural flow from the outside world into Korea, from prehistoric times until the mid-nineteenth century, was from China to Korea to Japan. After 1850 the tide turned. Japan became the recipient of Western culture and an agent for its transmission to more conservative Asiatic nations around her. Korea was the first. The Japanese from their legation in Seoul helped progressive young Korean nobles in their attempt to seize the government in 1884, and although this first coup failed, the Japanese continued to help Korean radicals in order to overthrow the monarchy.

Another source of Western influence was Christianity. French Catholic missionaries worked secretly in Korea throughout most of the century. There were severe persecutions of Christians, among the worst in the whole history of Christianity, during which about a score of the foreign priests and many thousands of natives were martyrized. French Catholic priests earned the respect of the Koreans, however, for the fortitude they showed in sharing with the native Christians the tortures that were inflicted upon them by the Confucian officials. American missionaries came into the country as soon as an ambassador was established there (1883), and after that churches, schools, and hospitals were built by various Protestant and Catholic missions. The Koreans were avid for educational missionaries and for modern medical help, and the American mission boards met this desire by sending trained educational and medical personnel. These first Americans rescued the native alphabet from the discard into which the Korean literati had thrown it, and translated the Bible and various other religious and literary classics into Korean without admixture of the Chinese ideogram.

This promotion of easy reading created an upsurge of interest in Western learning and started the Koreans upon the codification and standarization of the spelling system which prepared the language for the service it is rendering the nation at the present time. Newspapers using the onmun or *hangul*, as it is now called, were started in the 1890's, and various other weekly and monthly papers were launched soon after. Novels like Yi In-jik's *Hyolyu* (Bloody Tears), Yu Kil-chun's *Soyu Kimun* (Accounts of Travel in the West), and *Tongnip Chongsin* (Spirit of Independence), written by Syngman Rhee while he was in prison in 1904 for revolutionary activity against the old monarchy, all employed the revived onmun.

A word about the total personality of the Confucian-trained individual is in order here, since in the nineteenth century the pressure of competition for rank and position greatly increased, so that the scholar who emerged a successful candidate was likely to have advanced physical and nervous complaints. Scholars sometimes competed at the national examinations again and again until they were white-haired. Under this system, it is not surprising to find that Confucianism was literally ground into them, every educated man in the country sharing similar learning, having similar prejudices and roughly similar "blind spots." Korea had become, during its long peace, an ingrown nation. Little change was tolerated. All the members of the educated classes were trained in the same way, just as in the West a similar situation was perhaps achieved when all educated people studied theology only. All competed for one type of job after a twenty- or thirty-year course of study. Confucian culture therefore produced a special type: the scholar, round-shouldered, anemic, unable to walk far without help from his servants. Withdrawal from the world on the national level was all too easily reflected in the individual. If a dominant type could be selected to represent the whole class it would be the aloof individual who tended to be compartmentalized, alternately gentle and cruel.* It is this kind of yangban that modern Koreans react against with dislike.

ART      Artists continued to show an interest in all styles and to experiment even more with Western methods, oil paintings, and Christian art. There was less interest in the smooth flowing calligraphic styles, more in deliberately jagged, erratic, and uneven compositions. However, a conservative preoccupation with the old art symbols still dominated painting, and most artists, though refreshed by contacts with new sources of inspiration, such as the Japanese color prints, still did their best work in traditional media. The chief artists of the nineteenth century were Kim Chong-hi (Ch'usa), Chang Sung-op (Owon), Cho Sok-chin (Sorim), and An Chung-sik (Simjon). The latter two lived twenty years into the twentieth century. Also notable for their specialties were Hosan, Puksan, and Irho, whose works are mentioned below.

Kim Chong-hi (Ch'usa or Wandang) was the outstanding calligrapher of the nineteenth century. His dexterity in both handwriting and painting demonstrates the ease with which skill in writing—which demands greater control over the brush than even artists in the West usually achieved—can be transmitted into skill in painting. Wandang was born in Kyongjo in 1786. He was studious as a boy and had no trouble passing his examinations and then rising in official position to the rank of *pyongjo ch'amp'an* (staff member, military board, second rank, junior grade).

When he was twenty-four years old, he accompanied his father on a mission to Peking. There he met the great Chinese scholars Juan Yuan (Wan Won in Korean) and Weng Fang-kang (Ong Bang-gang), who were such high-ranking officials that it was difficult to arrange to see them. After Wandang and his father had met them, however, and had discussed Chinese history with them for some time, the Chinese, we are told, became quite affable. This was the beginning of what became a lifelong friendship for Wandang, who took the character *wan* from Wan Won's name to use in his own pen name.

In 1840, Wandang was implicated in a plot. He pleaded his case so clearly before the magistrate that "even those who were jealous of him could not see any basis upon which to judge him guilty." But there was no help for him. His family was out of favor, and he was banished to Cheju Island. Then an unusual thing happened. Many people, bringing their books with them, braved the fifty-mile trip by sea to the island to visit him and consult him, and it was not long before his house was as "busy as a crowded market." Signs of civilized living appeared within a few months, and even "Seoul fashions could be seen in this remote spot."[1]

After ten years of this exile another scandal occurred in Seoul. A minister was degraded, and it was thought at court that Wandang had had a hand in it; so he and his two brothers were taken away from their beautiful southern island and were sent to the cold north to

* Dr. K. Horney, *Our Inner Conflicts* (New York, 1945), p. 106, presents a stimulating analysis that is helpful in arriving at a more sympathetic understanding of the society that produced the artists of nineteenth-century Korea. Descriptions of this society as "degenerate, corrupt, and decadent" tend to obscure the fact that many individuals were vigorous and productive in spite of the dominant trend.

a worse place of exile. All three men were in their late sixties by that time, and Wandang soon died at the age of seventy.

As for his personal characteristics, he was said to have been clear-minded and tender-hearted, his usual manner towards everyone so mild that people "approached him with joy." However, when he was aroused about anything, particularly about the maladminis-tration of justice, his voice became penetrating "like a thunder-bolt, like a sword, like a spear, and everyone trembled with fear."

Wandang made a special study of inscriptions in order to trace the history of the forma-tion and changes in the writing of ideograms. He mastered the four main styles and wrote a simple and lucid essay on the derivations of the styles. This essay was included in the *Wandang Chip* (The Collected Works of Wandang). Some comments from it are as follows:

"So what the Chinese discard, our people still admire as if it were divine and still respect as if it were a great treasure. It is as if the rat challenged the phoenix. Is it not ridiculous? . . . Recently one of our calligraphers has become an authority, insisting upon the slogan, 'Concentrate all strength in the brush,' and overlooking the first step to good calligraphy, which is that the ink must be good, well ground, dark, thick, and lustrous. . . . The origin of calligraphy was in the Ye style, which, to be well imitated now, should appear square, ancient-looking and awkward. . . . But unless one has a refined and noble taste, one cannot do this well. . . ."

(On how to apply the brush:) "If one merely grasps the brush holder tightly, one applies pressure to it rather than to the brush itself. In these days those who study calligraphy neglect the ink stick and concentrate only on the brush. . . . In judging calligraphy or painting, one should look at it with the eye of a superior man and with the hand of a cruel official."[2]

In Wandang's "Orchid" *(Plate 221)* one sees the strength of his calligraphic style. Here the forceful brush strokes seen in both flower and ideogram show a boldness and a diversity that seem to defy the smooth and silky harmonies of line that were so popular with all the mediocre calligraphers. The orchid is painted in conjunction with the fungus that symbolizes long life. The orchid itself was the emblem of the Confucian "superior man."[3]

Wandang himself commented upon the way to paint an orchid:

"The part of painting the orchid is similar to the art of writing in the Ye style: unless one brings to it the fragrance of literature, and unless the love of books is in one's heart, one cannot paint it well. . . . Certainly one cannot paint it by following the rules in the painting manuals. . . . It is difficult to depict more than three or four orchids at a time. . . . We cannot expect masterpieces unless spirit and mind and hand are in accord. . . . The painting of orchids needs this accord more than calligraphy. Those who are paid for painting orchids may paint a thousand pieces at a time. . . . To paint the most delicate orchid, one should not forget the three aspects. In these days most painters who try to paint it do not know the delicate beauty of these aspects and paint in vain."[4]

Cho Hi-ryong (Hosan), a devoted follower of Wandang, was born in 1797. He became skilled in the three arts of painting, poetry, and calligraphy and made a specialty of painting the plum blossom. His "Plum Blossoms in the Snow" *(Plate 222)* is one of the most admired pieces in the Chun collection. It is a large hanging scroll done in ink on paper. There are terra-cotta washes and dots of white pigment in addition to the black ink. The picture is meant to be viewed from the top down; the eye begins with the faint moon—actually depicted instead of merely indirectly indicated—and travels down the immense rugged cliff through flurries of snow and petals to the center of interest: the hermit seated tranquilly and cosily inside his warm hut. Protected from the storm, he is absorbed in his books. The mood of this picture is very different from that of An Kyon's "Fisherman." Here the gentleman is protected from the threatening powers of nature by the roof of his hut and by the spell of his books.

Kim Su-ch'ol (Puksan), who was born about 1819 and died around the turn of the century, is a landscapist also very much admired by present-day Koreans. Puksan abandoned the formulas and depicted his scenes in his own somewhat erratic, blunt manner, as displayed in his "Landscape" *(Plate 223)*. Light and dark areas are placed in arresting contrast in a way that attracts the attention of the spectator to something compelling that the artist is trying to say but never expresses either succinctly or exactly. His painting was highly charged with emotion: restlessness, dissatisfaction, perhaps rebellion. His art was an expression of his personality and is held in high regard among his countrymen today.

The direct opposite to Puksan in his approach to his work was the artist Nam Ke-u (Irho), who limited himself to subjects which he could describe with impersonal, scientific accuracy. He was born in 1811. His specialty was the painting of butterflies, called in Korean *nabui*. Reference to his work, therefore, is usually shortened to the term *Nam nabi*. The two panels of butterflies and flowers *(Plate 224)* from an eight-panel set illustrate his technique. Grotesque rocks suggest a nobleman's garden. Small bright flowers are growing near the rocks: pinks, orchids, asters. Their colors complement and set off the bright hues of the fifteen or so butterflies arranged in the air above the rock in each panel. Details differ in the panels. Some of the species of butterflies seem to be extinct at the present time. Irho had a flair for decorative effect that was close to that of the Japanese print.

Chang Sung-op (Owon) was the outstanding painter of the period. He was born in Taewon in 1843 and died in 1897. He served during his lifetime as kamch'al (inspector) and was also a member of the Academy. But he was no scholar. He had an excellent memory and could paint accurately and without error something that he had seen years before, but he had no taste for book learning and did not even like to read. Other peculiarities noted by his biographers were his drinking habits and his insistence upon going his own way. Otherwise he was good company, very willing to oblige his friends by painting pictures for them on the spur of the moment and never standing upon ceremony. His "Galloping Horses" *(Plate 225)* is a panel from a series of four depicting the "Eight Horses of Wu Wang."* Two small animated horses are shown in full gallop, and everything in the painting underlines the feeling of free movement: waving willows, waving manes and tails, all unrestrained as the wind and bringing to mind some ancient memory of life on the Asiatic steppes. The movement of the horses establishes a parabola which carries the eye in and out of the frame of the picture twice. The horses are rendered with Western-style

* Wu Wang was the fifth sovereign of the Chou dynasty in China. See C.A.S. Williams, *Outlines of Chinese Symbolism and Art Motives* (Shanghai, 1932), p. 223.

modeling, and the colors are fresh and lively. Nevertheless, there seems to be some deliberate incoherence in the composition. The horses are the obvious center of interest, but they are pictured as small creatures in a landscape that defies analysis.

Owon's "Landscape" is a hand scroll done in lively colors on silk: a revival of a classic form in the hard and deliberate but very decorative manner of later Ch'ing.

Cho Sok-chin (Sorim), born in 1853, studied in China and devoted his life to reviving, in the face of the crumbling Confucian culture, nostalgic memories of the best in the old styles. His grandfather was also an artist of note. Sorim died in 1919, already long out of his own century and out of step with the times. Two fan paintings *(Plates 226, 227)* show his talent. In the "Country Scene" he has painted a simple Korean subject: a farmer and his cow against a background of a low hill dotted by graves. In the Sogwang-sa scene depicting the Sogwang Temple near the east coast, he has indicated the temple roofs and superstructure only. The foreground, in dark ink, is clear; the background, dim and lightly fading out. The whole piece is quietly elegant, like Sorim himself.

An Chung-sik (Simjon) was born in 1861 and died in 1919. He was livelier than Sorim, much more interested in the new trends and in experimenting with Western ideas. His "Mountain Retreat" *(Plate 228)* is a large hanging scroll done in colors on silk and elegantly mounted. He has attempted Western perspective and a Western method of depicting clouds and indicating depth. The painting is an autumn landscape, and its general impression is somber, as if something precious were slowly dying. But the lively colors of the turning leaves give the painting a cheerful, almost hopeful look, suggesting a mood of sadness mixed with courage that is of a remarkably sturdy sort, like that of Korea itself.

# CHAPTER SIXTEEN

# Yi Dynasty Architecture
# and Minor Arts

SECULAR ARCHITECTURE    During the early years of the Yi dynasty a tremendous amount of building took place. A new capital was erected on the banks of the Han River, fifty miles south of the old capital of Songdo, and much rebuilding of other towns and monastic establishments was undertaken as peace and order were gradually restored.

PALACES: In the new capital (modern Seoul) the forty-acre palace area of Kyongbok-kung was laid out in 1395, and a number of handsome buildings were constructed within the grounds. In spite of several great fires and some periods of neglect, the Kyongbok Palace has remained a show place of Korea to the present day. Another palace built by the founder of the dynasty was the Ch'angdok-kung, situated upon more hilly terrain farther to the east. This palace and the nearby Ch'anggyong-gung were generally the favorite palaces throughout the dynasty. A fourth palace, the Toksu-gung, in the southwest corner of the city, was a detached palace ordinarily used by a prince or a dowager queen. The Toksu Palace served twice as a royal residence for the king himself: once after the Japanese invasion of the sixteenth century and once again around the beginning of the present century. In the latter case, since the palace was located in the legation quarter between the American and British embassies, it was refitted for King Kojong so that the close proximity of Western diplomats would give him greater security after his queen had been murdered.

The Toksu Palace, being the last built, contains two modern buildings, both used as museums at present. They are set in a Western-style garden with lawns, hedges, a pool, and a fountain. Next to this area is the former throne hall *(Plate 229),* built according to the traditional pattern with an entrance gate, a paved forecourt, and a congeries of residential halls and peony gardens. Two of the halls behind the throne room, the Chukcho-dang and the Soggo-dang, are over four hundred years old. These halls, made of wood, show the narrowness in relation to width that was typical of early Yi construction.

The Ch'angdok-kung *(Plate 230)* was first built (1396–98) as a detached palace. In contrast with the Kyongbok-kung, which more nearly approaches the Chinese mandala or magic square in form, the Ch'angdok-kung is extremely irregular in shape. Although destroyed several times by fire in the past, it was in each instance rebuilt and is now open to the public. The entrance to the palace is through the ancient Tonhwa Gate, which was

281

originally constructed sometime during the sixteenth century. Not far from the gate is the throne hall *(Plate 231)*, known as the Injong-jon or Hall of Benevolent Government. It is a large double-roofed building of imposing appearance and is surrounded by covered corridors which lead into modern carpeted reception rooms. The hall itself has a beautiful parquet floor and a high painted and gilded ceiling supported by a number of great red-lacquered pillars. First built in 1804, it is representative of the best construction of the later Yi period. Curtains, chandeliers, and chairlike thrones were added in 1907. The king's private residence behind the throne hall is reached by a covered corridor *(Plate 232)*. The building itself includes a series of semi-European reception rooms furnished with wall-to-wall carpeting, mirrors, upholstered chairs, and wallpaper. Heat was apparently supplied by large braziers. Gold screens in the Oriental style complete the furnishings.

Within the extensive palace grounds are secluded sections formerly reserved for the palace women and called Secret Gardens. A number of pleasure pavilions *(Plate 233)* are located among the ponds and streams of these gardens. Entertainments held there often featured dancers who performed along the terraces between the halls and the reflecting pool *(Plate 234)*. In an elbow of the wall, in a lonely, out-of-the-way wooded spot filled with forsythia, azalea, cherry, and mulberry, is a small palace called the Naksonje *(Plate 235)*. It was here that the last remaining queen of Korea, Dowager Queen Yun, lived until the Korean War and returned after the departure of President Rhee in 1960.

Adjoining the Ch'angdok Palace is the Ch'anggyong-gung, whose grounds have been converted into a zoological garden and park. The throne hall, which is still standing, dates from early Yi days and is the only example of an early throne hall still in existence. The Ch'anggyong Palace is noted for its acres of magnificent cherry trees whose springtime blossoming is the occasion for lighting them with lanterns and keeping the park open to the public at night.

The more formal palace, the Kyongbok-kung *(Plate 236)*, was rebuilt by the prince regent in 1867 and served as a residence for the royal family until the queen's assassination in 1895. After that, the royal family never lived in it again. It was built on the Chinese axial pattern in the shape of a mandala or magic square.[1] The king's and the queen's residences formerly occupied the center area of the grounds, but these two buildings were moved by the Japanese to the Ch'angdok Palace. The throne hall *(Plate 237)* just in front of the residence area still remains. This building, called the Kunjong-jon or Hall of Untiring Rule, is set upon double-tiered platforms of dressed stone which are surrounded on all four sides by carved railings and have stone steps at the center of each side. The hall itself is double-roofed and lofty, exhibiting in its spaciousness the complicated ceiling structure that rises from the walls into a central dome. The roof and ceiling, supported by tall pillars of varying heights, constitute more than half the height of the room. Aside from the high throne that occupies a portion of the back wall, facing south, there is nothing in the large room to block the view of the interlocking and interweaving system of ceiling brackets and their decoration in lively hues of blue, green, and vermilion. The hall is surrounded by a large paved square and by covered colonnades. Its total effect, though diminished by the tall European-style capitol building erected just in front of it twenty years ago, is still impressive, especially when the great curving double roof, with its banks of gray tiles, is seen against the background of the gray cliffs of the encircling mountains, which rise just behind the palace grounds. There is an admirable union of the far-projecting roof and the building itself in the row of harmoniously disposed exterior brackets and horns and their twinkling contrasts of light and shade, which produce an effect probably reached by the West only in the days of baroque art. "To crown all," writes one authority, "imagine an almost tropical sky, blue with the much-vaunted blue of Greece, and in the background, the steep declivity of the Pukak-san with its dark green pines and dark grey granite rocks."[2]

Behind and to the left of the throne hall is the Kyonghoeru or banquet hall, set in an artificial lake filled with pink lotuses which bloom every year in August. An ancient notion of the rice-growing peoples of north Asia is still reflected in the luxuriant growth of these flowers. It is the belief that the fertility of a country depends upon the symbols and symbolic activities of the king and those around him and that the pink lotus, which is associated with fertility (as is the lotus depicted on wedding garments), has the power of assuring an abundant harvest.

The Kyonghoeru is an imposing two-storied structure with the lower story open to the air. Forty-eight large tapered columns of granite support the upper story, which is provided with an inner and an outer veranda spacious enough to accommodate with ease a hundred guests at one time. A great curving roof caps it all. Three stone bridges connect the pavilion with the garden *(Plate 238)*. Behind this formal area is another garden with a pond and islands designed for the pleasure of the court ladies.

Pagodas dot the park of the present palace grounds. Some of these, dating from Koryo and Silla, are classified as national treasures. Everywhere, intriguing details meet one's eyes, particularly the sculptured details in tile or stone that have weathered the years. The meaning and use of these architectural adjuncts will be briefly indicated below.

GATES AND WALLS: Some dozens of what were once Korea's hundreds of town gates still stand. Of these, the Great South Gate of Seoul is certainly the most familiar. Not only is this gate one of the most noteworthy; it is also one of the oldest, having originally been erected when the city walls were first built in 1396. It has been renovated and strengthened from time to time since, but it retains its original proportions of the early Yi dynasty. The double-tiered roof above the massive masonry of the gate makes this a graceful as well as monumental construction. Another handsome Seoul gate is the triple Kanghwa-mun, which used to be the main entrance to the Kyongbok Palace. Unfortunately, the superstructure was destroyed during the Korean War.

The gates and watchtowers of Suwon, about fifty miles southeast of Seoul, are among Korea's most picturesque. The East Gate of Suwon *(Plate 239)* was built of great blocks of dressed granite surmounted by a single-roofed pavilion. Unfortunately, it was completely destroyed during the Korean War. The watchtowers and the West Gate of Suwon *(Plate 240)* are equally well built. With their protective side walls, these towers and gates stood guard over the great fertile plain below them and over the approaches to the capital. A striking example of architectural engineering in this area is the water gate of Suwon *(Plate 241)*, which was strategically placed to allow water into the city and to keep enemies out.

Another gate showing a double-roofed superstructure is still standing at Chonju *(Plate 242)*. Gates to temple compounds are generally smaller than town or palace gates and normally stand in a clump of great trees.

RELIGIOUS ARCHITECTURE    CONFUCIAN AND OTHER SHRINES: The holy of holies among the Confucian temples in Korea were two establishments in Seoul: the Chong-myo or ancestral shrine of the Yi household and the Sunggyong-gok of the Confucian College and temple on the eastern outskirts of the old city. Austere and plain, these buildings are set in spacious grounds which still harbor great trees: enormously ancient ginkgos and tall cypresses and cryptomerias. The main building of the Confucian temple *(Plate 243)* is still used for periodic Confucian ceremonies.[3]

Scattered about the provinces outside Seoul were literally hundreds of Confucian shrines called sowon. These functioned as clubs for the local literati and as examination centers for aspiring men of letters. Some three hundred of these establishments also served as county-seat centers for civil service examinations. One such shrine near Andong is still in good repair *(Plate 244)*. Most of these shrines were placed in scenic spots.

Among non-Buddhist buildings in Seoul, the temples of the war god, Kwan-u, were the best cared for. Small isolated shrines to local spirits may be found throughout the countryside, but they are usually low, dark, and entirely devoid of artistic interest. They are, however, built as miniatures of larger shrines and in exact replica. The tiles, of standard size, look ridiculously out of proportion on small and top-heavy roofs that crown tiny shrines only a few square feet in overall area. In Seoul, in what are now the gardens of the Choson Hotel, is a pagoda built in imitation of the Temple of Heaven in Peking *(Plate 245)*. It stands as a charming reminder of late nineteenth-century Korea in the heart of the bustling modern city.

TOMBS: It has often been said of Korean graves that they are better located—on sunny hillsides with good drainage and on other imposing sites—than are most Korean homes and that, once dead, a man is better cared for than in his lifetime. There is some ground for truth in the comment. Most ordinary graves are located on hillsides, and the great tombs are handsomely laid out in spots where nature and the geomancer have come to terms and where magnificent stands of old trees and great parks are kept in good condition by guardians who live on the premises.[4] One of the most spectacular of such sites is that of the Kwangnung Tomb *(Plate 246)*. Here the mounds are exceptionally high and steep, and the whole area is still thickly forested. Junipers line the road to the gate, and the tomb shrine and statues are in an excellent state of repair *(Plate 247)*. The tomb was originally built in 1468 for King Sejo. His queen is also buried in the same area. Nearby is the Buddhist temple of Pongson-sa, one of the more important temples of the Yi period.

As an example of tomb architecture at the end of the dynasty, the Hongnung, the double tomb of King Kojong and Queen Min about fifteen miles east of Seoul, is the most imposing. After entering the area through the Spirit Gate *(Plate 248)*, one follows a broad paved avenue lined by stone animal and human figures from six to twelve feet tall *(Plate 249)* to the shrine pavilion, which is called the Chongja-gak. The front steps of this pavilion, with their carved sides, were reserved for the use of the king or his representatives, while the plain back steps accommodated all other visitors. The building has four folding doors in front and one in the center of the back. The lower walls are of gray brick set in cement; the upper are finished in pink plaster. On each side a curved red wooden sheath protects the walls and shades the building. The roof is of tile, with the royal insignia stamped on all the finials. Behind the building is a small open receptacle of stone where papers conveying greetings to the spirits of the king and the queen and listing the participants in memorial ceremonies were burned.

To the right of the main pavilion is a small open building housing the great tombstone. On one face of the stone, carved in old-style, formal Chinese characters, are the posthumous names of King Kojong and Queen Min, as well as the name of the tomb. On the back of the slab are recorded some biographical facts regarding the rulers, together with the date when the stone was erected.

The large, steep mound, carefully smoothed and covered with grass, is surmounted by a smaller mound reached by three platforms containing a stone table, stone lanterns, various stone figures, and an imposing stone buttress—the whole half-encircled by a decorative brick wall. The table is a *honyusok* or "spirit-playing stone," and it is stated by those in charge of the tomb that this is literally what is meant: a stone where the spirits of the dead king and queen play. At many royal tombs there are separate mounds for the king and the queen. Here there is only one, since the queen was assassinated and her body burned directly afterwards, nothing being left, according to one report, but her little finger.

TEMPLES AND MONASTERIES: Many of the leading Buddhist establishments are north of the thirty-eighth parallel and will not be considered in the following brief review of some dozen of south Korea's chief temples and monasteries. The monasteries described here were nearly all founded early in Korea's Buddhist history—in Silla and Koryo days—and were selected for inclusion because of their antiquity, their continuity, and their overall interest.

Kyonggi Province has several dozen temples located within Seoul and its outskirts. Four of these are described here. Chondung-sa is the main monastery on Kanghwa Island. It is perched high on a hill overlooking the sea and forms a wide arc like a bird's wing against the sky. The façade in summer is hospitably opened by folding back the front doors, which may be hooked to the eaves *(Plate 250)*. The altar within is handsomely furnished with an intricate orange-red canopy, a mural, and a trinity of Buddhas *(Plate 251)*. The slope of the roof is supported on the inside by five tiers of brackets. Murals along the walls repeat the chief colors of the altar mural—orange and green—and show Tantric deities and the Buddhist Wheel of the Law *(Plate 252)*. Chondung-sa became important during the Mongol invasion when the court took refuge on the island.

Kyongguk-sa is a small temple in the eastern suburbs of Seoul whose murals, both inside and outside the three chief halls, have been painted since the close of World War II by the northern priest from the Diamond Mountains who calls himself Namsan *(Plate 253)*. He has also shown great patience and care in refurbishing the whole complex system of eaves and brackets *(Plate 254)*.

One of the larger monasteries of Kyonggi Province is Silluk-sa, near Yoju. The main altar is furnished with a brilliant mural and with an Amitabha and two standing Bodhisattvas. A graceful brick pagoda built during the period of United Silla is a part of this temple ensemble *(Plate 255)*. In both shape and materials it is a very rare type for Korea. A memorial stele, Naong's stupa, and a Koryo lantern decorated with intricately modeled figures and topped by a scalloped octagonal crown are also among the temple's treasures.

The small monastery of Yongju-sa is noted for its excellent murals, for which the artist Tanwon is given credit, although it is doubtful that he painted them himself. Brilliantly done in orange-red, green, black, and white, they portray the Buddhist pantheon *(Plate 256)*. The chief Buddha is the Yaksa Yorae (Bhaisajyaguru) or Buddha of medicine. The two Bodhisattvas are depicted as elegant courtiers and the attendants as court officials. The Four Deva Kings appear in the background, and the disciples are shown as small figures behind them. The highlights and the modeling, which display an attempt to give a third dimension to the figures, are an eighteenth-century departure from Asiatic norms: an experiment with chiaroscuro.

The buildings at Yongju-sa are somewhat small and boxlike *(Plates 257, 258)*, and they show in their decoration all the exaggeration of detail, design, and color that were typical of late Yi Buddhist architecture. The dragon-head finial *(Plate 259)* is an example of the floridness that was so often characteristic of architectual ornamentation during the period.

Without doubt, the province richest in Buddhist temples of the past was Kyongsang, the ancient center of the Silla kingdom. Among the venerable monasteries still functioning are Haein-sa (founded A.D. 803), near Taegu, and Pulguk-sa, near Kyongju. Haein-sa, like most monastic establishments in Korea, is located in a beautiful though remote spot in the mountains.[5] The main hall is built on a raised platform reached by two flights of stone steps with a terrace between *(Plate 260)*. In the courtyard, at the foot of the staircase, are a Silla pagoda and lantern. The pagoda is constructed in the traditional Three Kingdoms pattern with a pedestal, three stories, and a ball-and-crown spire. The altar in the main hall is occupied by a trinity of Buddhas, the chief of which wears an unusual ornate crown *(Plate 261)*.

Behind the main hall is a library which houses the Koryo dynasty set of wood blocks inscribed with the Tripitaka—one of the most valuable editions of the ancient Buddhist canon in Asia.[6] The library building, long and low, is kept scrupulously free of insects and dust. In the surrounding woods of the temple area are found the sari-t'ap or relic containers of the monastery's priests of distinction.

Not the least important part of every monastery in Korea is the side temple. Several of these at Haein-sa are located high up on the mountainside and command the breath-taking views that are regarded as an integral part of the religious atmosphere of such Buddhist establishments. The usual side shrine to the mountain spirit is also found here, displaying a better-than-average tiger mural *(Plate 262)*. Other murals in the main hall and in the entrance gate include those of the Sa Chon Wang (Four Deva Kings) and are vigorously and gaudily painted in the flamboyant style of this type of Buddhist painting *(Plate 263)*.

One of the most attractive of the Buddhist temples in south Korea is the well-kept Eunhae-sa. The high roof of the main hall, with its unusually wide-flaring eaves, and the central staircase flanked by two banana trees, give it a special charm *(Plate 264)*. On its

286

altar a trinity of Buddhas sit upon large magenta silk cushions *(Plate 265)*. An example of the more hieratic and formal mural is to be seen in the Paekhung Shrine of the same temple *(Plate 266)*.

At Kumsan-sa, in North Cholla Province, an unusual three-storied main hall is a central feature *(Plate 267)*. It houses a colossal Buddha. Each story is walled in by gaily painted hinged doors. Near this building is a stone pagoda with a pedestal and six stories (in contrast with the usual three of early Silla pagodas), and adjoining it is a broad platform with a sari-t'ap urn pagoda in its center. A pedestal for an image, shaped like a lotus, stands in a small courtyard of Kumsan-sa *(Plate 268)*. An urn dating from A.D. 1111 is one of the particularly treasured monuments of this monastery.

The lecture hall at Kumsan-sa is long. It has seven spans instead of the usual three or five *(Plate 269)*. On an altar running the length of the building are seated five imposing Buddhas flanked by attendant Bodhisattvas in an altar set that is probably the most imposing in Korea *(Plate 270)*.

In South Cholla Province is located another old and famous monastery, the Hwaom-sa. Its main building is a great double-roofed structure of seven spans centered upon a broad platform which the worshipper reaches after a steep climb up a flight of stone steps *(Plate 271)*. On the platform before the main hall is a giant lantern, the largest in Korea, dating from the Koryo dynasty *(Plate 134)*. On the level below the lantern stands a great pagoda dating from an even earlier period *(Plate 272)*. The pagoda has the double pediment and five stories of the typical Silla pagoda, with the addition that here the pediment slabs are decorated with carvings of Buddhist deities. On the edge of the main courtyard overlooking the valley is a lion pagoda, also of United Silla derivation. Four lions function as caryatids supporting a superstructure of several stories topped by a ball-and-crown finial. A standing image of a Buddhist deity is placed in the center of the main story *(Plate 273)*.

In South Kyongsang Province the largest monastic establishments are T'ongdo-sa, P'yoch'ung-sa, and Pomo-sa. T'ongdo-sa is about twenty miles northwest of Pusan. It boasts a Silla pagoda *(Plate 274)* with the conventional Silla pediments and three stories, all in excellent condition of repair. There are also several examples of the Buddhist temple garden with flowering trees, waterfalls, and bridges *(Plate 275)*. These gardens are regarded as vehicles of religious teaching in the Son (Zen) sects. Another special feature of T'ongdo-sa is its gatehouse containing gaudily painted giant clay statues of the Four Deva Kings *(Plates 276, 277)*. The Eastern King generally holds a spear and a magic sword. He has a white face and a wiry beard. The Western King carries a four-stringed guitar or lute and has a blue face. The red-faced Southern King is armed with an umbrella which, when unfurled, causes thunderstorms and earthquakes. The Northern King, whose face is black, may carry a snake or some other monster, a pearl, two whips, and a panther-skin bag.[7] In a Taoist version these four kings carry a pagoda, a sword, two swords, and a spiked club, respectively.

P'yoch'ung-sa, near Miryang, is in comparatively good repair. Lying remote from the battle areas of the Korean War, it escaped the worst of the depredations, although its location in the mountains has made it vulnerable to visits by undercover agents from the north. This feature of all remote monasteries has induced the government to protect them by posting small garrisons in the vicinity. P'yoch'ung-sa, however, continues its peaceful life undisturbed, and the broad road leading to it is seldom without visitors. The entrance through a gatehouse is somewhat unusual *(Plate 278)*. The main buildings are located around a spacious courtyard *(Plate 279)*. A Silla pagoda, overgrown with lichen, stands before a side temple *(Plate 280)*. The altar murals display an unusual and striking representation of a sunburst halo done in dominating yellows and blues *(Plate 281)*. The spatial arrangement of side temples, gardens, and drums and bells used in daily ceremonies is pleasing *(Plate 282)*. The wooden drum in the shape of a fish *(Plate 283)*, formerly quite common in Korean temples, is now rarely found. The fish drum and the beam above it are decorated in the soft earth colors used everywhere before mineral paints took their place.

Pomo-sa, just outside Pusan, is another ancient foundation containing Silla relics. The monastery itself is an excellent example of the mountainside arrangement of various buildings in rising tiers connected by stairs and steep paths that take the worshipper up in a stiff climb to the ultimate temple at the top. There the pilgrim is confronted with a breathtaking view of the world, which now appears far away, somewhat dusty and much diminished, beneath him.

Kangwon-do, the province to the east of the capital, has several noted monasteries, the chief of which located below the thirty-eighth parallel are Sangwon-sa, Naksan-sa, and Woljung-sa. The ceiling of the Gate of the Deva Kings at Naksan-sa is decorated with charming paintings in the early Yi style that depict servants bearing baskets of fruit *(Plate 284)*. Sangwon-sa, one of the most notable monasteries in Korea, was unique in many of its architectural features as well as its treasures. Unfortunately, because of its location near the thirty-eighth parallel, it was destroyed during the Korean War. Its height and size, the layout of its side wings, its colonnades, and its inner construction were all out of the ordinary *(Plate 285)*. One of its relics, a handsome Silla bell, dated 725, was rescued from the ashes and has since been rehoused, but unluckily it cannot be restored to its former flawless condition.

CONSTRUCTION TECHNIQUES AND ORNAMENTATION    To conclude this description of Yi architecture, a word about construction techniques and methods of inspection is in order. Also, something should be said about architectural ornamentation and its symbolic connotations. Early in the dynasty, in order to exercise some control over the spate of building that attended the erection of the new capital, a government office was created for the supervision of construction and the inspection of materials. This office continued to operate throughout the dynasty. Certain subfunctions, such as that of inspecting tile accessories, were important enough to rate a special office like the Tile Bureau, which at the close of the dynasty employed forty-four tile experts.[8] All substandard products were officially broken in a special annual ceremony held at the close of the ninth month.

In construction itself, many ancient methods were (and still are) used to accomplish such universal tasks as that of nailless jointure both in major projects and in cabinet work *(Figures 6–8)*. Complicated jointure techniques were required in the solution of how best to achieve the safe interlocking of pillars and brackets in the larger halls *(Figures 9–11)*. The

288

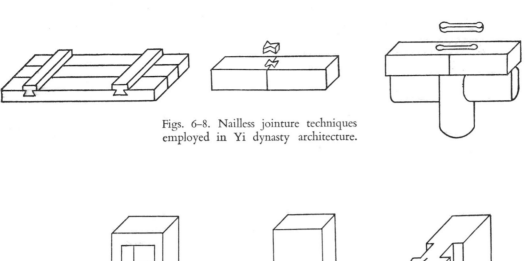

Figs. 6–8. Nailless jointure techniques employed in Yi dynasty architecture.

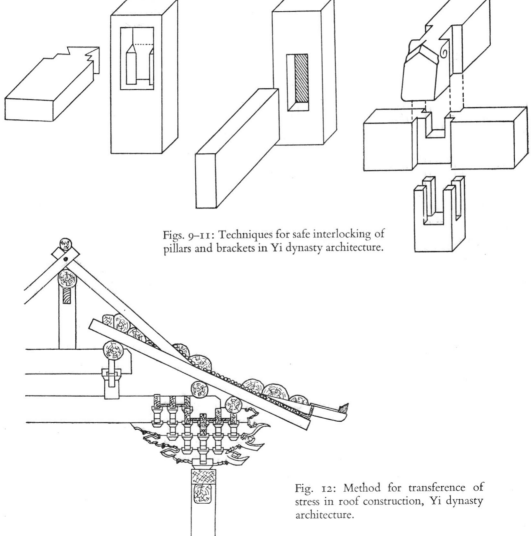

Figs. 9–11: Techniques for safe interlocking of pillars and brackets in Yi dynasty architecture.

Fig. 12: Method for transference of stress in roof construction, Yi dynasty architecture.

289

Figs. 13, 14: Examples of wing and gable construction in Yi dynasty architecture.

Fig. 15: Interior of study wing, showing bookcases, armrests, brush containers, charcoal brazier, etc. Yi dynasty.

methods for the transference of stress in roof construction through the building up of crossbeams and the use of a series of poles *(Figure 12)* were thoroughly time-tested and standardized. Where maximum outside lighting was required, architects and builders developed a variety of methods of roof construction to accommodate buildings with wings and gables. These additions to the basic structure were especially popular for study pavilions and schools, where access to outside light was essential *(Figures 13, 14)*. An interior sketch of a study wing of this kind shows the furnishings: bookcases, armrests, brush containers, charcoal brazier, and so forth *(Figure 15)*.

The ornamentation of important buildings was generally done in carved or painted wood, sometimes in both. A common design used for decorating beams or brackets was the scroll. Stylized lotus, peony, and vine were also found everywhere with little variation

290

in form or color *(Plate 286)*. As noted earlier, many of the decorations used on the walls, eaves, and ceilings were symbolic: animal, floral, and geometric. Among the animal symbols, the most frequently used were the dragon, the tiger, the phoenix, and the tortoise or "black warrior," which have been employed from antiquity to represent the four directions of the compass. In Korean as well as in Chinese cosmology, time and space were at first symbolically divided into four sections.

These sections or directions, and later the four seasons, were assigned to the above-named four animals, which represented east, west, south, and north respectively. Later, time and space came to be divided into twelve sections, and the twelve animals of the zodiac came to be associated with them. These symbols figured even more prominently in Korean art than in Chinese. Not only did they appear in the Koguryo tombs but continued to be used down to modern times. Their use in the tombs of United Silla is especially notable. The throne hall of Kyongbok Palace, built as late as 1870, features them; the four deities are found on the posts of the stair railings on each side of the upper terrace, and the twelve deities on the posts of the lower terrace. According to one authority, there appears to have been no palace in China where the zodiacal animals were so placed.[9]

The dragon in association with the tiger represented spiritual in contrast with physical strength. In Korea the dragon representing the king was sometimes shown with seven claws, whereas the Chinese imperial dragon had five. Sometimes the dragon is shown holding a pearl, the symbol of changelessness, while the dragon itself represents change. Flames rising from either or both indicate their supernatural aspects. The tiger is the symbol par excellence of bravery and military prowess. In Korea, where the Siberian tiger has been at home and uncontested for centuries, this symbol has had a real meaning. In antiquity the tiger was worshipped before Chinese civilization ever entered the country. When it appears in tomb murals or on garden walls, it is to be regarded as a protector against evil. The phoenix represents a sun bird as well as a combination of other fantastic birds. It stands for the second in power in any pair of relationships, symbolizing, for example, the queen or the empress. The *chirin* (in Chinese, *ch'i-lin*), a fabulous one-horned creature that is part deer, indicates an auspicious event. Another ancient Chinese mythical animal, the *hae-t'ae* (in Chinese, *chieh-chai*), is supposedly able to tell the innocent from the guilty and to eat fire, and for this reason is used as a symbol on ridgepoles and the fronts of buildings to ward off fire. Other symbols that supposedly possess the ability to protect against fire are the little clay figures called *chapsang* that are found along the lower roof lines. These prophylactic images also appear outside the the gates and on the railing posts of palaces, where they have been placed to scare off fire demons. Another architectural adjunct of charm and picturesqueness is the waterspout or end-tile of a ridgepole in the form of a dragon's head *(yongdu)*, a well-preserved example of which may be seen near the water gate at Suwon *(Plate 287)*.

Among Buddhist symbols extensively used in Korean architecture are the lotus and the Eight Treasures, which comprise a pair of books, rhinoceros-horn cups, a jewel, a lozenge, a painting, a jade chime, an artemisia leaf, and a coin. The lotus is an ancient Indian symbol encompassing all existence, blossoming as it does out of primal waters and therefore signifying all phenomena, good as well as bad. Thus the pink lotus, on the one hand, symbolizes fertility and passion while the white lotus, on the other, signifies purity and passionless·ess. The Eight Treasures are frequently found on ceramics, mats, chests, and scores of o her objects.

The popular symbols of longevity are Taoist rather than Buddhist in origin. They include the crane, the tortoise, the deer, a spray of fungus, the pine, the peach, and sometimes the red ball of the sun. The tortoise has other meanings besides that of longevity, one of these being destructive force. Gunpowder cases, for example, were made in the shape of a tortoise.

The *sagunja* or "four gentlemen"—the orchid, the plum, the bamboo, and the chrysanthemum—are Confucian symbols of the four qualities of the superior man. The orchid represents refinement associated with disinterested friendship; the plum, courage; the bamboo, integrity; and the chrysanthemum, a productive prime of life.

These two sets of symbols, those for longevity and those denoting the qualities of the superior man, are often found together on screens, brass-bound boxes, trays, and other furnishings. They are also often found painted on the white-plastered inside walls of many upper-class residences. Tortoise-shell designs, in their simplest connotation of long life, are immensely popular in Korea, where they frequently appear on the brick walls of palaces, on pavements, and on a great variety of homely objects.

Several other geometric patterns which also appear on walls, mats, and pavements are the thunder pattern (Greek fret); the weaving pattern, an ancient universal symbol for the making whole of that which is divided; and the symbol that is perhaps the oldest of all—even older than Buddhism in Korea—the swastika. Associated with the king and his palace, this symbol probably denoted the radiation of divine power from the king in all directions and in all seasons.* Among these semimagical geometric symbols must be included several Chinese ideograms representing good fortune, long life, happiness, wealth, and the like. The bat symbolized good fortune because its name, *pok,* is pronounced the same way as the ideogram for good fortune in Korean. Thus a group of five bats decorating a screen or a chest symbolized five different kinds of good fortune, while a group of three might mean long life, wealth, and many sons.

Two semipolitical symbols also deserve mention: the plum blossom and the *t'aeguk.* The stylized plum blossom formed the crest of the Yi household, and the t'aeguk still forms the central design of the Korean flag. The t'aeguk (in Chinese, *t'ai-chi)* is made up of two comma-shaped figures representing the principles of yang and yin and indicating the interaction of such opposites as good and evil, light and darkness, and so on, as well as symbolizing the creation of the cosmos and the reciprocal action of these principles in the phenomena of daily life. In China the yang or male principle is represented by the color black and the yin or female principle by the color red, and the juxtaposition of the two in the t'aeguk symbol signifies continual change, or the world in flux. When the Koreans adopted the symbol for their flag, they used a blue for the yang principle to connote a

* Yoshimitsu Hamaguchi, *Chosen no Komoyo* (Old Korean Designs) (Seoul, 1942). The names of the main gates of the palaces contain the character *hwa* (meaning "transform"), which symbolizes a very important idea in the Chinese theory of government. The power of the king, so long as he remained a proper conductor for divine influences, was thought capable of transforming the people—this power flowing out through the gates of the palace.

weaker yang and thereby show respect to China. The comma shape of the yang and yin signifies that one is always changing with respect to the other; therefore a weaker or a stronger member is always possible. Logically one would suppose that the Korean flag should display a larger yin area and a smaller yang area if Korea's weaker status vis-à-vis China is to be shown, but the Koreans chose to use the symbol as it stood. The flag was not created until 1878.

The lines in the corners of the flag represent a further symbolization of the diverse phenomena found in the tangible world. For example, three unbroken lines stand for the earth or transitory power; two unbroken lines with a broken line between signify water, whereas the opposite arrangement denotes fire. Literally hundreds of identifications with the phenomena of life can be read into these trigrams, which are among the most ancient of symbols to be found on the flags of the present-day world.[10]

MINOR ARTS    During the Yi dynasty period, the crafts of Korea, even more than those of China and Japan during their dynastic periods, were directed toward supplying the needs of the court, and their products were therefore skillfully and painstakingly turned out.[11] Furniture consisted largely of carved, lacquered, or inlaid chests for storage; tables of a similar variety of materials and makes; and folding screens. The chests remain one of Korea's specialties, ranging from ceiling-high wardrobes to small and delicate boxes such as cosmetic boxes equipped with drawers and small mirrors and writing boxes fitted with trays. One such writing box in the National Museum of Korea *(Plate 288)* is carved with floral sprays, birds, and rocks symbolizing mountains—all worked into borders in the most vigorous and elegant fashion. Although the designs are conventional enough, there is no trace here of the flabbiness and degeneration that characterized much of the craftsmanship seen in popular ware during late Yi. A small durable box covered with tortoise shell *(Plate 289)* represents a popular size of container for small articles like purses, fans, silver and gold hairpins, and tortoise-shell tobacco canisters. This type of small chest was often made in red lacquer. One of these in the museum of the Seoul National University *(Plate 290)* is decorated with black bands and brass studs and has a small hinged door with a brass lock. Two handles in the shape of bats complete the decoration. Two brush holders—one with a blue underglaze design and the other in red lacquer with brass ornaments—are shown with the lacquer chest.

Folding screens were usually painted or embroidered. Favorite subjects were hunting scenes, Chinese palace scenes *(Plate 291),* and rural scenes. The embroiderer's art was highly developed, and here the symbols and designs described above may be seen in their most personal rendition. Children's festival clothes, wedding garments, and other formal wear, as well as screens for inner apartments, scrolls for women's rooms, and the like, fall into this category of embroidered articles of great elaboration and cost. The bride's costume, like the formal European wedding gown, retains features of an ancient court dress. One of these features is the kimono sleeve, now seldom used in Korea in any dress but still retained in Japan *(Plate 292).* The color of the wedding garment is always red, and much of the embroidery on it is in cerise and pink to depict the lotus and its buds. The many colors on the sleeves denote good fortune, as they do on the sleeves of all formal children's wear.

The bottom of the robe is embroidered in waves and growing lotus to symbolize the miracle of life.

Among the products of the metalwork crafts, in which the Koreans maintained a lead, especially in brass and bronze casting, such implements as a dragon-decorated water clock *(Plate 293)* and dozens of Yi dynasty temple bells are the best examples. Table services in brass were universally used by the yangban class and the richer peasants. Hundreds of containers and accessories used in palaces and temples were of a high-grade brass: an alloy containing a small amount of gold to heighten its color, along with hardening metals to enhance its deep-toned ring when struck. Old Korea was a nation of bells—literally millions of them, fashioned mostly out of brass, to hang from the bridle of every horse and from the corners and eaves of every pagoda and temple. The bells used in Buddhist establishments had cutout sheet-metal clappers in the form of a fish—another symbol of Buddhism.

The arts of shamanism, on a craft level, were not entirely wanting in artistic merit. Many of the masks used in spring festivals and at royal funerals were transient creations of considerable esthetic interest. Shaman masks, the simple stock in trade of the exorcists, should also be noted in passing. A few of these in the museum of the Seoul National University were used in dealing with evil spirits *(Plates 294–99)*. One, in particular, is striking in its adaptation to its function as a mask for exorcising the pimple demon *(Plate 296)*. Another very ancient prophylactic symbol of sufficient merit to be mentioned here is the formerly ubiquitous devil post, of which there were several hundred thousand throughout the countryside at the end of the dynasty, although they have nearly disappeared by now. They came in pairs, one symbolizing the Upper Spirit or male principle and the other the Lower Spirit or female principle. They usually stood at the entrance of a village in order to ward off the evil that might enter that way. Many of these devil posts were done with an unmistakably jaunty air *(Plate 300)*.

It is pertinent here to put in a word about the Korean village house. Over ninety percent of the housing in Korea still consists of the small thatch-roofed mud-and-stone house with one, two, or three wings, a courtyard, and a gate *(Plate 301)*. Houses are always fenced off, even if the fence is only made of pine brush or kaoliang stalks. The ordinary house must be rethatched annually. In the countryside, it fits into the landscape, usually facing south, and always manages to be comfortable and cosy in any weather.

Yi dynasty ceramics show a distant kinship with Koryo prototypes but convey a very different total effect. Blue and white glazes and underglaze-painted pottery came into fashion. The class of wares with the lustrous green-blue glazes was no longer produced during the Yi dynasty, although an inferior celadon-type glaze was still used on the new wares from time to time. The decorations were generally bold and splashy, with designs that were disintegrated rather than precise, especially on jars and vases, although a certain pictorial daintiness could also be found in refined types used for tableware. A covered rice bowl in the Chun collection is a transition piece (late fourteenth or early fifteenth century) showing a broad, shallowly incised pattern of a peony arabesque covered with a grayish celadon glaze *(Plate 302)*.

A new technique called *punch'ong* was introduced: a process of incising and stamping a design in the clay and then brushing white slip across the whole pattern and allowing it to fill the depressions. The piece was then wiped, and the higher parts of the design were freed from the slip. A common pattern used in this technique was a simple crosshatching called the "rope curtain" design. A delightful drinking bowl in the Korean National Museum displays this pattern *(Plate 303)*. Around the rim is a band in a grasslike design. Below this appears a wide band in the rope-curtain pattern, then a ring of stamped discs, a band of chrysanthemum petals, and a bottom ring filled with overlapping chrysanthemum flowers among which are characters reading *naesom,* the name of the office in charge of palace food and drink. A shallow bowl of white porcelain painted with an overall design of three roses in underglaze blue is one of the most attractive of the finer pieces of Yi white ware *(Plate 304)*. It is about three inches in height and nearly eleven inches in diameter. The base is inscribed with a name and a date.

The bottle or narrow-necked vase was a popular type of ware upon which pictorial decoration was frequently used. One such bottle in the Chun collection is a heavy white stoneware wine jug of the type often used on outdoor occasions *(Plate 305)*. The decoration, in underglaze blue, depicts scholars enjoying a picnic in characteristic surroundings: mountains, rocks, pine, bamboo, birds, musical instruments, and books. The thick, smooth glaze is pitted with minute bubbles. The bottle is nearly sixteen inches in height and over seven inches in diameter at its widest point. A remarkably graceful but undecorated white vase with a narrow neck is covered with a blue-white glaze that was popular toward the end of the dynasty *(Plate 306)*.

A cream-colored porcelain jug decorated in underglaze blue and iron is an example of another utilitarian vessel, the water bottle *(Plate 307)*. The decoration combines orchids, butterflies, and rocks with dragonflies that figure prominently in cobalt blue. Still another example of the bottle is a wine container whose flat sides and hexagonal outline reproduce the shape of a pilgrim flask *(Plate 308)*. The broader surfaces carry decorations of carnations and bees, while the narrower ones are embellished with six bats, the symbols of good fortune, and have modeled ceramic loops to accommodate a cord. Since this piece is only seven inches in height, it may have been used as a honey container as well as a wine jug. Another bottle of the same height, now in the Chun collection, has squared sides and is decorated with landscape patterns in underglaze blue *(Plate 309)*. The lines of the decoration appear blurred, partly because of the different shades of blue employed and partly because there are no sharp transitions. The white is of a grayish tone that is characteristic of Yi ware. Stylized waves at the bottom and clouds at the top indicate the sea and the heavens. A wine bottle of the transition period (early fifteenth century) still shows the use of the celadon glaze over incised and stamped patterns filled with black and white slip *(Plate 310)*. The bottle, nearly twelve inches in height, is decorated with large and small medallions containing fish, willow trees, and a rain pattern against an overall background of stylized waves. The base is encircled by a band of twenty-two lotus petals; the neck, by another band of chrysanthemum petals.

A common shape for food jars in the Yi period was the globe with a wide mouth. A jar from a kiln at Keryong-san in South Ch'ungch'ong Province illustrates the type *(Plate 311)*. It is a vessel of punch'ong ware decorated in white slip and painted with a leaf-and-scroll design in underglaze iron. The jar is thought to date from the late fourteenth or the early fifteenth century. Another food jar, dating from a period about two hundred years later, is painted in underglaze iron and blue on a whitish paste *(Plate 312)*. The decoration pictures a grapevine, grape clusters, and broad grape leaves. The inscription on the shoulders of the jar hints at how a human being can become immortal.

Ceramic water containers, penholders, small boxes, and flower vases were popular accessories for the scholar's desk. Furniture and decorative objects for the desk were highly valued, and no pains were spared in devising beautiful and amusing ware for the use of the scholar. A box and a penholder *(Plates 313, 314)* are representative examples of desk furniture from this period. The box, a three-inch cube, is of Yi white stoneware with a blue cast, smooth and unmarred. The glaze is thick, opaque, and slightly greasy-looking. The penholder (in the Chun collection) is of white and reddish purple, with rings of blue at top and bottom. The form is a simple cylinder in an openwork basketware design.

178: "SAGE IN MEDITATION." KANG HUI-AN, 1419–65 (page 235). Album
leaf, ink on paper. Height: 9 1/4"; width: 6 1/4". Early Yi dynasty.
National Museum of Korea.

歲丁卯四月二十日夜余方就枕精神遽栩

298

179: "SPRING DREAM." AN KYON, 15TH CENTURY (page 236). Horizontal scroll, ink and color on silk. Height: 1 1/2'; length: 4 1/2'. Collection of Mr. Junkichi Mayuyama.

180: "THE FISHERMAN." AN KYON, 15TH CENTURY (page 236). Fragment, ink and color on silk. Height: 4″; width: 6″. Collection of Mr. Chun Hyung-pil.

181: "MOON VIEWING." YI
SANG-JWA, ACTIVE MID-16TH
CENTURY (page 242). Vertical
scroll, ink and color on silk.
Height: 74 9/16"; width:
32 5/16". Toksu Palace Museum

182: "TEMPLE IN THE MOUNTAINS." MUNCH'ONG, ACTIVE MID–16TH CENTURY
(page 243). Horizontal scroll, ink and color on paper. Height: 12 5/16";
width: 16 3/4". National Museum of Korea.

師任堂水墨葡萄　東谿趙龜命題　金履慶書　盒光圖觀

183: "GRAPES." SA IM-DANG (MADAME SIN), 1512–59 (page 245). Vertical scroll, ink on silk. Height: 12 1/2"; width: 8 5/8". Collection of Mr. Chun Hyung-pil.

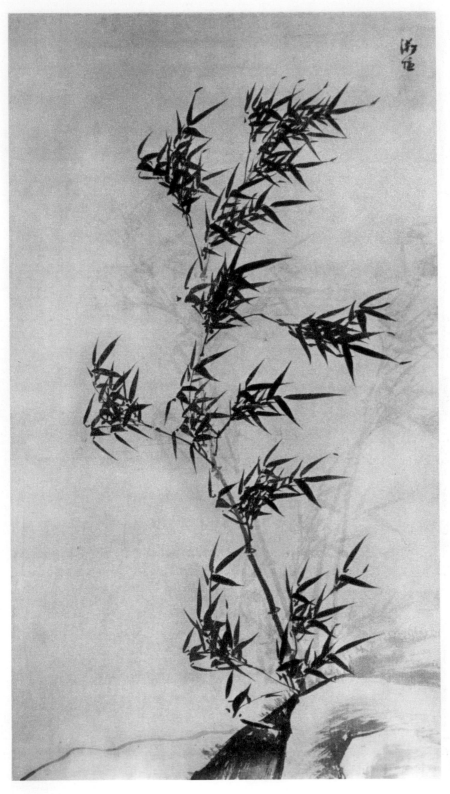

184: "BAMBOO." YI CHONG (T'ANUN), 1541—? (page 247). Vertical scroll, ink on silk. Height: 50 3/8"; width: 28". Collection of Mr. Chun Hyung-pil.

187: "BIRDS IN A TREE." CHO SOK, 1595—? (page 252). Vertical scroll, ink and color on silk. Height: 44 1/4"; width: 22 1/2". Toksu Palace Museum of Fine Arts.

188: "THE GOD OF LON-
GEVITY." KIM MYONG-GUK
(YONDAM), ACTIVE FIRST
HALF OF 17TH CENTURY
(page 253). Vertical scroll,
ink on paper. Height: 41
1/2″; width: 20 7/8″. Collection of Mr. Chun
Hyung-pil.

308

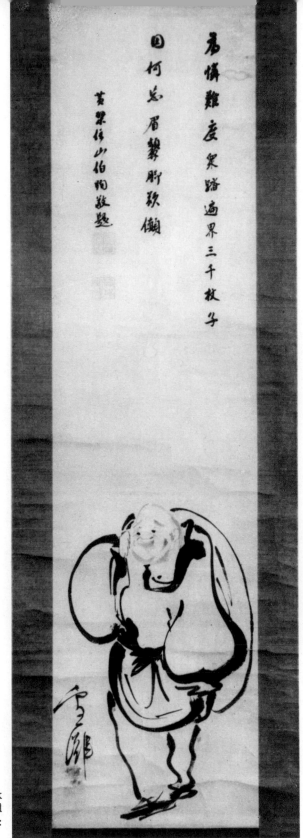

189: "THE MONK PODAE." HAN SI-GAK (SOL'TAN), 1621–*ca.* 1670 (page 255). Vertical scroll, ink on paper. Height: 46 1/2"; width: 11 1/2". Collection of Mr. Chun Hyung-pil.

190: "DIALOGUE BETWEEN THE FISHERMAN AND THE WOODCUTTER." YI MYONG-UK, *ca.* 1665–1725 (page 255). Vertical scroll, ink and color on paper. Height: 68 1/8"; width: 37 3/16" Collection of Mr. Chun Hyung-pil.

191: "MOUNTAIN RETREAT
AT LOSAN." CHONG SON
(KYOMJAE), 1676–1759
(page 263). Vertical scroll,
color on silk. Height:
48 3/4"; width: 27". Col-
lection of Mr. Chun
Hyung-pil.

311

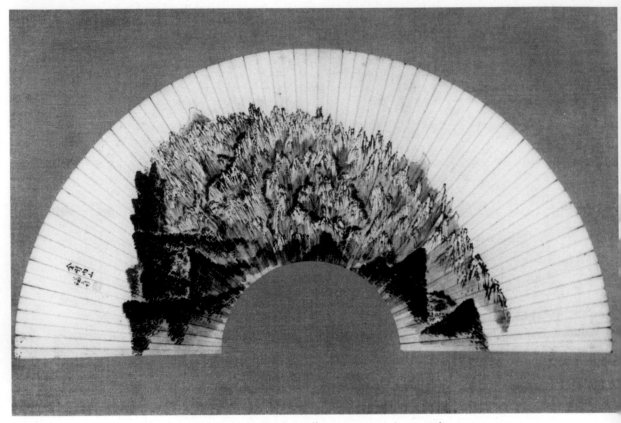

192: "DIAMOND MOUNTAIN SCENE." CHONG SON (KYOMJAE), 1676–1759
(page 263). Fan painting, ink on paper. Height: 11 1/6"; width: 31 9/16".
Collection of Mr. Chun Hyung-pil.

193: "WINTER LANDSCAPE." CHONG SON (KYOMJAE), 1676–1759 (page 263).
Vertical scroll, ink on paper. Height: 35 1/2"; width: 22 3/4". Collection
of Mr. Chun Hyung-pil.

194: "INWANG MOUNTAIN." CHONG SON (KYOMJAE), 1676–1759 (page 264).
Horizontal scroll, ink and color on paper. Height: 31 3/8"; length: 54 7/16".
Collection of Mr. Sohn Jai-hyung.

195: "VIEWING THE SPRING BLOSSOMS." SIM SA-JONG (HYONJAE), 1707–69 (page 265). Album leaf, ink and color on paper. Height: 10 15/16"; width: 6 9/16". Collection of Mr. Chun Hyung-pil.

196: "FALCON AND PHEAS-
ANT." SIM SA-JONG (HYON-
JAE), 1707–70 (page 265).
Vertical scroll, ink and
color on paper. Height:
51 7/16"; width: 23 15/16".
Collection of Mr. Chun
Hyung-pil.

316

柴門月色
辛巳九秋為
玄齋
岱山下寫

197: "MOONLIGHT THROUGH
A BRUSHWOOD GATE." SIM
SA-JONG (HYONJAE), 1707–70
(page 265). Vertical scroll,
ink on paper. Height:
21 1/2″: width: 10 1/2″.
Collection of Mr. Chun
Hyung-pil.

198: "WINTER LANDSCAPE." SIM SA-JONG (HYONJAE), 1707–70 (page 266). Vertical scroll, ink and color on silk. Height: 55 7/8"; width: 27 7/8". Toksu Palace Museum.

318

199: "STORM ON THE MOUNTAIN PASS." YUN TU-SO (KONGJAE), 1668–*ca.* 1730 (page 267). Vertical scroll, ink on silk. Height: 22 1/2″; width: 18 5/8″. Collection of Mr. Chun Hyung-pil.

200: "FOWLS." PYON SANG-BYOK (HWAJAE), *ca.* 1695–*ca.* 1750 (page 268).
Vertical scroll, ink and color on paper. Height: 11 3/4"; width: 18 1/4".
Collection of Mr. Chun Hyung-pil.

起未笄侍松檀
影衣
半月湖湘未平

堂生職

201: "PAVILION AND LAND-
SCAPE." CH'OE PUK (HO-
SAENGGWAN), *ca.* 1720–70.
(page 269). Vertical scroll,
ink and color on paper.
Height: 43 7/8"; width:
20". National Museum of
Korea.

観北齋

202: "LANDSCAPE." CHO YONG-U (KWANAJAE), 1687–
1761 (page 269). Vertical scroll, ink on paper.
Height: 58″; width: 12″. Collection of Mr. Chun
Hyung-pil.

203: "OLD MAN VIEWING A PAINTING." YI KWANG-SA (WONGYO), 1705–77 (page 269). Illustration for a text on calligraphy, ink on silk. Height: 9 1/2"; width: 8 3/4". Collection of Mr. Chun Hyung-pil.

204: "SPRING RIVER." YUN YONG (CH'ONGGO), 1708–*ca.* 1770 (page 270).
Album leaf, color on paper. Height: 8 13/16″; width: 5 5/8″. Collection of
Mr. Chun Hyung-pil.

324

205: "WOMEN'S VISITING HOUR." SIN YUN-BOK (HEWON), 1758-*ca.* 1820 (page 270). Album leaf, ink and color on paper. Height: 8 1/4"; width: 11 7/16". Collection of Mr. Chun Hyung-pil.

206: "LADIES' SCHOOL." SIN YUN-BOK (HEWON), 1758–*ca.* 1820 (page 271).
Album leaf, ink and color on paper. Height: 10 1/4"; width: 12 1/4".
Collection of Mr. Chun Hyung-pil.

207: "GIRL STRINGING A LUTE." SIN YUN-BOK (HEWON), 1758-*ca.* 1820
(page 271). Album leaf, ink and color on silk. Height: 10 7/8"; width:
8 9/16". Toksu Palace Museum.

208: "BOATING SCENE." SIN YUN-BOK (HEWON), 1758–*ca.* 1820 (page 271).
Album leaf, ink and color on paper. Height: 11 1/8"; width: 13 7/8".
Collection of Mr. Chun Hyung-pil.

209: "KISAENG PARTY." SIN YUN-BOK (HEWON), 1758–*ca.* 1820 (page 271).
Album leaf, ink and color on paper. Height: 11 1/8″; width: 13 7/8″. Collection of Mr. Chun Hyung-pil.

210: "THRESHING SCENE." KIM TUK-SIN (KUNGJAE), 1754–1822 (page 271).
Album leaf, ink and light wash on paper. Height: 12 1/2″; width: 14 1/16″.
Collection of Mr. Chun Hyung-pil.

211: "EVENING RAIN ON LAKE HSIAO-HSIANG." KIM TUK-SIN (KUNGJAE), 1754–
1822 (page 271). Vertical scroll, ink on paper. Height: 40 1/4"; width:
20 3/4". Collection of Mr. Chun Hyung-pil.

212: "HAN RIVER SCENE." KIM SOK-SIN (CHOWON), 1758–*ca.* 1824 (page 271). Vertical scroll, ink and color on paper. Height: 12 5/8"; width: 18 5/16". Collection of Mr. Chun Hyung-pil.

213: "RIVER IN SPRING." YI IN-MUN (YUCH'UN), 1746–1825 (page 272).
Vertical scroll, ink and color on paper. Height: 23 3/4"; width: 15 1/2".
Collection of Mr. Chun Hyung-pil.

214: "MOUNTAINS AND RIVERS WITHOUT END." YI IN-MUN (YUCH'UN), 1746–1825 (page 272). Section of horizontal scroll, ink and color on paper. (Scroll) Height: 17 9/16″; length: 30 3/4″. Toksu Palace Museum.

215: "LOTUS." KIM HONG-DO (TANWON), 1760–*ca.* 1820 (page 273). Vertical scroll, color on paper. Height: 13″; width: 18 1/2″. Collection of Mr. Chun Hyung-pil.

216: "SPRING JOURNEY."
KIM HONG-DO (TANWON),
1760–*ca.* 1820 (page 273).
Vertical scroll, ink on
paper. Height: 46 1/4";
width: 20 1/2". Collection
of Mr. Chun Hyung-pil.

217: "FALCON HUNT." KIM HONG-DO (TANWON), 1760–*ca.* 1820 (page 273).
Album leaf, ink and color on paper. Height: 10 15/16"; width: 13 1/4". Collection of Mr. Chun Hyung-pil.

218: "SEA GULLS AND WAVES." KIM HONG-DO (TANWON), 1760–*ca.* 1820 (page 273). Vertical scroll, ink and color on paper. Height: 14 3/4"; width 19 1/2". Collection of Mr. Chun Hyung-pil.

219: "THE PICNIC." KIM HONG-DO (TANWON), 1760–*ca.* 1820 (page 274). Album leaf, ink and color on paper. Height: 10 15/16"; width: 13 11/16". Collection of Mr. Chun Hyung-pil.

武夷歸棹

月沜

220: "WU-I SAILING HOME." KIM HONG-DO (TANWON), 1760–*ca.* 1820 (page 274). Vertical scroll, ink and color on paper. Height: 44 3/8"; width: 20 3/4". Collection of Mr. Chun Hyung-pil.

340

221: "ORCHID." KIM CHONG-HI (WANDANG), 1786–1856 (page 278). Vertical scroll, ink on paper. Height: 9"; width: 10 9/16". Collection of Mr. Chun Hyung-pil.

222: "PLUM BLOSSOMS IN THE
SNOW." CHO HI-RYONG (HO-
SAN), 1797–*ca.* 1870 (page 278).
Vertical scroll, ink and color
on paper. Height: 41 1/2";
width: 18". Collection of
Mr. Chun Hyung-pil.

223: "LANDSCAPE." KIM SU-CH'OL (PUKSAN),
*ca.* 1819–*ca.* 1900 (page 279). Vertical scroll,
ink and color on paper. Height: 59 1/4";
width: 18". Collection of Mr. Chun
Hyung-pil.

343

224: "BUTTERFLIES." NAM
KE-U (IRHO), 1811–*ca.* 1880
(page 279). Two panels of
a set for a screen, color on
paper. Height: 48 1/4";
width: 11 1/2". Collection
of Mr. Chun Hyung-pil.

344

225: "GALLOPING HORSES." CHANG SUNG-OP
(OWON), 1843–97 (page 279). Vertical
scroll (from four-scroll set, "Eight Horses
of Wu Wang"), ink and color on paper.
Height: 64"; width: 15". Collection of
Mr. Chun Hyung-pil.

345

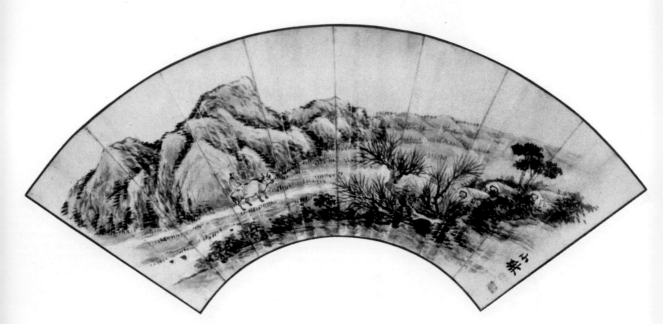

226: "COUNTRY SCENE." CHO SOK-CHIN (SORIM), 1853–1920 (page 280).
Fan painting, ink and color on paper. Height: 6 11/16″; width: 20″. Collection of Mr. Chun Hyung-pil.

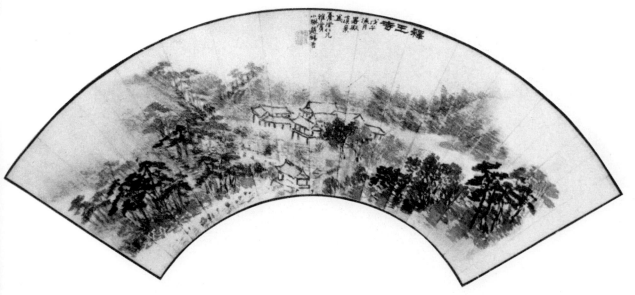

227: "SOGWANG TEMPLE." CHO SOK-CHIN (SORIM), 1853–1920 (page 280).
Fan painting, ink and color on silk. Height: 5 1/4"; width: 17 7/8". Collection of Mr. Chun Hyung-pil.

228: "MOUNTAIN RETREAT."
AN CHUNG-SIK (SIMJON),
1861–1919 (page 280). Vertical scroll, color on silk.
Height: 57 13/16"; width:
20 3/4". Collection of Mr.
Chun Hyung-pil.

229: THRONE HALL, TOKSU PALACE (page 281). Seoul. Late Yi dynasty, 1902; burned and rebuilt, 1906.

230: CHʻANGDOK PALACE (page 281). Seoul. Early Yi dynasty, 14th century (rebuilt).

231: THRONE HALL, CH'ANGDOK PALACE (page 282). Seoul. Late Yi dynasty, 19th century.

232: CORRIDOR, CH'ANGDOK PALACE (page 282). Seoul. Late Yi dynasty, 19th century (rebuilt).

233: "SECRET GARDENS," CH'ANGDOK PALACE (page 282). Seoul. Late Yi dynasty, 19th century.

234: TERRACE AND REFLECTING POOL, CH'ANGDOK PALACE (page 282). Seoul.
Late Yi dynasty, 19th century.

235: NAKSONJE, CH'ANGDOK PALACE (page 282). Late Yi dynasty, 19th century (rebuilt).

236: KYONGBOK PALACE (page 282). Seoul. Early Yi dynasty (rebuilt in 1867).

237: THRONE HALL, KYONGBOK PALACE (page 282). Seoul. Early Yi dynasty, 14th century (rebuilt in 1867).

238: BRIDGE, KYONGBOK PALACE (page 283). Seoul. Early Yi dynasty, 14th century (rebuilt in 1867).

239: EAST GATE, SUWON (page 283). Kyonggi Province. Yi dynasty, 17th–18th century.

240: WEST GATE AND WATCHTOWERS, SUWON (page 283). Kyonggi Province.
Yi dynasty, 17th–18th century (first built in early Yi dynasty *ca.* 1500; rebuilt after Hideyoshi invasion).

241: WATER GATE, SUWON (page 283). Kyonggi Province. Yi dynasty, 1794.

242: DOUBLE-ROOFED GATE, CHONJU (page 284). North Cholla Province.
Yi dynasty, 18th century (rebuilt in 19th century).

243: CONFUCIAN TEMPLE: SUNGGYONG-GOK (page 284). Seoul. Early Yi
dynasty, 15th century (rebuilt in 1600).

244: CONFUCIAN SHRINE (page 284). Near Andong, North Kyongsang
Province. Yi dynasty, 1541; rebuilt later.

245: "TEMPLE OF HEAVEN" PAGODA (page 284). Choson Hotel gardens, Seoul. Height: about 50′. Late Yi dynasty, 1896–98.

246: KWANGNUNG: TOMB OF KING SEJO (page 284). Kyonggi Province, near Seoul. Early Yi dynasty, 15th century.

247: GUARDIAN FIGURES, TOMB OF KING SEJO (page 284). Kyonggi Province, near Seoul. Height: about 6′. Early Yi dynasty, 15th century.

248: HONGNUNG: TOMB OF KING KOJONG AND QUEEN MIN; SPIRIT GATE (page 284). Kyonggi Province, near Seoul. Late Yi dynasty, 19th–20th century.

249: GUARDIAN FIGURE, TOMB OF KING KOJONG AND QUEEN MIN (page 284).
Granite. Kyonggi Province, near Seoul. Height: about 11′. Late Yi dynasty,
20th century.

250: MAIN HALL, CHONDUNG-SA (page 285). Kanghwa Island, Kyonggi Province. Yi dynasty, 17th century.

251: ALTAR, CHONDUNG-SA (page 285). Kanghwa Island, Kyonggi Province.
Yi dynasty, 17th century (rebuilt in 20th century).

252: MURAL, CHONDUNG-SA: TANTRIC DEITIES (page 285). Kanghwa Island, Kyonggi Province. Yi dynasty, 18th century.

253: MURALS, KYONGGUK-SA (page 285). Seoul. Height: about 8'; width: about 5' (in two sections). 20th century (after 1945).

254: DETAIL OF EAVES AND BRACKETS, KYONGGUK-SA (page 285). Seoul. 20th century.

255: PAGODA, SILLUK-SA (page 286). Kyonggi Province. Height: about 32'.
United Silla, 8th century.

256: MURAL, YONGJU-SA: BHAISAJYAGURU, BODHISATTVAS, AND ATTENDANTS (page 286). Kyonggi Province, near Suwon. Yi dynasty, 18th century.

257: MAIN HALL, YONGJU-SA (page 286). Kyonggi Province, near Suwon. Yi dynasty, 18th century.

258: SIDE TEMPLE, YONGJU-SA (page 286). Kyonggi Province, near Suwon.
Yi dynasty, 18th century.

259: DRAGON–HEAD FINIAL, YONGJU–SA (page 286). Kyonggi Province, near
Suwon. Yi dynasty, 18th century.

260: MAIN HALL, HAEIN-SA, WITH SILLA PAGODA AND LANTERN (page 286).
North Kyongsang Province, near Taegu. Yi dynasty, 1769 (main hall).

261: ALTAR AND BUDDHAS, HAEIN-SA (page 286). North Kyongsang Province, near Taegu. Yi dynasty, 18th century.

262: TIGER MURAL, HAEIN-SA (page 286). North Kyongsang Province, near Taegu. Yi dynasty, 19th century (retouched).

263: DETAIL FROM MURAL, HAEIN-SA: DEVA KING (page 286). North Kyong-sang Province, near Taegu. Yi dynasty, 18th century (retouched in 19th century).

264: MAIN HALL, EUNHAE-SA (page 286). North Kyongsang Province, near
Taegu. Yi dynasty, 18th century.

265: ALTAR AND BUDDHAS, EUNHAE-SA (page 287). North Kyongsang Province, near Taegu. Yi dynasty, 18th century.

266: DETAIL FROM MURAL, EUNHAE-SA (page 287). North Kyongsang Province, near Taegu. Yi dynasty, 19th century.

267: MAIN HALL, KUMSAN-SA (page 287). North Cholla Province. Height: 40–50′. Yi dynasty.

268: LOTUS PEDESTAL, KUMSAN-SA (page 287). North Cholla Province.
Height: about 5′. Koryo, 12th century.

269: LECTURE HALL, KUMSAN-SA (page 287). North Cholla Province. Yi dynasty, 17th century.

270: ALTAR, KUMSAN-SA (page 287). North Cholla Province. Yi dynasty, 17th century.

271: MAIN HALL, HWAOM-SA (page 287). South Cholla Province. Yi dynasty, 1703.

272: PAGODA, HWAOM-SA (page 287).
South Cholla Province. Height: about
22′. United Silla, 8th century.

273: PAGODA (LION PAGODA), HWAOM-SA
(page 287). South Cholla Province. Height:
about 22′. United Silla, 8th century.

274: PAGODA, T'ONGDO-SA (page 287). South Kyongsang Province. Height: about 12′. United Silla, 8th century.

275: GARDEN, T'ONGDO-SA (page 287). South Kyongsang Province. Yi dynasty, 16th century.

276, 277: FUOR DEVA KINGS, TʻONGDO-SA (page 287). Painted clay. South
Kyongsang Province. Height: about 10′. Yi dynasty, probably 18th century.

278: ENTRANCE GATE, P'YOCH'UNG-SA (page 288). South Kyongsang Province, near Miryang. Yi dynasty, 19th century(?).

279: COURTYARD, P'YOCH'UNG-SA (page 288). South Kyongsang Province, near Miryang. Yi dynasty, 19th century.

280: PAGODA, P'YOCH'UNG-SA (page 288). South Kyongsang Province, near
Miryang. Height: about 12'. United Silla, 8th century.

281: ALTAR MURAL, P'YOCH'UNG-SA (page 288). South Kyongsang Province, near Miryang. Yi dynasty, 18th century (retouched in 20th century).

282: DRUM AND BELL, P'YOCH'UNG-SA (page 288). South Kyongsang Province, near Miryang. Yi dynasty, probably 18th century.

283: FISH-SHAPED DRUM, P'YOCH'UNG-SA (page 288). South Kyongsang Province, near Miryang. Yi dynasty, probably 18th century.

284: CEILING MURALS, GATE OF THE DEVA KINGS, NAKSAN-SA (page 288).
Kangwon Province. Yi dynasty, probably 19th century (retouched 17th-
century design).

404

285: MAIN HALL, SANGWON-SA (page 288). Kangwon Province. Yi dynasty, 17th century. Destroyed *ca.* 1950.

286: DETAIL FROM DOOR PANEL (page 291). Yi dynasty, 19th century.

291: DETAIL FROM SCREEN: CHINESE PALACE SCENE (page 293). Painting on silk. Height: 60″; width: 20″. Modern. National Museum of Korea.

292: BRIDAL KIMONO WITH LOTUS DESIGN (page 293). Embroidered silk.
Yi dynasty, probably 19th century. Museum of Cologne.

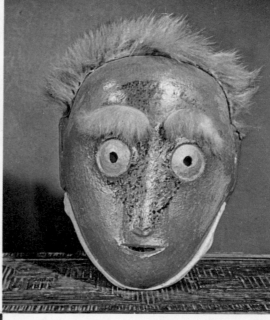

294–99: SHAMANISTIC MASKS (page 294). Painted wood. 294, 297–99. Carnival masks (monks). 295. Good-luck mask (old man). 296. Mask for exorcising pimple demon. 298. Monkey mask for carnival. 20th century, modeled on ancient designs. Museum of the Seoul National University.

300: DEVIL POST (page 294). Carved and painted wood. 20th century.

416

301: FARMHOUSES (page 294). 20th century.

302: COVERED RICE BOWL (page 294). Exterior painted in white slip. From kiln in Muan district, South Cholla Province. Height: 6 3/8"; diameter: 6 3/8". Yi dynasty, 14th century. Collection of Mr. Chun Hyung-pil.

303: DRINKING BOWL (page 295). Punch'ong ware; celadon glaze over stamped decoration filled with white slip. Height: 3 3/8"; diameter: 7 3/4". Yi dynasty, late 14th–early 15th century. National Museum of Korea.

304: SERVING BOWL (page 295). White porcelain painted in underglaze blue. Height: 2 3/4″; diameter: 10 15/16″. Yi dynasty, *ca.* 18th century. Collection of Mr. Chun Hyung-pil.

305: WINE JUG (page 295). White stoneware painted in underglaze blue. Height: 15 7/8″; widest diameter: 7 3/8″. Yi dynasty, 18th–19th century. Collection of Mr. Chun Hyung-pil.

420

306: VASE (page 295). Blue-white glaze, undecorated. Height: 12″; diameter: about 7″. Yi dynasty, 19th century. Museum of the Seoul National University.

307: WATER JUG (page 295). Cream-colored porcelain painted in underglaze blue and iron. Height: 6 11/16″; diameter: 3 3/4″. Yi dynasty, 17th–18th century. Collection of Mr. Sohn Jai-hyung.

308: WINE BOTTLE (page 295). White porcelain painted in underglaze blue. Height: 7 1/4″; width: 7″. Yi dynasty, 17th–18th century. Toksu Palace Museum.

309: WATER BOTTLE (page 295). White stoneware painted in underglaze
blue. Height: 7″; width: 4 1/4″; depth: 3″. Yi dynasty, 18th–19th century.
Collection of Mr. Chun Hyung-pil.

310: WINE BOTTLE (page 295). Celadon glaze; incised and stamped decoration filled with black and white slip. Height: 11 1/2"; diameter at base: 3 1/4". Yi dynasty, early 15th century. Toksu Palace Museum.

311: FOOD JAR (page 295). Punch'ong ware decorated in white slip and painted in underglaze iron. From kiln at Keryong-san, South Ch'ung-ch'ong Province. Height: 6 3/16"; diameter at base: 2 5/8". Yi dynasty, late 14th–early 15th century. National Museum of Korea.

312: FOOD JAR (page 296). Whitish porcelain painted in underglaze blue and iron. Height: 12 11/16"; diameter at base: 5 3/16". Yi dynasty, 17th–18th century. Toksu Palace Museum.

313: CERAMIC BOX (page 296). White stoneware. Height, width, and depth: 3″. Yi
dynasty, 18th century. Collection of Mr.
Chun Hyung-pil.

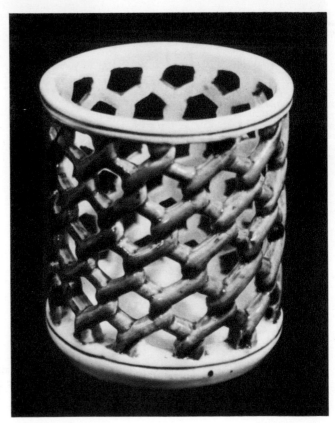

314: PENHOLDER (page 296). White and
reddish-purple stoneware; openwork basket pattern. Height: 4 3/4″; diameter: 4″.
Yi dynasty, 18th century. Collection of
Mr. Chun Hyung-pil.

428

# Appendix: Chronological Table
# of Major Events in Far Eastern History

| CHINA | KOREA | JAPAN |
|---|---|---|
| | 2333: Mythical founding of the Korean nation by Tangun | |
| *ca.* 1122: Shang superseded by Western Chou dynasty | | |
| 206: Han dynasty established | | *ca.* 200: Transition from Jomon to Yayoi culture |
| | 108: Kingdom of Choson overcome by Han armies; Lo-lang and three other Chinese colonies established | |
| | 57: Silla established (traditional date) | |
| | 37: Koguryo established (traditional date) | |
| | 18: Paekche established (traditional date) | |

B.C.

---

| CHINA | KOREA | JAPAN |
|---|---|---|
| A.D. 8: Uprising of Wang Mang; end of Former Han | | |
| 25: Later Han established | | |
| | 42: Principality of Karak established (traditional date) | |
| | 204: Control of Lo-lang by Kung-sun family; colony of Tai-fang established | |
| 222: Dissolution of Later Han; beginning of Three Kingdoms | | |
| 265–589: Six Dynasties in south, nomad dynasties in north (Northern Wei, 386–535) | | |
| | 313: Fall of Lo-lang to Koguryo and Paekche | |
| | 372: Introduction of Buddhism to Koguryo | |
| | 384: Adoption of Buddhism by Paekche | |
| | 405: Wani and Achiki sent as envoys to Japan | *ca.* 405: Official adoption of the Chinese written language |
| | 424: Buddhism introduced to Silla by Mukhoja | |
| | 524: Buddhism officially adopted by Silla court | |
| | | 552: Buddhism officially adopted; beginning of Asuka period |
| | 562: Karak absorbed by Silla | |
| 581: Sui Established | | |
| 618: T'ang established | | |
| | | 646: Taika Reforms by Prince Shotoku; beginning of Nara period |
| | 663: Paekche defeated by Silla | |
| | 668: Koguryo defeated by Silla; United Silla period begins | |

430

| CHINA | KOREA | JAPAN |
|---|---|---|
| | | 794: Heian period begins |
| | | 866: Fujiwara ascendancy established; Late Heian begins |
| 906: Dissolution of T'ang | | |
| | 918: Koryo founded by Wang-gon | |
| 960: Sung established | 935: End of United Silla | |
| 1126: End of Sung; Chins active in north China (1113–1234) | 1097: Zen introduced to Korea | |
| | | 1156: Taira family rule established |
| | | 1185: Kamakura period begins |
| 1206–36: Mongols supersede the Chin in north China | 1206–36: First Mongol invasions; period of Mongol domination begins | |
| | 1236–70: Court in refuge on Kanghwa Island | |
| 1271: Yüan established | | 1274, 1281: Mongol attacks |
| 1368: Ming established | 1392: Yi dynasty established; state organized on Confucian principles | 1392: Ashikaga (Muromachi) period begins |
| | 1443: *Chongun* alphabet completed | |
| | 1541: First *sowon* (literary school) established | |
| | | 1549: Arrival of Saint Francis Xavier; first contact with Christianity |
| | | 1568: End of Ashikaga; Nobunaga rule established |
| | | 1582: Hideyoshi comes to power |
| | 1592, 1598: Hideyoshi's invasions | 1603: Ieyasu comes to power; Edo (Tokugawa) period begins |
| 1644: End of Ming; Ch'ing established | | |
| 1839–44, 1856–60: Western wars and treaties | 1775: Christian conversions start | |
| | | 1854: Treaty with U.S. concluded by Commodore Perry |
| | | 1868: Meiji Reformation |
| | 1883: First American embassy established | |
| | 1894: Sino-Japanese War | |
| | 1904: Russo-Japanese War | |
| 1911: End of Ch'ing; Republic established | 1910: Annexation by Japan; end of Yi dynasty | |

# Notes

CHAPTER 1

1. Carl W. Bishop, "Historical Geography of Early Japan," *Report of the Smithsonian Institution*, Vol. LXVI (1925), p. 553.

2. Sueji Umehara, *Chosen Kodai no Bosei* (Funerary Practices of Ancient Korea) (Kyoto, 1947), pp. 18–28.

3. Kim Che-won, "Han Dynasty Mythology and the Korean Legend of Tangun," *Archives of the Chinese Art Society of America*, Vol. III (New York, 1948–49), p. 44.

4. *Ibid.*, p. 46.

5. *Ibid.*, p. 47.

6. James S. Gale, "A History of the Korean People," *The Korean Mission Field* (Seoul, July, 1924—September, 1927), chap. vii, p. 6.

7. Sueji Umehara, *Chosen Kodai no Bunka* (The Ancient Culture of Korea) (Kyoto, 1946), pp. 34–40.

CHAPTER 2

1. G. B. Sansom, *Japan: A Short Cultural History* (rev. ed., New York, 1943), p. 11.

2. Umehara, *Chosen Kodai no Bunka*, pp. 50 ff.

3. Han Hung-su, "Studies on the Megalithic Culture of Korea," *Chindan Hakpo* (Seoul, July, 1935), pp. 36–37.

4. George M. McCune, "Notes on the History of Korea: Early Korea," *Research Monographs on Korea*, Series I, No. 1 (Ypsilanti, Michigan, 1952), p. 9.

5. Umehara, *Chosen Kodai no Bunka*, pp. 47–48.

6. Esson M. Gale, "Discourses on Salt and Iron: A Debate on State Control of Commerce and Industry in Ancient China," *Sinica Leidensia*, Vol. II (Leyden, 1931).

7. Sueji Umehara and R. Fujita, *Chosen Kobunka Sokan* (Selected Specimens of the Ancient Culture of Korea) (Kyoto, 1947), Vol. I, p. 6. Umehara, *Chosen Kodai no Bunka*, pp. 50 ff.

8. Umehara, *Chosen Kodai no Bunka*, chap. iv.

9. Ryuzo Torii, "Populations Préhistoriques de la Mandchourie Orientale," *Journal of the College of Science*, Vol. XXXVI, No. 8 (Tokyo, 1915), pp. 55–56.

10. Bishop, *op. cit.*, p. 558.

11. Alexander Slawik, "Die Chinesische Präfekturen (Kün) in Korea zur Han-, Wei-, und Tsinzeit," *Wiener Beiträge zur Kunst- und Kultur-Geschichte Asiens*, Vol. VII (1933), pp. 5–13. E. H. Parker, "On Race Struggles in Corea," *Transactions of the Asiatic Society of Japan*, Vol. XVIII (Tokyo, 1890), pp. 157–228.

12. Bishop, *op. cit.*, p. 561.

CHAPTER 3

1. Torii, *op. cit.*, p. 70.

2. Hiroshi Ikeuchi, "A Study on Lo-lang and Tai-fang, Ancient Chinese Prefectures in the Korean Peninsula," *Memoirs of the Research Department of the Toyo Bunko*, Series B, No. 5 (Tokyo, 1930), p. 89.

3. Chosen Government-General, *Hakubutsukan Chinretsuhin Zukan* (Museum Exhibits Illustrated) (Seoul, 1928–43), Vol. VIII, p. 4.

4. Umehara, *Chosen Kodai no Bunka*, chap. v.

5. Chosen Government-General, *Chosen Koseki Zufu* (Album of Korean Antiquities) (Seoul, 1915–35), Vol. I. (Hereinafter to be referred to as *CKZ*.)

6. Umehara, *Chosen Kodai no Bunka*, p. 15.

7. Akio Koizumi, *Rakuro Saikyo-zuka* (The Painted Basket Tomb of Lo-lang) (Seoul, 1934), Plates 86–88.

8. Lacquer decorates, protects, and cements. See Otto Maenchen-Helfen, "Zur Geschichte der Lackkunst in China," *Wiener Beiträge zur Kunst- und Kultur-Geschichte Asiens*, Vol. XI (1937), p. 59.

9. Yoshito Harada and Kingo Tazawa, *Rakuro* (Lo-lang) (Tokyo, 1930), Plates 21–25 and p. 14 for evidence of the local use of lacquer. This book is a report on the excavation of Wang Hsü's tomb in Lo-lang. See also Maenchen-Helfen, *op. cit.*, footnote 116.

10. Henri Maspero, "La vie privée en Chine à

l'époque des Hans," *Revue des Arts Asiatiques,* Vol. VII (Paris, 1931–32), p. 186.

11. For illustrations of the two types, see Umehara, *Chosen Kodai no Bunka,* Plates 9–10.

12. Tadashi Sekino and Others, "Rakuro-gun Jidai no Iseki" (Remains of the Lo-lang Period), Vol. IV of the series *Koseki Chosa Tokubetsu Hokoku* (Special Report on the Investigation of Ancient Remains) (Seoul, 1927). For a description of the buckle, see Tadashi Sekino, *Chosen Bijutsu Shi* (History of Korean Art) (Kyoto, 1932), Plate 9.

13. Viktor von Griessmaier, "Die Granulierte Goldschnalle," *Wiener Beiträge zur Kunst- und Kultur Geschichte Asiens,* Vol. VII (1933), pp. 31–38.

14. Harada and Tazawa, *op. cit.,* Plates 80, 104–7 and p. 29.

15. Maenchen-Helfen, *op. cit.,* footnote 104.

16. Koizumi, *op. cit.,* Plates 68–69.

17. *Ibid.,* Plates 80–82. See also H. Haguenauer, "Les récentes fouilles japonaises en Corée," *T'oung Pao,* Vol. XXIII (Leyden, 1948).

18. Laurence Sickman and Alexander Soper, *The Art and Architecture of China* (London and Baltimore, 1956), pp. 34–35.

19. Kyoichi Arimitsu and Evelyn McCune, "New Discoveries in Korean Archeology" (unpublished lecture delivered at the University of California, July 24, 1951).

20. For a good discussion of the Chinese mirrors found in Korea, see Kurt von Blauensteiner, "Die Spiegel," *Wiener Beiträge zur Kunst- und Kultur-Geschichte Asiens,* Vol. VII (1933), pp. 14–30.

21. Wilma Fairbank, "A Structural Key to Han Mural Art," *Harvard Journal of Asiatic Studies,* Vol. VII, No. 1 (April 1942), Figure 12. See also the Ku K'ai-chih scroll and the Koguryo murals in Hiroshi Ikeuchi and Sueji Umehara, *Tsuko* (T'ung-kou) (Tokyo, 1940), Vol. II, Plate 50.

22. Tsuneyoshi Oba and Kamejiro Kayamoto, *Rakuro Oko Bo* (The Tomb of Wang Kuang of Lo-lang) (Seoul, 1935), Plate 73.

23. Koizumi, *op. cit.,* Plates 108–9.

24. Oba and Kayamoto, *op. cit.,* Plate 38. Maspero, *op. cit.,* Plate 57.

25. Harada and Tazawa, *op. cit.,* Plates 116/1, 120, 121. Koizumi, *op. cit.,* Plates 83, 89.

26. Harada and Tazawa, *op. cit.,* Plates 85–96. For a study of the quatrefoil design like that found on the cover of this box, see Otto Maenchen-Helfen, "From China to Palmyra," *Art Bulletin,* Vol. XXV (New York, 1943).

CHAPTER 4

1. Chindan Hakhoe, ed., *Han'guk-sa Yonpy'o* (Korean History, Chronological Chart) (Seoul, 1959), p. 51.

2. Sansom, *op. cit.,* pp. 71–72, 87.

3. Masaharu Anesaki, *Buddhist Art in Its Relation to Buddhist Ideals* (Boston, 1923), p. 12.

4. Ernest Fenollosa, *Epochs of Chinese and Japanese Art* (Boston, 1913), Vol. I, p. 46.

5. *Ibid.,* p. 49.

6. Robert Paine and Alexander Soper, *The Art and Architecture of Japan* (Edinburgh and London, 1955), pp. 173–76.

7. Kim Che-won, "The Stone Pagoda of Koo Huang Li in South Korea," *Artibus Asiae,* Vol. XIII (Ascona, Switzerland, 1950), p. 27.

8. Paine and Soper, *op. cit.,* pp. 173–75, for description and diagrams.

9. National Gallery of Art and Other U.S. Museums, Catalog: *Masterpieces of Korean Art* (Boston, 1957), Nos. 20–23, p. 48. Umehara, *Chosen Kodai no Bunka,* chap. vii.

10. Sekino, *Chosen Bijutsu Shi,* p. 66.

11. *Ibid.,* p. 68.

12. Soper, *op. cit.,* p. 174.

13. Sekino, *Chosen Bijutsu Shi,* p. 63, and Tojin Kayamoto, "Tamamushi-zushi no Baai: Nihon Bijutsu ni oyoboshita Chosen no Eikyo" (The Tamamushi Shrine: Korean Influence on Japanese Art), *Museum,* No. 23 (Tokyo, 1953).

14. Imperial Japanese Government, Department of Education, *Japanese Temples and Their Treasures* (Tokyo, 1915), p. 107. Fenollosa, *op. cit.,* pp. 50 ff.

15. *Japanese Temples and Their Treasures,* pp. 110–111. See also Langdon Warner, *The Craft of the Japanese Sculptor* (New York, 1936).

16. Josef Stryzygowski, "Perso-Indian Landscape in Northern Art," in *The Influence of Indian Art* (London, 1925).

CHAPTER 5

1. Sueji Umehara, "Newly Discovered Tombs with Wall Paintings of the Kao-kou-li Dynasty," *Archives of the Chinese Art Society of America,* Vol. VI (1952), pp. 8–9.

2. Ikeuchi and Umehara, *op. cit.,* Vol. I, chaps. iii–iv, pp. 7–13.

3. Yoshio Yonezawa, *Painting in the Ming Dynasty* (Tokyo, 1956), p. 1.

4. Ikeuchi and Umehara, *op. cit.,* Vol. II, chap. ii.

5. *Ibid.,* Vol. I, chap. ii and Plates 9–11.

6. Umehara, *Chosen Kodai no Bunka,* chap. vi.

7. Ikeuchi and Umehara, *op. cit.,* Vol. II, p. 5.

8. *Ibid.,* Vol. II, chap. ii and Plates 9–11, 43.

9. *Ibid.,* Vol. II, chap. v. The paintings of the Four Spirits were done directly upon the stone faces, which had been carefully dressed for this purpose. The Japanese artist Tsunekichi Oba was commissioned to make copies of these murals in 1938. His copies in color have been reproduced in *Tsuko.*

10. Umehara, "Newly Discovered Tombs with Wall Paintings of the Kao-kou-li Dynasty," pp. 12 ff.

11. Andreas Eckhardt, *A History of Korean Art* (London, 1929), pp. 122 ff. for easy reference.

12. Sickman and Soper, *op. cit.*, Plate 54*a*.

13. Umehara, "Newly Discovered Tombs with Wall Paintings of the Kao-kou-li Dynasty," pp. 8 ff.

14. Kim Che-won, "Two Old Silla Tombs," *Artibus Asiae,* Vol. X (Ascona, Switzerland, 1947), pp. 184–85.

15. Umehara, *Chosen Kodai no Bunka,* chap. vi.

16. Cf. 451, dated image of Southern Sung in the Freer Gallery of Art.

17. Osvald Sirén, "Indian and Other Influences in Chinese Sculpture," in *Studies in Chinese Art* (London, 1936), Figures 49–50 (Buddha statues from the Musée Albert Sarraut, Pnom Penh) and pp. 15–36.

18. Alice Getty, *The Gods of Northern Buddhism* (Oxford, 1928), pp. 18–24, 90–91.

19. Sekino, *Chosen Bijutsu Shi,* p. 55 and Plate 11.

CHAPTER 6

1. The introduction to Umehara's *Chosen Kodai no Bunka* contains an excellent account of Japanese archeological activities in Korea from 1905 to 1945.

2. Sueji Umehara, "Deux Grandes Découvertes Archéologiques en Corée," *Revue des Arts Asiatiques,* Vol. III (Paris, 1926), pp. 24–33.

3. Helen Chapin, "Ancient Capital of Silla," *Asian Horizon,* Vol. I, No. 4 (London, 1948), p. 44.

4. Harada and Tazawa, *op. cit.,* p. 44.

5. National Gallery of Art and Other U.S. Museums, *Masterpieces of Korean Art,* pp. 43–44.

6. Kosaku Hamada and Sueji Umehara, *Keishu Kinkan-zuka to Sono Iho* (The Gold Grown Tomb at Kyongju and Its Treasures) (Seoul, 1924–27), Vol. III, Part 1, Plates 38–44, 51–68.

7. Albert von Le Coq, *Chotscho* (Berlin, 1913), Plate 30. See also A. Grünwedel, *Altbuddhistische Kultstätten in Chinesischen Turkestan* (Berlin, 1912), p. 335, Figure 666.

8. Hamada and Umehara, *op. cit.,* pp. 124 ff.

9. Kim Che-won, *Two Old Silla Tombs* (Seoul, 1948), Figure 17.

10. Josef Stryzygowski, *Altai-Iran and Völkerwanderung* (Leipzig, 1917), p. 112, Figure 32.

11. Wilhelm A. Jenny, *Die Kunst der Germanen in Frühen Mittelalter* (Berlin, 1940), p. 62.

12. Sueji Umehara, "Kodai Chosen ni okeru Hoppa-kei Bumbutsu Konseki" (Traces of Northern Culture in Ancient Korea), *Seikyu Gakuso,* Vol. VII (Seoul, February 1932), pp. 16 ff.

13. Jenny, *op. cit.,* p. 12.

14. Umehara, "Deux Grandes Découvertes Archéologiques en Corée," p. 29 and Plate 16.

15. Kim, "Two Old Silla Tombs," *Artibus Asiae,* Vol. X, Figure 21.

16. *Japanese Temples and Their Treasures,* p. 107.

17. National Gallery of Art and Other U.S. Museums, *Masterpieces of Korean Art,* p. 58.

18. *CKZ,* Vol. III, p. 328.

CHAPTER 7

1. Gabriel Ferrand, "Arab Accounts of the Geography of Korea," arranged and translated by Shannon McCune, *Research Monographs on Korea,* Series G, No. 1 (Ypsilanti, Michigan, 1948), pp. 2–7.

2. *Korean Studies Guide* (Berkeley and Los Angeles, 1954), p. 146. Kim Hyong-gyu, "The Past and Future of the Korean Language," *Choson Munhak Ch'ongsol* (Essays on Korean Culture) (Seoul, 1947).

3. Edwin O. Reischauer, *Ennin's Travels in T'ang China* (New York, 1955), pp. 276–81. This is an excellent account of Koreans in China written by a Japanese traveler of the ninth century.

4. James S. Gale, *op. cit.,* chap. xv, p. 14.

5. Much has been written on this interesting subject. See Yi Son-gun, *Hwarangdo Yongu* (Study of the Way of Hwarang) (Seoul, 1949); Chu Yo-sop, *Kim Yu-sin* (Seoul, 1947), pp. 35 ff.; and a comparative study of *hwarang* and similar institutions in Japan and Formosa and among the Amerinds of the United States: Akihide Mishina, *Chosen Kodai Kenkyu Dai-ichi-bu: Shiragi Karo no Kenkyu* (Study of Ancient Korea, Part One: Study of the Hwarang of Silla) (Tokyo, 1943), chaps. i and ii.

6. Sansom, *op. cit.,* pp. 121–28, for a short account of the exchange of Buddhist priests between Japan and Korea during this period.

7. Getty, *op. cit.,* p. 31.

8. Sansom, *op. cit.,* p. 125.

9. Eckhardt, *op. cit.,* p. 66.

10. Chapin, *op. cit.,* p. 40.

11. Eckhardt, *op. cit.,* inset Plate D, Figures 11 and 13.

12. Chosen Government-General, *Chosen Hobutsu Koseki Zuroku* (Illustrated Catalog of Korean Treasures and Relics) (Seoul, 1938–40), Vol. I: "Bukkokuji to Sekkutsu-an" (Pulguk-sa and Sok-kuram), Plates 28–30.

13. *Ibid.,* Plates 43 and 65.

14. W. J. Evans-Wentz, *The Tibetan Book of the Dead* (Oxford and London, 1958), pp. 74–75.

15. For a comparative study of Korean pagodas, see Ko Yu-sop, *Choson T'app'a ui Yongu* (Study of Korean Pagodas) (Seoul, 1948) and Chosen Government-General, *Chosen Kinseki Soran* (Complete Survey of Korean Stone Monuments), 2 vols. (Seoul, 1919).

16. Kim, "The Stone Pagoda of Koo Huang Li in South Korea," p. 28.

17. *Ibid.*, p. 31.

18. Edouard Chavannes, "Le cycle turc des douze animaux," *T'oung Pao,* Series 2, Vol. VII (Paris, 1897), p. 122.

19. Maurice Courant, "Korea up to the Ninth Century," *T'oung Pao,* Series 1, Vol. IX (Paris, 1899), p. 13.

20. Kayamoto, *op. cit.,* pp. 6–11.

21. Alexander Soper, "The Rise of Yamato-e," *Art Bulletin,* Vol. XXIV (December, 1942), p. 359.

22. Chapin, *op. cit.,* p. 45.

23. James S. Gale, *op. cit.,* chap. xiv, p. 7.

CHAPTER 8

1. *Korean Studies Guide* (Berkeley and Los Angeles, 1954), pp. 182–83, presents a convenient tabulation of the reigns of Koryo kings and the various suzerains to whom they declared vassalage.

2. Paik Nak Choon (George Paik), "Tripitaka Koreana," *Transactions of the Korea Branch of the Royal Asiatic Society,* Vol. XXXII (Seoul, 1951), p. 67.

3. Sohn Pow-key, "Early Korean Printing," *Journal of the American Oriental Society,* Vol. LXXIX, No. 2 (April–June, 1959), p. 96.

4. James S. Gale, *op. cit.,* chap. xxi, p. 3, presents a well-reasoned memorial by Yi Che-hyon.

5. Talbot Hamlin, *Architecture through the Ages* (New York, 1940), p. 411.

6. Warren Viessman, "Ondol Radiant Heat in Korea," *Transactions of the Korea Branch of the Royal Asiatic Society,* Vol. XXXI (Seoul, 1948–49), p. 14.

7. William Willets, *Chinese Art* (Harmondsworth, England, 1958), Vol. II, p. 668.

8. *Ibid.,* p. 684, for a translation of Emperor Kang Hsi's opinion of Western cities.

9. See James S. Gale, *op. cit.,* Chap. xvi, p. 20, for translation of a poem *(circa* 1200) extolling the comforts of *ondol* heating. See also Viessman, *op. cit.*

10. Yi Pyong-do, ed., *Koryo-sa* (Annals of Koryo) by Chong In-ji, 139 vols. (Seoul, 1949). Eckhardt, *op. cit.,* p. 22.

11. Gaijiro Fujishima, *Chosen Kenchiku Shiron* (History of Korean Architecture), reprinted from articles in *Kenchiku Zasshi* (Magazine of Architecture), Nos. 530–36 (Tokyo, 1930), pp. 341 ff.

CHAPTER 9

1. See the translation in Getty, *op. cit.,* for an account of the iconography of the Kuan-yin. The curls are also a characteristic feature of a Southern Ch'i Kuan-yin dated 494.

2. Chosen Government-General, *Hakubutsukan Chinretsuhin Zukan,* Vol. XIII, Nos. 5, 7–8, 10–13.

3. *Ibid.,* Vol. VI, No. 9.

4. *Ibid.,* Vol. XV, No. 11.

5. *Ibid.,* Vol. XVI, No. 11.

6. National Gallery of Art and Other U.S. Museums, *Masterpieces of Korean Art,* p. 72, for easy reference. See also *CKZ,* Vol. IX, No. 4072.

7. Kojiro Tomita, "A Han Lacquer Dish and a Koryo Silver Ewer from Korea," *Bulletin of the Museum of Fine Arts,* Vol. XXXIII, No. 199 (Boston, 1935), pp. 64–69.

8. *Ibid.,* pp. 68–69.

9. The scroll of 1007 is in the collection of Judge Kim Wan-sop, Seoul.

CHAPTER 10

1. Ken Nomori, "Korai Seiji" (Koryo Celadon), in *Sekai Toji Zenshu* (Ceramics of the World) (Tokyo, 1955), Vol. XIII: "Korea: Pre-Koryo and Koryo Periods," p. 227. (This work will hereinafter be referred to as *STZ,* Vol. XIII.)

2. William B. Honey, *Corean Pottery* (London, 1947), p. 7. Sensaku Nakagawa, "Korai Zogan Seiji no Moyo ni tsuite" (Concerning the Patterns of Inlaid Koryo Celadons), in *STZ,* Vol. XIII.

3. William B. Honey, *The Ceramic Art of China and Other Countries of the Far East* (London, 1945), p. 167.

4. Ken Nomori, "Korai Toyasho no Chosa" (Research on Koryo Kiln Sites), in *STZ,* Vol. XIII. See also Gregory Henderson, "Korean Ceramics: Problems and Sources of Information," *Far Eastern Ceramics Bulletin,* Vol. X, Nos. 1–2 (Ann Arbor, 1958), p. 24.

5. *STZ,* Vol. XIII, pamphlet in English, pp. 3–11. Henderson, *op. cit.,* p. 18.

6. *STZ,* Vol. XIII, p. 3.

7. The gray paste gave way to a coarse reddish one toward the close of the Koryo dynasty. *STZ,* Vol. XIII, p. 4.

8. Lorraine Warner, "Korean Grave Pottery of the Korai Dynasty," *Bulletin of the Cleveland Museum of Fine Art,* Vol. VI., No. 3 (April, 1919), p. 46.

9. Masahiko Sato, "Meiki no Aru Korai Toji" (Specimens of Dated Koryo Ceramics), *STZ,* Vol. XIII, pp. 300–9.

10. Honey, *Corean Pottery,* p. 8.

11. Nomori, "Korai Seiji," pp. 227 ff. See also his *Korai Toji no Kenkyu* (Research on Koryo Pottery) (Tokyo, 1944), an authoritative account in Japanese.

12. Warner, *op. cit.,* p. 46. *STZ,* Vol. XIII, Plates 1, 6–17.

13. Honey, *Corean Pottery,* p. 7. Cf. Nomori, *Korai Toji no Kenkyu,* pp. 131–35.

14. *STZ,* Vol. XIII, Plate 4.

15. *Ibid.,* Plate 5.

16. See Stephen W. Bushell, *Description of Chinese*

*Pottery and Porcelain* (Oxford, 1910), for a reference to the secret color of Yüeh-chou. See also W. Hough, "The Bernadou, Allen, and Jouy Collections in the United States National Museum," *Report of the U.S. National Museum, 1891* (Washington, D.C., 1892), p. 435, for a poem referring to the Korean "secret color" glaze.

17. *STZ*, Vol. XIII, Plate 8.

18. See Henderson, *op. cit.*, p. 27, for an account in English.

19. *STZ*, Vol. XIII, Plate 16. About five of these bowls, and probably no more, are in existence.

20. *Ibid.*, frontispiece and Plate 11.

21. *Koku Yao-lun*. See Honey, *Corean Pottery*, p. 8.

CHAPTER 11

1. See Homer B. Hulbert, *The History of Korea* (Seoul, 1905), Vol. I, p. 300. See also *Koryo-sa*, Vol. LXXVIII, section on food and goods.

2. Yi Sang-baek, "A Problem Pertaining to the Causes of Discriminatory Treatment of Illegitimate Descendants," *Chosen Munhwa Yongu Nongyo* (Some Studies in Korean Civilization) (Seoul, 1947), Vol. II, pp. 173–204.

3. George M. McCune, "Korean Relations with China and Japan, 1800–1864," (Ph.D. thesis, University of California, Berkeley, 1941), pp. 230 ff. (Two parts of this thesis have been published: *Far Eastern Quarterly*, Vol. V, May, 1946, and *Korea Review*, Vol. I, 1948).

4. George M. McCune, "The Exchange of Envoys between Korea and Japan during the Tokugawa Period," *Far Eastern Quarterly*, Vol. V (May, 1946).

5. Kim Won-yong, *Early Movable Type in Korea* (Seoul, 1954), pp. 8 ff.

6. James S. Gale, *op. cit.*, chap. xxv, for translations of a few of the songs.

7. Pyon Sang-byok was awarded the title for his work in portraiture. See *Kunyok Sohwajang* (Sourcebook of Painters and Calligraphers of Korea), ed. O. Se-ch'ang (Seoul, 1928), pp. 176 ff. (Hereinafter to be referred to as *Kunyok.)*

8. See Ludwig Bachhofer, *A Short History of Chinese Art* (New York, 1944), p. 119, for a good brief discussion of this point.

9. Cho Sik, *Nammyong Chip* (The Collected Works of Nammyong), quoted in *Kunyok*, p. 50.

10. *Chinhwi Sokko* (Supplement to Collected Korean Writings), quoted in *Kunyok*, p. 52.

11. This picture was published in *CKZ*, Vol. XIV, No. 5851. It is now owned by Mr. Junkichi Mayuyama of Tokyo.

12. George Rowley, *Principles of Chinese Painting* (Princeton, 1947), p. 18.

13. Yi Hwang. See *Kunyok*, p. 51.

CHAPTER 12

1. René Grousset, *The Rise and Splendour of the Chinese Empire* (London, 1952), p. 220.

2. Brewster Ghiselin, *The Creative Process* (Berkeley, 1952), pp. 14–30.

3. Translation in James S. Gale, *op. cit.*, chap. xxvii.

4. William Cohn, *Chinese Painting* (London, 1948), p. 91.

5. See *CKZ*, Vol. XIV, Nos. 5868, 5869, 5873, 5874, 5894.

6. Yi Household, *Selected Paintings from the Museum Collections* (Seoul, 1921), No. 15. See also Charles Hunt, "Some Pictures and Painters of Corea," *Transactions of the Korea Branch of the Royal Asiatic Society*, Vol. XIX (Seoul, 1930), facing p. 22, and *CKZ*, Vol. XIV, Nos. 5876, 5877. (No. 5877 is upside down.)

7. *P'aegwan Chapki* (Miscellaneous Minor Official Writings) and *Kunyok*, p. 84.

8. *Kanidang Chip* (The Collected Works of Kanidang), quoted in *Kunyok*, pp. 95 ff.

9. *Kunyok*, pp. 96 ff.

10. Nam T'ae-ung, *Ch'ongjuk Hwasa* (History of the Bamboo Painters) (early eighteenth century), quoted in *Kunyok*, p. 124.

11. *Yolsong Oje* (Collected Prose and Poetry). The *Yolsong Oje* is an anthology of selected prose and poetry from Taejong to Sukchong. Nos. 1 to 8 were compiled by Nangson-gun and Nos. 9 to 17 by Song Sang-gi and Yi Kwan-myong, including the poetry of King Sukchong. See *Kunyok*, p. 124.

CHAPTER 13

1. For easy reference, see Sansom, *op. cit.*, pp. 411–13, 439–40.

2. Hendrik Hamel, "An Account of the Shipwreck of a Dutch Vessel," *A Collection of Voyages and Travels* (London, 1744); reprinted in *Transactions of the Korea Branch of the Royal Asiatic Society*, Vol. IX (Seoul, 1918). Hamel was in Korea for eighteen years, from 1653 to 1670.

3. Nam T'ae-ung, *op. cit.*, quoted in *Kunyok*, p. 138.

4. Yun Tu-so, *Hwadan* (How to Judge Painting), quoted in *Kunyok*, p. 138.

5. *Wanam Chip* (The Collected Works of Wanam), quoted in *Kunyok*, p. 137.

6. See *CKZ*, Vol. XIV, No. 5910.

7. *Samyon Chip* (The Collected Works of Samyon), quoted in *Kunyok*, p. 137.

CHAPTER 14

1. Charles Dallet, *Histoire de l'Église en Corée* (Paris, 1874), Vol. I, Introduction.

2. *STZ,* Vol. XIII, Introduction, p. 3.

3. *Wolsa Chip* (The Collected Works of Wolsa), translated by James S. Gale, *op. cit.,* chap. xxx. (Slightly revised by the author of the present volume.)

4. Soetsu Yanagi, *Chosen to Sono Geijutsu* (Korea and Its Arts) (Tokyo, 1922), for a sympathetic discussion of this point.

5. For an analysis of Korean flowering see *Kunyok,* pp. 165 ff.

6. Pak Yon-am, *Yorha Ilgi* (Jehol Diary), quoted in *Kunyok,* p. 167.

7. *Songho Chip* (The Collected Works of Songho), quoted in *Kunyok,* p. 167.

8. *Kyomjae Hwach'op* (Collection of Commentaries on Kyomjae's Paintings), quoted in *Kunyok,* p. 166.

9. Yi Household, *Selected Paintings from the Museum Collections,* No. 38.

10. *CKZ,* Vol. XIV, No. 5923.

11. Laurence Binyon, "Chinese Painting," in *The Romance of Chinese Art* (London, 1936), p. 54.

12. *CKZ,* Vol. XIV, No. 6065.

13. Ko Yu-sop and Others, *Choson Myongin Chon* (Biographies of Distinguished Koreans) (Seoul, 1939), Vol. II, pp. 301–10.

14. Cho Hi-ryong, *Sogu Mangnyon-nok* (Record of Yearly Memoranda), in *Kunyok,* p. 204. Cho's pen name was Hosan, and he was an artist of note.

15. *Ige Chip* (The Collected Works of Ige), quoted in *Kunyok,* p. 205.

CHAPTER 15

1. *Wandang Chip* (The Collected Works of Wandang), quoted in *Kunyok,* p. 219.

2. *Ibid.,* pp., 220–21.

3. C.A.S. Williams, *Outlines of Chinese Symbolism and Art Motives* (Shanghai, 1932), p. 298.

4. From a letter to a friend, included in the *Wandang Chip* (The Collected Works of Wandang) and quoted in *Kunyok,* p. 222.

CHAPTER 16

1. For a good summary in English of the Chinese concept of the socio-magic influences emanating from the royal family as an aid to the people, see Helen Chapin, "Palaces in Seoul," *Transactions of the Korea Branch of the Royal Asiatic Society,* Vol. XXXII (Seoul, 1951), p. 26.

2. Eckhardt, *op. cit.,* p. 26.

3. Life Magazine, *The World's Great Religions* (New York, 1957), pp. 82–83.

4. Wilbur Bacon, "Tombs of the Yi Dynasty Kings and Queens," *Transactions of the Korea Branch of the Royal Asiatic Society,* Vol. XXXIII (Seoul, 1957), p. 4.

5. Helen Chapin, "A Little-known Temple in South Korea and Its Treasures," *Artibus Asiae,* Vol. XI, No. 3 (Ascona, 1948), pp. 189–95.

6. Paik Nak Choon (George Paik), *op. cit.,* p. 73.

7. Williams, *op. cit.,* pp. 193–95.

8. Tomo Imamura, "Kaoku Kenchiku ni kansuru Chosen no Fushu Ippan" (Some Korean Customs of House Building), *Seikyu Gakuso,* Vol. V (Seoul, 1931), and National Museum of Korea, *Korean Vocabularies in the Fields of Art and Archeology, Part I: Architecture* (Seoul, 1955).

9. Chapin, "Palaces in Seoul," p. 36.

10. *Ibid.,* p. 25.

11. Williams, *op. cit.,* pp. 146–48. International Publicity League of Korea, *Pictorial Korea* (Pusan, 1951–52), p. 12.

# Bibliography

Anesaki, Masaharu: *Buddhist Art in Its Relation to Buddhist Ideals,* Boston, 1923

Arimitsu, Kyoichi, and McCune, Evelyn: "New Discoveries in Korean Archeology," unpublished lecture delivered at the University of California, 1951

Bachhofer, Ludwig: *A Short History of Chinese Art,* New York, 1944

Bacon, Wilbur: "Tombs of the Yi Dynasty Kings and Queens," *Transactions of the Korea Branch of the Royal Asiatic Society,* Vol. XXXIII, Seoul, 1957

Binyon, Laurence: "Chinese Painting," *The Romance of Chinese Art,* London, 1936

Bishop, Carl W.: "Historical Geography of Early Japan," *Report of the Smithsonian Institution,* Vol. LXVI, 1925

Blauensteiner, Kurt von: "Die Spiegel," *Wiener Beiträge zur Kunst- und Kultur-Geschichte Asiens,* Vol. VII, Vienna, 1933

Bushell, Stephen W.: *Description of Chinese Pottery and Porcelain,* Oxford, 1910

Chapin, Helen: "Ancient Capital of Silla," *Asian Horizon,* Vol. I, No. 4, London, 1948

——: "A Little Known Temple in South Korea and Its Treasures," *Artibus Asiae,* Vol. XI, No. 3, Ascona, Switzerland, 1948

——: "Palaces in Seoul," *Transactions of the Korea Branch of the Royal Asiatic Society,* Vol. XXXII, Seoul, 1951

Chavannes, Edouard: "Le cycle turc des douze animaux," *T'oung Pao,* Series 2, Vol. VII, Paris, 1897

Cheng Te-k'un: "Archeology in China," *Prehistoric China,* Vol. I, Cambridge, England, 1959

Chindan Hakhoe, ed., *Han'guk-sa Yonpy'o* (Korean History, Chronological Chart), Seoul, 1959

Chosen Government-General: *Chosen Hobutsu Koseki Zuroku* (Illustrated Catalog of Korean Treasures and Relics), 2 vols., Seoul, 1938–40

——: *Chosen Kinseki Soran* (Complete Survey of Korean Stone Monuments), 2 vols., Seoul, 1919

——: *Chosen Koseki Zufu* (Album of Korean Antiquities), 15 vols., Seoul, 1915–35

——: *Hakubutsukan Chinretsuhin Zukan* (Museum Exhibits Illustrated), 22 vols., Seoul, 1928–43

Chu Yo-sop: *Kim Yu-sin,* Seoul, 1947

Cohn, William: *Chinese Painting,* London, 1948

Courant, Maurice: "Korea up to the Ninth Century," *T'oung Pao,* Series 2, Vol. IX, Paris, 1899

Dallet, Charles: *Histoire de l'Église en Corée,* Paris, 1874

Dubs, Homer: "Wang Mang and His Economic Reforms," *T'oung Pao,* Vol. XXV, Leyden, 1940

Eckhardt, Andreas: *A History of Korean Art,* London, 1929

Evans-Wentz, W. Y.: *The Tibetan Book of the Dead,* Oxford and London, 1958

Fairbank, Wilma: "A Structural Key to Han Mural Art," *Harvard Journal of Asiatic Studies,* Vol. VII, No. 1, 1942

Fenollosa, Ernest: *Epochs of Chinese and Japanese Art,* 2 vols., Boston, 1913

Ferrand, Gabriel: "Arab Accounts of the Geography of Korea," arranged and translated by Shannon Mc-Cune, *Research Monographs on Korea,* Series G, No. 1, Ypsilanti, Michigan, 1948

Fujishima, Gaijiro: *Chosen Kenchiku Shiron* (History of Korean Architecture), Tokyo, 1930

Gale, Esson M.: "Discourses on Salt and Iron: A Debate on State Control of Commerce and Industry in Ancient China," *Sinica Leidensis,* Vol. II, Leyden, 1931

Gale, James S.: "A History of the Korean People," *The Korean Mission Field,* Vols. XX–XXIII, Seoul, 1924–27

Getty, Alice: *The Gods of Northern Buddhism,* Oxford, 1928

# BIBLIOGRAPHY

Ghiselin, Brewster: *The Creative Process*, Berkeley, 1952

Goodrich, L. Carrington: *A Short History of the Chinese People*, rev. ed., New York, 1951

——: "Sino-Korean Relations at the End of the Fourteenth Century," *Transactions of the Korea Branch of the Royal Asiatic Society*, Vol. XXX, Seoul, 1940

Gowland, W.: "Notes on the Dolmens and Other Antiquities of Korea," *Journal of the Anthropological Institute*, Vol. XXIV, 1890

Griessmaier, Viktor von: "Die Granulierte Goldschnalle," *Wiener Beiträge zur Kunst- und Kultur-Geschichte Asiens*, Vol. VII Vienna, 1933

Grousset, René: *The Rise and Splendour of the Chinese Empire*, London, 1952

Grünwedel, A.: *Altbuddhistische Kultstätten in Chinesischen Turkestan*, Berlin, 1912

Haguenauer, H.: "Les récentes fouilles japonaises en Corée," *T'oung Pao*: Vol. XXIII, Leyden, 1948

Hamada, Kosaku, and Umehara, Sueji: *Keishu Kinkan-zuka to Sono Iho* (The Gold Crown Tomb at Kyongju and Its Treasures), 3 vols., Seoul, 1924–27

Hamaguchi, Yoshimitsu: *Chosen no Komoyo* (Old Korean Designs), Seoul, 1942

Hamel, Hendrick: "An Account of the Shipwreck of a Dutch Vessel," *A Collection of Voyages and Travels*, London, 1744; reprinted in *Transactions of the Korea Branch of the Royal Asiatic Society*, Vol. IX, Seoul, 1918

Hamlin, Talbot: *Architecture through the Ages*, New York, 1940

Han Hung-su: "Studies on the Megalithic Culture of Korea," *Chindan Hakpo*, Seoul, July, 1935

Harada, Yoshito, and Tazawa, Kingo: *Rakuro* (Lo-lang), Tokyo, 1930

Harrington, Fred H.: *God, Mammon, and the Japanese*, Madison, Wisconsin, 1944

Henderson, Gregory: "Korean Ceramics: Problems and Sources of Information," *Far Eastern Ceramics Bulletin*, Vol. X, Nos. 1–2, Ann Arbor, 1958

Honey, William B.: *Corean Pottery*, London, 1947

——: *The Ceramic Art of China and Other Countries of the Far East*, London, 1945

Horney, K.: *Our Inner Conflicts*, New York, 1945

Hough, W.: "The Bernadou, Allen, and Jouy Collections in the United States National Museum," *Report of the U.S. National Museum, 1891*, Washington, D.C., 1892

Hulbert, Homer B.: *The History of Korea*, Seoul, 1905

Hunt, Charles: "Some Pictures and Painters of Korea," *Transactions of the Korea Branch of the Royal Asiatic Society*, Vol. XIX, Seoul, 1930

Ikeuchi, Hiroshi: "A Study on Lo-lang and Tai-fang, Ancient Chinese Prefectures in the Korean Peninsula," *Memoirs of the Research Department of the Toyo Bunko*, Series B, No. 5, Tokyo, 1930

—— and Umehara, Sueji: *Tsuko* (T'ung-kou), Tokyo, 1940

Imamura, Tomo: "Kaoku Kenchiku ni kansuru Chosen no Fushu Ippan" (Some Korean Customs of House Building), *Seikyu Gakuso*, Vol. V, Seoul, 1931

Imanishi, Ryu: *Chosen Shi no Shiori* (A Guide to Korean History), Seoul, 1935

Imperial Japanese Government, Department of Education: *Japanese Temples and Their Treasures*, Tokyo, 1915

Jenny, Wilhelm A.: *Die Kunst der Germanen in Frühen Mittelalter*, Berlin, 1940

Kayamoto, Tojin: "Tamamushi-zushi no Baai: Nihon Bijutsu ni oyoboshita Chosen no Eikyo" (The Tamamushi Shrine: Korean Influence on Japanese Art), *Museum*, No. 23, Tokyo, 1953

Kim Che-won: "Han Dynasty Mythology and the Korean Legend of Tangun," *Archives of the Chinese Art Society of America*, Vol. III, New York, 1948–49

——: "The Stone Pagoda of Koo Huang Li in South Korea," *Artibus Asiae*, Vol. XIII, Ascona, Switzerland, 1950

——: "Two Old Silla Tombs," *Artibus Asiae*, Vol. X, Ascona, Switzerland, 1947

——: *Two Old Silla Tombs*, Seoul, 1948

Kim Hyong-gyu: "The Past and Future of the Korean Language," *Choson Munhak Ch'ongsol* (Essays on Korean Culture), Seoul, 1947

Kim Won-yong: *Early Movable Type in Korea*, Seoul, 1954

Kim Yong-gi: *Choson Misul-sa* (History of Korean Art), Seoul, 1947

Ko Yu-sop: *Choson T'app'a ui Yongu* (Study of Korean Pagodas), Seoul, 1948

—— and Others: *Choson Myongin Chon* (Biographies of Distinguished Koreans), Seoul, 1939

Koizumi, Akio: *Rakuro Saikyo-zuka* (The Painted Basket Tomb of Lo-lang), Seoul, 1934

*Korean Studies Guide*, Berkeley and Los Angeles, 1954

Le Coq, Albert von: *Chotscho*, Berlin, 1913

Life Magazine: *The World's Great Religions*, New York, 1957

Maenchen-Helfen, Otto: "From China to Palmyra," *Art Bulletin*, Vol. XXV, New York, 1943

——: "Zur Geschichte der Lackkunst in China," *Wiener Beiträge zur Kunst- und Kultur-Geschichte Asiens*, Vol. XI, Vienna, 1937

Maspero, Henri: "La vie privée en Chine à l'époque des Hans," *Revue des Arts Asiatiques*, Vol. VII, Paris, 1931–32

McCune, George M.: "Korean Relations with China and Japan, 1800–1864," Ph.D. thesis, University of California, 1941; published in part in *Far Eastern Quarterly*, Vol. V, May, 1946, and *Korea Review*, Vol. I, 1948

——: "Notes on the History of Korea: Early Korea," *Research Monographs on Korea*, Series I, No. 1, Ypsilanti, Michigan, 1952

——: "The Exchange of Envoys between Korea and Japan during the Tokugawa Period," *Far Eastern Quarterly*, Vol. V, May, 1946

Mishina, Akihide: *Chosen Kodai Kenkyu Dai-ichi-bu: Shiragi Karo no Kenkyu* (Study of Ancient Korea, Part I: Study of the Hwarang of Silla), Tokyo, 1943

Nakagawa, Sensaku: "Korai Zogan Seiji no Moyo ni tsuite" (Concerning the Patterns of Koryo Inlaid Celadons), in *Sekai Toji Zenshu* (Ceramics of the World), Vol. XIII: "Korea: Pre-Koryo and Koryo Periods," Tokyo, 1955

National Gallery of Art and Other U.S. Museums: Catalog: *Masterpieces of Korean Art*, Boston, 1957

National Museum of Korea: *Korean Vocabularies in the Fields of Art and Archeology, Part I: Architecture*, Seoul, 1955

Nomori, Ken: "Korai Seiji" (Koryo Celadon), in *Sekai Toji Zenshu* (Ceramics of the World), Vol. XIII: "Korea: Pre-Koryo and Koryo Periods," Tokyo, 1955

——: *Korai Toji no Kenkyu* (Research on Koryo Pottery), Tokyo, 1944

——: "Korai Toyasho no Chosa" (Research on Koryo Kiln Sites), in *Sekai Toji Zenshu* (Ceramics of the World), Vol. XIII: "Korea: Pre-Koryo and Koryo Periods," Tokyo, 1955

O Se-ch'ang, ed.: *Kunyok Sohwajang* (Sourcebook of Painters and Calligraphers of Korea), Seoul, 1928

Oba, Tsuneyoshi, and Kayamoto, Kamejiro: *Rakuro Oko Bo* (The Tomb of Wang Kuang of Lo-Lang), Seoul, 1935

Paek Nam-un: *Chosen Hoken Shakai Keizai Shi* (Social and Economic History of Feudalistic Korea), Tokyo, 1933

Paik Nak Choon (George Paik): "Tripitaka Koreana," *Transactions of the Korea Branch of the Royal Asiatic Society*, Vol. XXXII, Seoul, 1951

Paine, Robert, and Soper, Alexander: *The Art and Architecture of Japan*, Edinburgh and London, 1955

Parker, E. H.: "On Race Struggles in Corea," *Transactions of the Asiatic Society of Japan*, Vol. XVIII, Tokyo, 1890

Reischauer, Edwin O.: *Ennin's Travels in T'ang China*, New York, 1955

Rowley, George: *Principles of Chinese Painting*, Princeton, 1947

Sansom, G. B.: *Japan, a Short Cultural History*, rev. ed., New York, 1943

Sato, Masahiko: "Meiki no Aru Korai Toji" (Specimens of Koryo Ceramics), in *Sekai Toji Zenshu* (Ceramics of the World), Vol. XIII: "Korea: Pre-Koryo and Koryo Periods," Tokyo, 1955

Sekino, Tadashi: *Chosen Bijutsu Shi* (History of Korean Art), Kyoto, 1932

—— and Others: *Rakuro-gun Jidai no Iseki* (Remains of the Lo-lang Period), Vol. IV of the series *Koseki Chosa Tokubetsu Hokoku* (Special Report on Investigation of Ancient Remains), Seoul, 1927

Shiratori, Kurakichi: "The Legend of King Tung-Ming, the Founder of Fuyo-kuo," *Memoirs of the Research Department of the Toyo Bunko*, Series B, No. 10, Tokyo, 1938

Sickman, Laurence, and Soper, Alexander: *The Art and Architecture of China*, London and Baltimore, 1956

Sirén, Osvald: *History of Early Chinese Art*, 2 vols., London, 1930

——: "Indian and Other Influences in Chinese Sculpture," *Studies in Chinese Art*, London, 1936

——: *The Chinese on the Art of Painting*, Peiping, 1936

Slawik, Alexander: "Die Chinesische Präfekturen (Kün) zur Han-, Wei-, und Tsin-Zeit," *Wiener Beiträge zur Kunst- und Kultur-Geschichte Asiens*, Vol. VII, Vienna, 1933

Sohn Pow-key: "Early Korean Printing," *Journal of the American Oriental Society*, Vol. LXXIX, No. 2, April-June, 1959

——: "The Opening of Korea: A Conflict in Tradition," *Transactions of the Korea Branch of the Royal Asiatic Society*, Vol. XXXVI, Seoul, 1960

Soper, Alexander: *The Evolution of Buddhist Architecture in Japan*, Princeton, 1942

——: "The Rise of Yamato-e," *Art Bulletin*, Vol. XXXIV, 1942

# BIBLIOGRAPHY

Stryzygowski, Josef: *Altai-Iran und Völkerwanderung,* Leipzig, 1917
——: "Perso-Indian Landscape in Northern Art," *The Influence of Indian Art,* London, 1925
Tabohashi, Kiyoshi: *Kindai Nissen Kankei no Kenkyu* (Study of Japanese-Korean Relations in Modern Times), 2 vols., Seoul, 1940
Tomita, Kojiro: "A Han Lacquer Dish and a Koryo Silver Ewer from Korea," *Bulletin of the Museum of Fine Arts,* Vol. XXXIII, No. 199, Boston, 1935
Torii, Ryuzo: "Populations Préhistoriques de la Mandchourie Orientale," *Journal of the College of Science,* Vol. XXXVI, No. 8, Tokyo, 1915
Umehara, Sueji: *Chosen Kodai no Bosei* (Funerary Practices of Ancient Korea), Kyoto, 1947
——: *Chosen Kodai no Bunka* (The Ancient Culture of Korea), Kyoto, 1946
——: "Deux Grandes Découvertes Archéologiques en Corée," *Revue des Arts Asiatiques,* Vol. III, Paris, 1927
——: "Kodai Chosen ni okeru Hoppa-kei Bumbutsu Konseki" (Traces of Northern Culture in Ancient Korea), *Seikyu Gakuso,* Vol. VII, Seoul, 1932
——: "Newly Discovered Tombs with Wall Paintings of the Kao-kou-li Dynasty," *Archives of the Chinese Art Society of America,* Vol. VI, 1952
—— and Fujita, R.: *Chosen Kobunka Sokan* (Selected Specimens of the Ancient Culture of Korea), Kyoto, 1947
Viessman, Warren: "Ondol Radiant Heat in Korea," *Transactions of the Korea Branch of the Royal Asiatic Society,* Vol. XXXI, Seoul, 1948–49
Wagner, Edward: "The Purge of Korean Literati," Ph.D. thesis, Harvard University, 1959
Warner, Langdon: *The Craft of the Japanese Sculptor,* New York, 1936
Warner, Lorraine: "Korean Grave Pottery of the Korai Dynasty," *Bulletin of The Cleveland Museum of Art,* Vol. VI, No. 5, April, 1919
Willetts, William: *Chinese Art,* Harmondsworth, England, 1958
Williams, C. A. S.: *Outlines of Chinese Symbolism and Art Motives,* Shanghai, 1932
Yanagi, Soetsu: *Chosen to Sono Geijutsu* (Korea and Its Arts), Tokyo, 1922
Yi Household: *Selected Paintings from the Museum Collections,* Seoul, 1921
Yi Pyong-do, ed.: *Koryo-sa* (Annals of Korea) by Chong In-ji, 100 vols., Seoul, 1949
Yi Sang-baek: "A Problem Pertaining to the Causes of Discriminatory Treatment of Illegitimate Descendants," *Choson Munhwa Yongu Nongyo* (Some Studies in Korean Civilization), Seoul, 1947
Yi Son-gun: *Hwarangdo Yongu* (Study of the Way of Hwarang), Seoul, 1949
Yonezawa, Yoshio: *Painting in the Ming Dynasty,* Tokyo, 1956

# Index

NOTE: *Numbers in italics indicate pages on which plates appear; all other numbers indicate text pages. Chinese characters are given for a number of important Korean names and special terms.*

443

INDEX

452

# DATE DUE

| APR 1 3 | | | |
|---|---|---|---|
| | | | |
| | | | |
| | | | |
| | | | |
| | | | |
| | | | |
| | | | |
| | | | |
| | | | |
| | | | |
| | | | |
| | | | |
| | | | |
| | | | |
| | | | |
| | | | |
| | | | |

1969

71

71

71

Demco, Inc. 38-293